PENGUI

BLISS

Osho's unique contribution to the understanding of who we are defies categorization. Mystic and scientist, he is a rebellious spirit whose sole interest is to alert humanity to the urgent need to discover a new way of living. To continue as before is to invite threats to our very survival on this unique and beautiful planet.

His essential point is that only by changing ourselves, one individual at a time, can the outcome of all our 'selves'—our societies, our cultures, our beliefs, our world—also change. The doorway to that change is meditation.

Osho the scientist has experimented and scrutinized all the approaches of the past and examined their effects on the modern human being, and responded to their shortcomings by creating a new starting point for the hyperactive twenty-first-century mind: OSHO Active Meditations.

Once the agitation of a modern lifetime has started to settle, 'activity' can melt into 'passivity', a key starting point of real meditation. To support this next step, Osho has transformed the ancient 'art of listening' into a subtle contemporary methodology: the OSHO Talks. Here words become music, the listener discovers who is listening, and the awareness moves from what is being heard to the individual doing the listening. Magically, as silence arises, what needs to be heard is understood directly, free from the distraction of a mind that can only interrupt and interfere with this delicate process.

These thousands of talks cover everything from the individual quest for meaning to the most urgent social and political issues facing society today. Osho's books are not written but are transcribed from audio and video recordings of extemporaneous talks to international audiences. As he puts it, 'So remember: whatever I am saying is not just for you . . . I am talking also for the future generations.'

Osho has been described by the *Sunday Times* of London as one of the '1000 Makers of the 20th Century', and by American author

Tom Robbins as 'the most dangerous man since Jesus Christ'. *Sunday Mid-Day* (India) has selected Osho as one of ten people—along with Gandhi, Nehru and Buddha—who have changed the destiny of India.

About his own work, Osho has said that he is helping to create the conditions for the birth of a new kind of human being. He often characterizes this new human being as 'Zorba the Buddha'—capable both of enjoying the earthy pleasures of a Zorba the Greek and the silent serenity of a Gautama the Buddha.

Running like a thread through all aspects of Osho's talks and meditations is a vision that encompasses both the timeless wisdom of all ages past and the highest potential of today's (and tomorrow's) science and technology.

Osho is known for his revolutionary contribution to the science of inner transformation, with an approach to meditation that acknowledges the accelerated pace of contemporary life. His unique OSHO Active Meditations™ are designed to first release the accumulated stresses of body and mind so that it is then easier to take an experience of stillness and thought-free relaxation into daily life.

Two autobiographical works by the author are available: *Autobiography of a Spiritually Incorrect Mystic*, St Martin's Press, New York (book and e-book), and *Glimpses of a Golden Childhood*, OSHO Media International, Pune, India (book and e-book).

BLISS

LIVING BEYOND
HAPPINESS AND MISERY

OSHO

PENGUIN
ANANDA

An imprint of Penguin Random House

PENGUIN ANANDA

USA | Canada | UK | Ireland | Australia
New Zealand | India | South Africa | China

Penguin Ananda is part of the Penguin Random House group of companies
whose addresses can be found at global.penguinrandomhouse.com

Published by Penguin Random House India Pvt. Ltd
7th Floor, Infinity Tower C, DLF Cyber City,
Gurgaon 122 002, Haryana, India

First published in Penguin Ananda by Penguin Books India 2016

10 9 8 7 6 5 4 3 2

ISBN 9780143426271

For sale in the Indian Subcontinent only

Typeset in Sabon by Manipal Digital Systems, Manipal
Printed at Repro Knowledgecast Limited, India

www.penguin.co.in

Contents

Contents

1

Your Desires Are Your Hell

Om
I bow down to Blessed Shiva,
the wondrously beautiful
who delights in the luminous bliss
of his own being.

Now begins the Shiva Sutra:

Consciousness is being.
Knowledge is bondage.
The body is a union of nature and ego, the doer.
Endeavour is bhairava, Brahman.
The world ceases to be for one whose circle of energy is
complete.

THE SEARCH FOR the truth of life can be done in two ways. One is the way of the man: of aggression and attack, grabbing, snatching and taking away. The other is the way of the woman: of surrender and going in.

Science is the male path, the path of aggression; religion is the female path, the path of surrender.

Try to understand this very clearly.

1

This is why all the Eastern scriptures begin with a salutation to the divine. This salutation is not just a formality, it is not the mere following of some tradition or convention. This salutation points to the fact that surrender is the path we will be entering, and only the humble will be able to arrive there.

People who are aggressive, full of ego, people who want to arrive even at truth by seizing it, people who try to possess truth—who arrive at the door of truth like soldiers, with an attitude to conquer—will be defeated. They may succeed in possessing the trivial, but the vast—the whole—will never be theirs. They may succeed in stealing the worthless, but what is valuable will never be a part of their spoils.

This is why science discovers everything that is non-essential while missing the essential. It succeeds in gathering facts about soil, rocks, matter—but an understanding of consciousness, of godliness, eludes it. It is the same as if someone attacks a woman who is passing by: he can manage to rape her, he can have her body, but he will never have her being, he will never be able to win her love.

People who approach existence aggressively are rapists. They may come to control matter, the visible world of nature that is all around, the body of existence. They can manage to dissect and analyse it, they can discover a few secrets about it, but just as when a man attacks a woman, this will be pointless. The man may be able to possess the woman's body, but it will be pointless because he will never be able to touch her being. And if her being remains untouched, the potential for love that is hidden within her like a seed cannot sprout. He will never be showered by her love.

Science is a rape. It is an assault upon nature—as if nature is an enemy, an enemy that has to be conquered and defeated. This is why science believes in dividing and analysing. Analysis cuts and divides; it depends on division.

If you ask a scientist, 'Is this flower beautiful?' he will pick the flower, take it apart and dissect it, but he has no understanding that the beauty of the flower will disappear when you tear it to pieces. The beauty was in its wholeness; it will not be found in its pieces. Yes, by analysing the flower the scientist will find some chemical components; he will find different minerals and everything the flower is made of. He can even put them in separate bottles and label them correctly, but he will not be able to say, 'This bottle contains the beauty of the flower.' The beauty will have disappeared.

If you dissect the flower, you will not find the essence of the flower, you will only come across its physical components. This is why science does not know consciousness—how can it? Even after so much effort there will not be even a glimpse of consciousness—there cannot be. And it is not because there is no consciousness, but because the scientist has chosen the wrong method. The method he uses is not the right way to discover consciousness. He approaches through the door that leads to the non-essential.

Whatever is of value will never be known through aggression. Only when you enter through the door of humbleness will you be able to know the mystery of life. Only if you are ready to bow down, if you are prayerful will you be able to touch the very centre of love. To penetrate the heart of existence is almost like seducing a woman. As you come close to her, you will need a very loving, humble and prayerful heart. This is not a moment for haste. If you are in a hurry, you will miss the ride. You will need tremendous patience. Hurry, and her heart will close, because hurry also indicates aggression.

So a seeker of truth lives a life of prayerfulness and patience. All scriptures begin with prayer and end with patience. Here too the search begins with prayer.

The first step of the journey in this scripture is:

Om
I bow down to Blessed Shiva,
the wondrously beautiful,
who delights in the luminous bliss
of his own being.

Now begins the Shiva Sutra:

Let this salutation penetrate deep within you, because if you miss this first door, you will not be able to understand when I describe the palace to you later on. Put the male in you aside, put away your aggressive attitude a little. This understanding is not going to come through your intellect; it is going to arise from your heart. This understanding will not depend on your logic; it will depend on your love.

You will be able to understand these sutras, but it will not be in the same way you understand a mathematics problem. It will be more like understanding poetry. You don't attack poetry—you savour it slowly, sip by sip, just like you enjoy sipping tea. You don't swallow it all at once as if it were a bitter medicine, no. You savour the taste little by little; you let the taste dissolve within you.

To absorb a poem, you have to read it again and again many times. With mathematics, once you have solved the problem, there is no need to solve it again and again. Then it is finished. But you can never reach the last stratum of a poem. The heart is boundless, so the more you love, the more your love will unfold.

This is why in the East they don't just read a scripture once, they do *paath*—they read it over and over again. Scriptures are not meant for simple reading; you cannot merely read a scripture. Reading means that once you have read it you can throw the book in the trash—finished. Now that you have read it once, why bother with it again?

'Paath', to read again and again, means that you will need to savour it slowly. If it were only a matter of intellectual understanding, you could have finished with it in one reading. But here you will need to savour it unhurriedly, reading it again and again and again. You will have to read it and reread it many times; you will have to enter it in moments of different feelings, in moments of different moods—sometimes when the sun is rising on the horizon, sometimes when the darkness of the night blankets everything, sometimes when the mind is cheerful and sometimes when the mind is filled with sadness. Only in this way, by and by, will all its nuances unfold to you. And yet you will never be able to say that you have exhausted it totally.

No words of a master can ever be exhausted in their entirety. The more you discover in them, the more you find still remains to be discovered. The deeper you dive into them, the deeper they become. No *paathi*—a person who repeats his readings of the scriptures—is ever able to have known them entirely. The very meaning of paath is to absorb again and again, many, many times.

The West has not understood this yet. They cannot understand why people have been reading the Gita for thousands of years. They wonder, 'Someone who reads the same Gita every morning . . . Have they gone crazy or something?' They have no idea that the whole process of paath is to allow the meaning to penetrate deep into your heart. It has more to do with savouring than understanding. It has nothing to do with your logic, mathematics and calculations. Its purpose is to bridge the gap between the heart and the message. The purpose is that, by and by, the real meaning of the words in the Gita will become merged with the reader to such an extent that no distance remains between the two. This is the feminine way, the way of surrender: remember it.

These Shiva Sutras can be understood only if you go into them with the attitude of surrender, 'let-go'. Allow them to enter into you. Don't be in a hurry to decide if they are right or wrong. Let this point be very clear to you: as far as the statements of the awakened ones are concerned, you cannot judge whether they are right or wrong. In the first place, how will you be able to decide?

How can a person who lives in darkness say anything about the light? How can a sick person, who has always been confined to a bed and never known health, understand what health is? A person who has never known love, who has always lived a life of hate, jealousy and enmity, can read love poems, because he can understand the words, but the deeper meaning will always remain hidden to him.

Don't judge right and wrong, simply imbibe these sutras.

I am not saying that you should understand them—just drink and savour their taste. If that taste begins to reveal secret dimensions which are hidden within you, if the taste of these sutras can give birth to a new fragrance within you and you find that the stench of your personality has started to disappear, and even if for a single moment, if you find that a flower has blossomed inside you and released its fragrance, that a light has been kindled within you and given you a glimpse beyond your darkness, like a flash of lightning in the dark, then this, this alone, will bring understanding to you. This understanding will not come through your intellect or reasoning, but through experiencing. Hence, remain in an attitude of let-go.

The second point is that 'sutra' means the most concise, quintessential, telegraphic. Each and every word of a sutra is highly condensed. A sutra is never long and elaborate; it is very short, atomic. It is like a small seed which contains the whole tree. A sutra is like a small seed: you cannot see the tree in the seed, even if you want to. You cannot see the tree in the seed because that will require very penetrating eyes. To see the tree in the seed, to see the future in the present, the tomorrow in the today, the invisible in the visible, you will need very, very penetrating eyes.

You don't have this penetrating vision yet. Right now you can only see the seed. The only way for you to see the tree is to plant the seed; there is no other way to see it. You will only be able to see the tree when the seed breaks open in the soil and sprouts.

These sutras are like seeds. Sow them deep in your heart without any judgement. Right now if you try to judge the seeds, you will only throw them away because they will look like rubbish to you.

In fact, there is not much difference between a seed and a pebble. Sometimes a pebble looks even more colourful, shining, beautiful—more precious than a seed. And yet there is a great difference between a seed and even the costliest diamond, a Koh-i-noor. If you plant the Koh-i-noor, nothing will sprout. Regardless of how costly the Koh-i-noor is, still, it is lifeless. No matter how precious fools may think it is, it is not alive. And no matter how ugly a seed may look—it may not even cost a penny—life is hidden within it.

If you sow a seed, it can give birth to a huge tree that will create millions of seeds. One small seed can make the whole earth green because a single seed can create millions more, and each of those millions of seeds will give birth to another million seeds. A small seed can contain the whole universe.

A sutra is like a seed: you cannot be in a hurry with it. Only when the seed that has been planted in your heart sprouts and flowers will you be able to *experience*, and only then can you come to any conclusion.

The third thing before we enter into these sutras: religiousness is a great revolution. What you understand as religion really has almost nothing to do with religiousness. Hence, these sutras of Shiva will even shock you. You may even become afraid because your idea about religion will be very disturbed. If you really understand these sutras, all your temples and mosques and churches will simply crumble. And don't try to save them, because even if they are saved, you have not understood anything through them. You are already going to these places, yet you are almost dead.

Your temples are very decorated, but they have not given even one ray of joy to your life. Your temples are well-lit, but this has not touched the darkness in your life. So don't be afraid of these sutras, although they will certainly create difficulties for you. Shiva is not some kind of a priest. A priest tries to console you because he is interested in exploiting you; he is not interested in your transformation. His interest is in keeping you the way you are. His very business depends on you remaining as you are—sick, full of diseases.

I have heard:

A doctor's son returned home after completing his education. His father was a busy doctor and had never been on a vacation, so he told his son, 'I would love to go on a vacation for three months and get some rest. Meanwhile, please take care of my practice. I have spent my whole life earning money and never taken a break.'

The father returned after a three-month world tour. He asked his son, 'How are things going?'

The son replied, 'Everything is just fine. You'll be surprised, but the patients you could not cure your whole life, I cured them in just three months!'

The father was shocked. He said, 'You idiot! They gave us all our business! Do you think I don't know how to cure them? How do you think I paid for your education? It depended on those patients! They could have paid for the education of your brothers and sisters as well. You've ruined the whole thing!'

The priest wants you to remain sick, the way you are: his whole business depends on it. Shiva is not a priest. Shiva is an awakened one, an enlightened one, an avatar. He is a revolutionary seer, a beacon of light. His words are like fire—come close to him only if you are ready to be burned. Accept his invitation only if you are ready to disappear as you are, because the new can arise only when you have ceased to be as you are. It is only from your ashes that the new life will emerge.

Keeping these things in mind, now try to understand each sutra.

The first sutra:
Consciousness is being.

Although consciousness is our very nature, we never come to experience our atman, our being. If consciousness is the being, then we all should have realized it already, because we *are* consciousness. So then what actually is meant by: 'Consciousness is being'?

The first meaning is that in this world, only atman, consciousness, belongs to you. The word 'atman' means 'that which is yours . . . and nothing else is yours'. Regardless of how much you may think you own, nothing is yours. What you believe to be yours—friends, loved ones, family, money, fame, respectability, power—is all illusion, because death will take it all away from you. Death is the criterion to judge what is really yours and what is not. Whatever death can take away from you is not yours, only what it can't take away is your own.

'Being' is the only thing that is your own. But the moment we think in terms of 'my own', in terms of 'mine', 'the other' comes in. 'Mine' means someone or something which belongs to me. You simply don't realize that, except for yourself, nothing belongs to you—it cannot. And as long as you go on believing in the idea that someone else belongs to you, you will be wasting precious time and life— just dreaming. In the same time, you could have become enlightened, and ultimate freedom could have been yours. Instead, you have collected only rubbish.

Only you are your own.

So the first thing to be remembered is: except for you, yourself, no one is yours.

This sutra is very revolutionary; it is very much against society. Society lives with the notion that other people are 'mine'—the people of the same race are 'mine'; the people of the same country are 'mine'—*my* country, *my* race, *my* religion, *my* family—and the whole game of 'mine' continues. Society thrives on the idea of 'mine'.

True religiousness is something contrary to society. It is freedom from society, it is freedom from 'the other'. Religiousness says that except for your own being, there is nothing else you can claim as your own.

If looked at superficially, this statement would appear to be very selfish. 'I alone am mine' immediately sounds like a selfish attitude, but there is nothing selfish in it. The truth is that this is the only understanding that can bring a real feeling of altruism and ultimate meaning into your life. Until you are filled with your own being, no altruism or ultimate meaning can be born in your life.

When you call others 'yours', what actually are you doing? By calling them yours, you are exploiting them.

Your 'mine' is nothing but an extension, a part of your exploitation of them. Whenever you call someone 'mine', you turn that person into a slave, you make that person one of your possessions. You say, 'my wife', 'my husband', 'my son', 'my father'—but what is your role in this 'my'-ness? Behind the screen of 'mine', what is the fundamental basis of your relationship? You exploit that person, you dominate that person, you use that person. If you call this exploitation of another 'altruism', then you are sadly mistaken.

An emperor had three sons. As he grew old, he became worried about which of his three sons would be worthy of inheriting his kingdom. All three were equally capable and qualified, and that made the choice very difficult. One day he called his sons and said, 'Tell me the most virtuous act you did last year.'

The eldest son said, 'Before leaving on a pilgrimage, the richest man in this city left his precious diamonds and jewellery worth tens of millions of rupees with me, without even counting them or making me sign a receipt. He asked me to keep them until his return. If I had wanted to, I could have stolen all his treasure, because the man had no documents or witnesses to prove that the treasure belonged to him. The man had not kept count, so I could have easily stolen at least a few diamonds for myself. Instead, I returned the treasure to him intact.'

The father said, 'You did good, but let me ask you one question: if you had kept some diamonds for yourself, wouldn't you have felt guilty and ashamed?'

The son replied, 'Yes, I would have felt guilty.'

Then the father said, 'You can't call this an act of altruism. What you did was just save yourself from feeling guilty. What is altruistic about it? Since stealing the diamonds would have given you a guilty conscience and caused you anguish, you decided to give them back to their owner. It was the right thing to do, but it had nothing to do with altruism. You were only thinking of yourself.'

When he heard this, the second son got a little worried. He said, 'One evening, as I was passing by a lake, I saw a man drowning. No one was around, so I could have easily ignored his cries for help and gone on my way. Instead, I immediately jumped into the lake and saved the man, risking my own life.'

The emperor said, 'You also did the right thing, but if you had walked away without rescuing the man, wouldn't the shadow of that man's death have followed you for the rest of your life? You could have ignored him, but you had already heard his cries for help. Wouldn't the ghost of his death have haunted you forever? It was only because of this fear that you jumped in and risked your life. But don't imagine this to be an act of altruism.'

The third son said, 'Once, as I was passing through a forest, I saw a man sleeping at the edge of a cliff. If he had turned over he would have fallen and been killed because there was a great abyss below. As I quietly moved closer, I discovered that this man was none other than my sworn enemy. When I recognized him, I could have quietly gone my way. Even if I had just passed on my horse, perhaps even that sound would have made him move in his sleep. He could have turned over and fallen into the valley. But instead, I walked towards him very silently, because any noise might have made him turn over, to his death. I knew he was a wicked man: I knew that he would curse me even if I saved his life. Still, I gently woke him up so that he was safe. Now this man is blaming me for having saved his life! He is saying that he went there to commit suicide and I followed him even there! That I won't let him live in peace, and I wouldn't let him die either.'

The emperor said, 'It is better than what the other two did, but this is not altruism either. Why? Because your ego is nourished, as if you have done something great. When you talk about it, I can see the shine in your eyes! Look at you! Your chest is puffed up. Anything that nourishes your ego like this cannot be an altruistic act. You have enhanced your ego in a very subtle way. You think that you have done something very religious, that you are better than the other two—but I will have to look for a fourth person to be the ruler of this kingdom.'

In fact, you are not really helping others, even when you think you are. You cannot help others, because how can someone who does not even know himself help others? Serving the poor and tending to the sick gives you the idea that you are serving, but if you look at it closely, you will find that only your ego is served. If, in the end, your ego is nourished by all your service, then your service is just another name for exploitation. Until you have known yourself, until you have experienced your own being, you cannot be authentically altruistic, because only when you know yourself does such a great transformation take place.

I have heard:

Mulla Nasruddin was having a fight with his wife.

The wife said to Mulla, 'This has to be settled once and for all—why do you hate all my relatives?'

Mulla said, 'That is completely wrong! The facts don't support your accusation and I can prove it. The proof is that I love your mother-in-law more than I do mine.'

This is how the ego functions. On the surface, it looks as if you are serving others, but deep down you are only nourishing your own ego. And the subtler the ways of the ego get, the more difficult it becomes to recognize it. Naturally, other people can't see it, but even you become incapable of seeing it. Others are fooled, but even you, yourself, are deceived by this facade you create for others. We have all ended up creating our own personal maze. We started the whole thing in order to be able to fool others, and we never thought that we ourselves would be lost in it. But we are lost.

So the first thing to remember is, except for yourself, no one else belongs to you. As this remembrance deepens in you—that the consciousness is atman, being; that except for consciousness, nothing else is yours; all else is extraneous, alien, other—the first ray of transformation will enter into your life.

With this remembrance, a gap will appear between you and society, between you and all your relationships. But people don't want to look at themselves. It is difficult also because it means that you will go through a process that is fatal.

A Marwari businessman from Rajasthan fell in love with a film actress. It is very rare, because Marwari businessmen are very notorious for avoiding love. But even the improbable sometimes happens! He fell in love, but because he had a very suspicious businessman's mind, he phoned a private detective to spy on the actress and find out if she was a good, moral woman. He wanted this to be very, very clear, in black and white, before he would propose marriage to her.

The detective started investigating and spying on the actress and, a week later, he sent in his report. The report said: 'The woman is absolutely moral, innocent, without a blemish. There is no evidence to doubt her character— except that recently she has been spending time with a dubious-looking Marwari.'

The businessman himself was that dubious-looking Marwari!

Your eyes can see others, your hands can touch others, your mind can think about others—but as far as you are concerned, you don't observe yourself. Your situation is like the darkness under a lamp: the light of the lamp shines everywhere, except directly under itself. This is how it is for you: the light of your own inner lamp, your own consciousness, shines all around—except on you. So you move everywhere in that light, in all directions. Only one thing remains unseen, undiscovered—that one is none other than you.

So this is the first sutra: *Consciousness is being.* Let this sutra penetrate like a seed deep within your heart. All your journeying through the whole world is meaningless if you remain unaware of your own self. Even if you gain all the knowledge in the world but remain ignorant of yourself, that knowledge in the final sense will prove to be your ignorance.

You may have seen the whole world, journeyed to the moon and the stars, but if you have not seen your own being, you are still blind. Because only if you have seen yourself can you claim to have sight; only if you have known your own being can you claim to have wisdom. Only someone who has bathed in his own luminous consciousness is holy. Consciousness alone is the holy place; there is no other holy place.

Consciousness is your intrinsic nature. You have not been away from it even for a moment. But your situation is like the darkness under the lamp. You can never go away from this light, this self-luminous consciousness, even if you want to, but you can live in the illusion that you have gone far away from it. In this world you can dream, but the dream can never be the reality. There is only one reality, and that is your consciousness, your true nature.

Consciousness is being. So the first thing to remember is that nothing is yours except for consciousness. The moment this feeling has crystallized in you, *sannyas* is born— because just the feeling that someone or something can be yours is the very meaning of *sansara*, the worldliness or unconsciousness.

This first sutra is a tremendous revolution. Shiva is throwing a glowing ember at you to ignite this awareness that you alone are yours, no one else is.

This realization will create anguish in you, because you have formed great relationships with others, and you have treasured great dreams around others. You have attached great hopes in others. A mother has high expectations of her son, a father has high ambitions for his son, and in all these hopes and expectations, you are lost. Your father may have spent his whole life working for his high hopes in you. And yet, what did he actually gain from all his hoping? You will be spent in a similar way, building hopes in your son and striving for them, ultimately gaining nothing. And your son will carry on this same stupidity—he will build expectations on his children.

No, this will not help. Look within, towards yourself— neither towards the past nor towards the future. No one is yours. No son can ever bring you fulfilment; no relationship can ever replace your connection with your own being. You are your only friend, but to realize this will create fear in you because you will feel very alone. People are so afraid to be alone that even when they walk down a dark, deserted alley, they begin to sing loudly. Hearing the sound of their own voice, they feel they are not alone.

This whole thing is the same as hearing your own voice. When a father weaves dreams around his son, the son is not a party to it. The father is just whistling alone in a deserted alley. He is destined for misery because he has spent his whole life weaving dreams, believing that his son is also dreaming the same dreams. No, the son has his own dreams—just as you have your dreams and your father was busy with his own dreams. And all these dreams never meet—anywhere.

Every father dies unhappy. Why? Because all the dreams he has been weaving his whole life fail. Here, everyone is to dream his own dreams, not yours. If you want to live a life of fulfilment, contentment, then you should never project your dreams on to anyone else; otherwise, you are bound to be disappointed.

The only meaning of worldliness is that you have tethered the boat of your dreams with others. And the meaning of 'sannyas', true renunciation, is that you have woken up to it and you have realized and accepted one thing—however painful and agonizing it may feel in the beginning—that you are alone; that all your relationships and friendships are false and superficial. This does not mean that you should escape to a cave in the Himalayas, because escaping to the Himalayas will show only one thing: that relationships and friendships are still real to you, that they have not yet lost their meaning for you.

If something has become false and meaningless for you, then there will be no point to run away from it. When you wake up in the morning you don't run away from your house because in the night you had a dream there that turned out to be false. Once you realize that the dream was false, the matter is over. What is there to run away from?

But there are people who are renouncing and running away from their families, from their wives and children. This very desire to escape only shows that they may have heard somewhere that dreams are unreal, but it is not their own experience. Until yesterday a man was chasing after his wife, today he is running away from her, but in both the instances his wife remains the focus.

There was a Jaina monk by the name of Ganesh Varni. He had left his wife many years before—naturally, after all, he was a holy man. Twenty years after becoming a monk, he was in Kashi when he got the news that his wife had died. When he heard this news, it is interesting to note what he said. He said, 'Good riddance!'

His disciples interpreted these to be words of great non-attachment. But if you think about it a little, you will see that this is not the case. He had renounced the relationship with his wife twenty years before, but it had continued to be a reality within him, and that is why he could make a statement like this. The very idea of 'riddance' only shows that he was still disturbed by his relationship with the wife. To him, it was still a reality.

The arithmetic is simple: the wife he had left twenty years ago must have been following him like a shadow. He must have felt haunted by her, burdened. Even after twenty years he had not become free of her. For all that time, his mind must have been debating about whether leaving her had been right or wrong. The words 'good riddance' reveal nothing about the wife, they reveal something about him: although he had escaped from the wife, he had not been able to let go of her.

Ganesh Varni was a so-called holy man—but, beware, because your holy men can also be living in great delusion. He was a man of impeccable character, of unerring behaviour. He was virtuous, upright, and yet he missed the point: he escaped to the Himalayas, but his inner troubles remained with him.

One more thing to be understood about this: the fact that the first thought that came to him when his wife died was 'good riddance' shows that unconsciously he must have been desiring the wife's death. Try to understand this: at some deep level, he must have wished her dead and finished forever—but this only exposes the violence he had buried within.

The words you speak don't come without a reason, just out of the blue. Each and every word comes from inside you. And in moments such as these, when you suddenly get the news of your wife's death, you don't react in your normal, controlled way. What comes out of you in such moments is your reality. An hour later you would have the opportunity to correct yourself and do a whitewash, but that statement would be false. But in a moment of immediacy, when Ganesh Varni was given the news, he exposed himself. In that moment, the whole mask of holiness that he had created and kept on for twenty years was completely forgotten. If this could happen to Ganesh Varni, it can very easily happen to you.

No, running away will not help. No one has ever been able to become free just by running away. But disciples cannot see this: they think Ganesh Varni's words show what a great man he is, that he is beyond attachment. They think his words are of great significance and they have included them in his biography.

You have no idea what it means to be beyond attachment. You live in a state of attachment, so you can understand non-attachment; you can understand opposites. You know very well that you can't leave your wife, but this man did it. Obviously, you consider him to be greater than you. But this man is only your opposite; he is not different from you. You are standing on your feet while he is standing on his head, but there is not one iota of difference between your mind and his mind. Just look at yourself: you all think that your wife is trouble. Can you find a single husband who can say that his wife is not a trouble? But, please, don't ask him in front of his wife; ask him when he is alone, with no else listening.

Mulla Nasruddin said to me, 'I was a happy man once, and I only came to know of it later on, after I got married—but by then it was too late because the happiness had already slipped through my fingers.'

If you look deeply into it, you will not find a single husband who has not thought sometimes of killing his wife, who has not dreamed of murdering his wife. In the morning he may be surprised at what a ridiculous dream he had, but deep down in his unconscious, the desire was hidden there. It is a simple logic: the mind always wants to destroy the source of trouble. But the truth is that the other is never the cause of trouble. If your wife were the cause of your troubles, you would have escaped to the Himalayas long ago—who could have stopped you? No, the wife is not the source of your troubles; even if you escape to the Himalayas, you will take another wife there.

The problem is in *you*. You cannot live alone, you need the other. You are afraid of aloneness. When there is someone else around, you are at ease. Why? The presence of the other reassures you that someone will be there in good times and in bad times; someone will be there for you to rely on in life and in death.

Aloneness is your intrinsic nature. Someone who has realized that nothing or nobody else other than his own being belongs to him is the person who has known his aloneness.

There is no need to escape, the problem will follow you wherever you go. Stay where you are. There is no need for you to make even the slightest change on the outside, but inside, become aware of your aloneness, experience the total aloneness within you. Experience that you are alone, that there is no friend or companion. But please don't make it into a mantra, that you sit down every morning and chant, 'I am alone, I have no friends, no companions.' No, this will not help. This repetition will only show that it has not yet become your realization. Try to make it your understanding; that you are alone is a fact.

Your difficulty lies in understanding this. This is what is meant by *tapascharya*, ascetic discipline. Ascetic discipline does not mean that you stand under the hot sun—no. Except for man, all other animals and birds live outside, under the sun, yet none of them attains ultimate liberation! Also, ascetic discipline does not mean fasting. As it is, half the world is starving, yet no one is attaining ultimate liberation because of that. Nothing will happen by tormenting and torturing the body in this way: that is just violence against yourself. It is the greatest sin—and only idiots do it. If you have even a small amount of awareness, you will not do such stupid things. If it is wrong to starve other people, how can starving yourself be right? If torturing others is violent, how can torturing yourself be non-violent?

Torturing, as such, is violence. What difference does it make as to whom you torture? Those who are more courageous torture others; those who are weak torture themselves. In torturing others there is the danger that the other can take revenge. There is no risk in torturing yourself—who will take revenge? So it is only the weak who torture themselves. Have you ever noticed that when a man gets angry he beats his wife, but when the wife gets angry she beats herself? These wives seem to be imitating the monks.

So the weak torture themselves—what else can they do? And the powerful torture others. Obviously, there is always some risk when you torture others, because who knows what the other will do, how the other will react. So the weak are violent towards themselves and the strong are violent towards others.

A religious person is someone who is non-violent: he neither tortures others nor himself. The very idea of hurting and torturing is unthinkable to such a person.

Ascetic discipline means that you have come to understand and accept the reality that you are alone, that there is no way to have a friend or companion. No matter how much you desire it, no matter how often you close your eyes and dream about it, you will remain alone. For so many lives you have built homes, you have created families, you have lost families, but through it all you have always remained alone. Your aloneness has never been touched in the slightest.

For the person who has realized this, has accepted this—that he is alone—there is a pointer in this sutra: *Consciousness is being.* Only your being is yours, no one else.

The second thing of significance in this sutra is consciousness.

Being is not a doctrine that you read in a scripture and believe in. It is not something like the theory of gravity. 'Being' is not a theory, it is an experience, and the experience is one of the immense intensity of consciousness. So the more conscious you become, the more you will know your being; the more unconscious you become, the more you will lose contact with your being. And as you are, you are almost in a coma.

If you want to know your being, you don't need any philosophy; what you need is a method to awaken your consciousness. You need a technique that can help you become more conscious. It is like stoking a fire: ashes are created, and as you shake off the ashes the hot coals begin to glow again. In the same way, you need a technique that can shake off the ashes and allow your embers to glow again, because only in the heat of your embers will you be ready to realize that *you* are consciousness.

And the more conscious you become, the more integrated you will be with your inmost being. The day you become totally conscious will be the day you realize your godliness. You will experience your being to the same extent that you grow in consciousness. But right now, you are almost unconscious. Right now, you are almost in a drunken state: you are walking, moving and working like a somnambulist, as if you are sound asleep. You are not aware.

Has it ever happened to you when reading a book, that you read a page and suddenly realize, 'My God! I have read the whole page and I don't remember a word of it!' What was happening while you were reading? You can read a book half-asleep—your mind must have been somewhere else. You read the whole page before you realized that you were not present, and now you don't remember any of it. In the same way, sometimes you walk down an entire street before you realize that you are walking. You work without being aware that you are working.

Consciousness is being. You go on living unconsciously and then you ask, 'What is soul?' You want someone else to give you evidence? You want someone to prove it to you, to explain it to you logically so you can just believe in it. Without such an explanation you may end up becoming an atheist. Atheism is a natural outcome of unconsciousness, just as theism is an outcome of consciousness. As your consciousness grows, there is no need for any belief in the existence of being.

There are many foolish people who believe in the soul, but that doesn't *solve* anything for them. Here in India, everyone believes in the soul—what difference has it made? It does not bring a revolution into people's lives. Perhaps you believe because this idea has been repeated for thousands of years and your ears have become tired of hearing the same repetition. You have completely forgotten that you need to seek and look into it for yourself. Through repetition you become hypnotized. If the same thing is repeated again and again, you easily forget that it can be doubted, that it can be questioned, that it has to be inquired into.

To believe in the existence of the being consoles you. You know your body will die: it gives you great solace to hear that your being will not die. It gives you consolation to hear that the inmost being never dies, that fire cannot burn it, that weapons cannot pierce it, that death cannot harm it. But consolation is not truth. No, it will not help you to just accept the existence of the being as a doctrine, nor will it help you to hypnotize yourself through constant repetition. Being can only be realized by rising in consciousness.

Live your life in such a way that ash doesn't gather on you. Live in a way that the fire within you shines bright and glowing. Live in a way that you are conscious moment by moment—never unconscious.

Mulla Nasruddin had his first son. He was immensely happy, so he invited his best friend to a tavern to celebrate the occasion . . .

You know only one way to celebrate your happiness, and that is by becoming unconscious. This is strange! Shiva, Mahavira, Buddha go on saying that there is only one bliss in existence, and this is the bliss of becoming conscious—but the only happiness you know is that of becoming unconscious. Either you are right or they are right: you both cannot be right.

So instead of going to the hospital first to see his newborn son, Mulla went straight to the pub. He wanted to celebrate right away—after all, a long-awaited dream had come true—so they both got drunk.

When they reached the hospital and Mulla looked at his son through the window, he started to cry. His friend asked him why he was crying and Mulla said, 'In the first place, he doesn't look like me . . .'

Now Mulla was drunk! He could not have recognized his own face, but he immediately said that the son didn't look like him.

'And not only that,' he said, 'this boy looks very small to me. What am I supposed to do with such a small child? Do you think he will survive?'

Mulla's friend said, 'Don't worry. When I was born, I also weighed only three pounds.'

Mulla asked him, 'Did you survive?'

His friend thought about it for a moment . . . he was also very drunk. Then he said, 'I can't say for sure.'

You are unconscious. All perspectives in your life, all vision, is dominated by your unconsciousness; everything gets blurred. You become unable to see anything as it is. You only know one happiness, and that is the happiness of forgetting yourself. You try to forget yourself by going to a movie, or by listening to music, or through sex. Wherever you have been able to forget yourself, you call it great joy!

You call forgetting yourself a joy? There is a reason for it: whenever you become a little conscious, you see that apart from misery there is nothing else in your life. With just a small awareness, you immediately see pain, misery, ugliness all around.

I have a friend who has been a bachelor his whole life. I asked him, 'What happened? How did you miss getting married?'

He said, 'There was a big problem: the woman I loved looked beautiful to me only when I was drunk. When I was drunk I was ready to marry her, but she refused. When I was sober she was willing to marry me, but then I wasn't. This is how I missed getting married. What to do? There was no common ground.'

Whenever you open your eyes, you will see that there is nothing but ugliness and misery everywhere. Everything appears to be beautiful when you are unconscious. This is why it is difficult for you to conceive that consciousness is being. You say, 'Impossible!' And that is why it is necessary for you to go through pain. This has been called 'arduous spiritual discipline'. Whenever someone starts to become aware, in the beginning he will have to face his pain. For many, many lives you have created only misery for yourself—who else, if not you, can pass through it? This is what the doctrine of karma is.

'Karma' simply means that for lives upon lives you have created only misery all around you. Knowingly or not, you have sown the seeds of misery—now who else can reap the crop? So whenever you start to become aware, you see the crop—a vast expanse of crop. You have to walk through this field, but in your fear you simply collapse in helplessness. Seeing this vast field and realizing what a great harvest of pain it is, you simply close your eyes and escape into drunkenness; you become unconscious. But the more unconscious you become, the bigger your crop of misery grows. Each life that you live adds something more to your chain of karma, it does not decrease it. You fall deeper and deeper into the ditch; hell comes closer and closer.

As you grow in awareness, the first thing that is bound to happen is you will begin to see the misery in your life, the hell that you have created. But if you take courage and pass through your miseries consciously, you will have harvested the crop. Whatsoever miseries you pass through consciously are a crop that has been harvested; you will not have to go through the same miseries again.

Once you have passed through this chain of karmic miseries—the chain that has remained tied around your being—if you can pass through this with awareness, courageously, 'No problem, I will go through all this misery that I myself have created; I will get to the bottom of it; I want to return to the time when I was innocent and this journey of misery had not yet started, when my being was still absolutely pure and I had not yet accumulated any misery. I am determined to go through all the pain and sorrow up to that point, regardless of the consequences,' if you have this much courage, then it won't be long before you are bound to arrive at the point where this sutra of Shiva—*Consciousness is being*—will be clear to you.

Once you have become centred in your consciousness within, then you will never create any more misery. Only an unconscious person goes on creating misery.

Have you ever seen a drunk staggering along the street? This is how your life is; you try to put your foot down in one place and it lands somewhere else; you intend to go to one place, but you arrive somewhere else. You want to say one thing, but you end up saying something else. You want to do one thing, but you end up doing something quite different. You see this happening every day, but you don't understand the reason for it. You want to apologize to someone but you end up fighting even more. You begin with words of love, but end up with hostility. Have you lost your senses?

A drunk was walking down the street, looking up at the sky, when a car passed, and the driver barely managed to prevent an accident. He stopped his car and shouted at the drunk, 'If you don't look where you're going, you're going to go where you're looking!'

You are all in the same situation: you have no idea where you are going, why you are going, where you are looking or why you are looking. You are just on the move, because there is a restlessness in you which doesn't allow you to stop. This inner restlessness keeps you going. Then, whatsoever you do, it is bound to have the opposite effect.

People come to see me and say, 'We never did any wrong to anybody. We only did good, but what comes back to us is evil.' But it is not possible that you do good and you get bad in return. It is impossible that you plant a mango seed and the tree that grows gives the bitter fruit of the neem tree. This is impossible. The only possibility is that you, in your unconscious state, must have sown the seed of the neem tree without realizing it. How can a tree lie? You must have sown the wrong seeds by mistake.

Even when you do some good, it is not that your intentions are necessarily good. Even when you speak the truth, you may do it to hurt the other person. You can speak the truth to insult somebody. It is as if you are using the truth as a deadly weapon of some kind. Your truths are bitter. The truth need not be bitter; but your joy is in the bitterness, not in the truth. Your lies are always sweet, your truth is always bitter. What is happening? Is bitterness the nature of truth? Is sweetness intrinsic to lie?

No, the fact is that you want your lie to work, so you make it sound sweet. You know perfectly well that, otherwise, it won't work. In the first place, you know that a lie will be difficult to spread unless you coat it with sweetness. It is like sugar-coating a bitter pill: a child will swallow it thinking that it is candy. And before the child has had a chance to discover the bitterness, the pill will be swallowed.

You make a lie sound sweet because you want to sell the lie. You make the truth sound bitter, not because you are interested in supporting the truth, but because you want to use it to hurt others. You only speak the truth when you can use it in such a way that it becomes even worse than a lie.

You are unconscious, you are completely unaware of your actions. It will be good if you can begin to watch this with awareness: did you say exactly what you intended to say, or did you end up saying something different? Was what you said really what you meant to say?

Mark Twain returned home one evening. His wife asked him, 'How did your speech go?'

He answered, 'Which one? The one I prepared, the one I actually gave, or the one that I now think I should have given?'

The speech you prepare to deliver, and what you actually end up delivering, are very different. Then on your way back home, as you think about what you should have said . . . These are all three very different things.

Are you in your right senses? It seems you go on missing all your targets. Have you ever hit a single target in your life? Even a man wearing a blindfold will hit the target sometimes if he just goes on shooting. Did you know that even a stopped clock will show the right time twice in twenty-four hours? But in your life there are not even two occasions when you get things right. Is your situation worse than a stopped clock? Even a man who goes on shooting arrows in the dark will manage to hit the target one day. You shoot arrows with your eyes open, in broad daylight, and yet you never hit the mark. What can be the reason for this?

Mulla Nasruddin liked to hunt deer. On his third hunting trip, when he reached the lodge and opened his suitcase, he found a large photograph, at the bottom of which his wife had written, 'Mulla dearest, this is what a deer looks like.'

Although Mulla loved to hunt deer, still, he had no idea about what a deer looked like. His wife just wanted to make sure that he didn't kill the wrong animal and bring it home as deer, hence the photograph.

You have missed the target every time and this is the misery of your life. And the only reason why you miss is that you are unconscious. So from now on, whatsoever you do, do it consciously. Rise with awareness, walk with awareness . . .

Mahavira has said, 'Walk with awareness, sit with awareness, eat with awareness, speak with awareness and even sleep with awareness.'

Someone asked Mahavira, 'Who is a holy man?'
And he said, 'One who is aware.'
And then he was asked, 'And who is a sinner?'
Mahavira answered, 'One who is unaware.'

The person who lives as if asleep is the sinner; the person who lives in awareness is the holy man.

This is exactly what Shiva means when he says, 'Consciousness is being.'

Keep growing in your consciousness and, by and by, you are bound to have a glimpse of being in your life.

The second sutra:
Knowledge is bondage.

This sutra is puzzling. But the word 'knowledge' has many meanings. One, as long as you are full of the knowledge that you 'are' you will remain in ignorance—because 'I', the ego, is ignorance. On the day you will be full of being, the 'am-ness' will remain, but the 'I-ness' will disappear.

You can try an experiment with this. Sit quietly under a tree and look inside yourself, search—where is the 'I'? You will not find it anywhere. You will find am-ness all over, but the 'I' is nowhere. 'Is-ness' you will find all over, but there will be no 'I' anywhere there with the is-ness.

The ego is your creation, it is of your own making. It is false, unreal; there is nothing more inauthentic than 'I'. It is functional, it is needed in the world, but it has no place anywhere in the world of truth.

So the knowledge based on the sense that 'I am' is one kind of knowledge, and is the cause of bondage. This knowledge has the sense of 'I', not the sense of am-ness. The sense of am-ness is pure, without any boundaries. When you say 'am', is there any difference between your am-ness and the am-ness of a tree? Is there any distinction between your am-ness and my am-ness? When you simply are, then you, the rivers, the mountains, the trees all become one. But as soon as you say 'I', you become separate from the whole. The moment you say 'I', you break yourself away, you alienate yourself and you disconnect yourself from existence.

Am-ness is Brahman, the absolute reality, and 'I' is man's state of ignorance. When you experience simple am-ness, then there is no separate centre within you. Then you are one with the whole existence. Then you are like a wave that has disappeared into the ocean. As you are now, you are like a wave that is frozen into ice and alienated from the ocean.

Knowledge is bondage. The first kind of knowledge, the knowledge that says 'I am' is one bondage. The second kind of knowledge that is bondage is all the knowledge that you have gathered from the outside, from others. This is the knowledge that you have stolen from the scriptures, that you have borrowed from the great masters—whatever is just memorized by you, all of that is bondage. It will not bring you liberation. This is why you will not find a man who is more in bondage than the pandit.

All kinds of people come to me, all sorts of patients, but none are more afflicted with the cancer of knowledge than the pandit, the scholar. There is no cure for him; he is beyond a cure. The trouble with the scholar is that he already knows, so he can neither listen nor can he understand. You say something to him and, before you have even finished your statement, he has already given it a meaning. You can say something to him and, even before you have finished speaking, he has given it his own interpretation. A mind that is filled with words is incapable of wisdom. The scholar knows so much without actually knowing anything, because all his knowledge is borrowed.

If knowing, wisdom, could be attained through scriptures then everyone would be wise because everyone has access to the scriptures. Knowing is found only when you have gone beyond words and become silent—when you have let go of all scriptures, when you give back to the world all the knowledge that you have got from others and seek the reality which is your own essential essence and not borrowed from anyone.

Try to understand this a little more deeply.

You have received your body from both your parents. In your body, nothing is yours: half of your body comes from your father and the other half comes from your mother. Then your body is made up of the food you eat every day, and then your body contains the five elements: air, fire and so on. You cannot claim any of these as yours. But your consciousness is none of these elements, nor have you received it from your parents.

Whatever you know, you have learned it from your schools and universities; you have heard it quoted from your scriptures; you have received it from your priests and religious teachers; but all this is part of your body, not of your being. Your being is that which you have received from no one. Your true essence is that which you have not received from anybody—your mother or father, the society, your religious teachers or the scriptures. And until you have discovered this true nature which is innately yours, not given to you by anyone . . .

Knowledge is bondage because it does not allow you to reach your true nature, your true essence. This is the knowledge that has divided man. You say you are a Hindu, but have you ever thought about why? You say you are a Mohammedan, but have you ever considered why? What is the difference between a Hindu and a Mohammedan? Can a physician decide from a blood test that this blood belongs to a Hindu and this to a Mohammedan? Can anyone ever determine whether a particular bone has been taken from the body of a Hindu or a Mohammedan? No, there is no way. You will not find out anything by doing an autopsy, because the bodies of both Hindus and Mohammedans are made of the same five elements.

But if you examine their minds, you will certainly know who is a Hindu and who is a Mohammedan, because their scriptures are different, their doctrines are different, their language is different. The difference between the two is just of words. You are a Hindu because you have received one kind of knowledge that is labelled 'Hindu'. Somebody is a Jaina because they have received a different kind of knowledge that is called 'Jaina'. All the differences between you, all the walls between you, are those of knowledge—and the knowledge is all borrowed.

If you raise a Mohammedan child in a Hindu household, the child will grow up to be a Hindu: he will wear the sacred thread of a Brahmin, he will quote from the Vedas and the

Upanishads. In the same way, let a Hindu child be brought
up in a Mohammedan household, and the child will begin
reciting verses from the Koran.

Knowledge divides you because it builds walls all
around you. It makes you fight with your fellow human
beings and brings hostility and conflict into your life. Just
think a little: if you were never taught that you are a Hindu,
a Mohammedan, a Jaina, a Zoroastrian or a Christian,
what would you be? You would grow up as a human being,
without any walls around you.

There are some three hundred religions in the world—
three hundred prisons. Each person is forced to be locked
up in one prison or the other as soon as he is born. And
the priests try their best to condition the child as early
as possible. They call it 'religious education', but there
is nothing more irreligious than this. The child is caught
early, before the age of seven, because after this it will be
more difficult to have control over the child. If the child
begins to understand even a little, the child will start raising
questions—and the pandits and the priests have absolutely
no answers to those questions.

The pandit can only satisfy idiots. The less intelligent
a person, the more easily he will be satisfied by the pandit.
He asks a question and the answer is provided. If you ask
a pandit, 'Who created the world?' he will answer, 'God
created the world.' You will go home happy and satisfied
without asking him, 'But who created God?' The pandit
would have been annoyed if you had asked this second
question because he doesn't know the answer himself.
The answer is not written in any book. It is a troublesome
question, this 'Who created God?' You can go on endlessly
asking this question, no matter what answer you are
given. If you look at it closely, you will find that your first
question was not answered at all: seeing that you are not

so intelligent, the pandit has merely put a cover over your curiosity.

Children are innocent. Their faculties of thinking and reasoning have not yet developed. They are not in a position to ask questions, so whatever garbage you dump in their brains, they accept it. Children are open to everything because they feel that whatsoever is being told to them must be right. A child cannot raise many questions, because to be able to raise questions you need a certain amount of maturity. This is why all the religions take a hold of children and virtually strangle their very potential. This strangling appears to be very decorative, very ornamental: one has a Bible hanging around his neck, another his *Samayasar* or his Gita. These 'decorations' are so endearing that later on it will need tremendous courage to get rid of them. And whenever you try to let go of them, you will face a very great fear: to let go of these scriptures will feel to you like becoming ignorant. You will discover that without them you know nothing. These scriptures were your only wealth, so you anxiously guard them with your life. They are your only means to hide your ignorance.

It would have been so simple if it were possible to destroy ignorance just by hiding it. The fact is that ignorance grows the more you hide it. It is like hiding a wound, but hiding a wound will not heal it. Instead, it will grow deeper and deeper inside and the pus will spread throughout the body.

Shiva says: *Knowledge is bondage.* The knowledge that is learned, borrowed or taken from others is the cause of your bondage. Drop everything you have acquired from others and go in search of something you have not received from anyone else. Search for your original face. There is a spring of consciousness hidden within which has not been given to you by anybody. It is your very nature, your own real treasure, your individuality—and this is your being.

The third sutra:
   The body is a union of nature and ego (the doer).
   The word 'yoni' (womb) means 'prakriti' (nature). This is why we call the woman also prakriti, nature. The woman gives birth to the body; she represents nature. The word 'kala' (art) means 'the sense of doing'. And there is only one art, and that is the art of entering into this world. In fact, you are born into a body only because of your belief in yourself as the doer.
   Your body is created from two things: your sense of being a doer, the ego, plus the physical form, which you get from nature. As long as you have a sense of 'doing', nature will go on providing you with an appropriate body. This is how you are born into a body again and again. Sometimes you were an animal, a bird or something else; at some other time you may have been a tree and, at yet another time, a human being.
   Whatever you have desired, you have received. The desire of 'doing' that you have carried has been actualized. Thoughts become real things, so be very alert when you desire something, because sooner or later it will materialize. If you enjoy watching birds fly and you think, 'How free! I wish I was a bird!' then sooner or later you will be a bird. If you see dogs mating and the thought arises in you, 'They are so free. What fun they must be having,' then sooner or later you will be born as a dog. Whatever desire you accumulate within you is like a seed.
   Nature only gives you the body; you are the artist, its creator. You have created your own body—that is the meaning of kala. No one else can give you a body: it is your very desire of doing that has created your body.
   Have you ever noticed how your last thought before you fall asleep at night becomes your first thought when you wake up in the morning? All night long, while you were sleeping, the thought remained within you like a seed. So your last thought at night is your first thought in the morning. At the

moment of death all desires from your lifetime will gather and become a seed. This seed will become the beginning of a new womb, of a new birth. You will just start again from where you had left off.

Whatever you are is your own doing. Don't blame anybody else for it. In the first place, there is no one else you can blame. It is just the cumulative effect of your own actions. Whatsoever you are—beautiful or ugly, happy or unhappy, man or woman—whatsoever you are is the cumulative outcome of your own actions. You are the architect of your life. Don't say that destiny has made you, because that will be simply deceiving yourself. That way you are dumping the responsibility on someone else. Don't say that existence has sent you as a body; don't dump the responsibility on existence. That is just a strategy to avoid taking your own responsibility. You are in this prison called body only because of yourself. For someone who understands this—that 'I am the cause of my being here in this world'—a revolution happens in his life.

Shiva is saying: *The body is a union of nature and ego, the doer.* Nature is just the womb, the field. It is your ego that becomes the seed in it. Your sense of doing, that 'I should do this and that, I should achieve this and that, I should become this and that,' functions as the seed. Whenever your art of being the doer meets with the womb of nature, a body is created.

This is why the buddhas say to drop all desires and only then will you be liberated. If you desire heaven, you will become a god—but even that is not liberation. The state of freedom from the need for a body does not happen through desire. All desires lead to the formation of a physical body.

As long as you have not become desire-less, as long as you have not left desiring completely, you will go on being born again and again into new bodies. And no matter how different the forms of these bodies may be, their basic reality is still the same. All bodies suffer in the same way.

Whether it is the body of a bird or of a human being, there is no difference in the suffering because, fundamentally, all suffering is one: the confinement of the being in a body, its entry into the prison of the body. Then whether the walls of the prison are circular or rectangular or triangular makes no difference—even if you think it makes a difference.

A friend of mine is an art teacher. He was sentenced to three years in prison. When he came out, I asked, 'How did it go? How was your time in prison?'

He said, 'Everything was okay, just that the corners of my prison cell were not at right angles.'

This is the mind of an art teacher: he was upset that the corners of his cell were not at ninety degrees! This was his real problem during those three years—staying in the same prison cell day in, day out, seeing the same corners of the cell again and again, and they were not at right angles.

So he said to me, 'Everything else was fine, there was no particular difficulty at all—just that the walls of the prison cell were not at a ninety-degree angle.'

What real difference does it make whether the corners are set at ninety degrees or not? A prison is a prison! So whether a body is that of a bird or a human being does not make much difference. The fact is that you are imprisoned, and that is the misery. You are in bondage, and that is the suffering.

Desire creates bondage. Desire is the rope that binds us. And remember, except for you, no one else is responsible.

The fourth sutra:
Endeavour is bhairava, Brahman.

Udyama is the endeavour by which you try to come out of this prison. This endeavour itself is bhairava. Bhairava is a technical term: *bha* means 'that which sustains and maintains', *ra* means 'that which destroys' and *va* means 'that which creates, expands'. So 'bhairava' means 'the Brahman, the ultimate truth which supports and sustains all, out of which we are born and into which we will eventually disappear; the expansion and eventual contraction, the collapse; that which is the origin, the birth of all, and into which all will dissolve'. This is the very source, the existence.

Shiva says the spiritual endeavour is bhairava, the original source. The day you begin your spiritual endeavour, you start becoming one with the original source of all existence. With the first rays of your endeavour, your journey towards the sun, its source, has begun. With the first thought of liberation that arises in you, the destination is not far away because the first step is almost half the journey.

Endeavour is bhairava . . . You will attain it, although it will take some time for you. It will take a little time before you reach the destination. But as soon as you have started making efforts and the seed is planted within you—'May I get out of this prison, may I become free of the body, may I be released from all desires, may I cease to behave in ways that increase my entanglement with this world, may I be free from the desire to come into this world again'—as soon you are afire with the longing to end your unconsciousness and become more and more conscious, you have already started to move closer to the original source, you have already started to become one with the Brahman.

In fact, you are already one with the Brahman, it only needs to be remembered. You are already intrinsically one with it. You are a stream of the same ocean, a ray of the same sun, a tiny part of the same vast sky. Once you begin to remember this and your prison walls begin to crumble, you are merged with infinite space.

Endeavour is bhairava . . . Great effort will be needed, because your sleep is very deep, and only a consistent effort will be able to break it. Being lazy will not do. If you dissolve your sleep today and you go back to sleep tomorrow, then you will continue to wander for life after life. If you break your sleep on the one hand and keep going back to sleep on the other, all your effort will have been in vain. So, 'udyama' means making an all-out effort.

People come to me and say, 'We make the effort, but nothing is happening.' When I look at their faces I can see that they make no effort at all, or even if they do, it is always just lukewarm. There is no intensity of life in their efforts: this is why nothing happens to them. But they come to me with an attitude, as if they are doing existence a big favour by making efforts, and yet nothing is happening. They come with a complaint that something fishy must be going on, that some injustice must be happening to them, otherwise, why is it that things happen to others, but not to them?

No injustice ever happens in this universe. Whatever happens is always just and right. There is nobody sitting up there meting out either justice or injustice. In existence there are certain basic laws, and these laws are called dharma. If you walk around scatterbrained, you are bound to fall down and break your leg. In that case you wouldn't go to the court to sue the Law of Gravitation. Gravity is not interested in either causing you to fall or in stopping you from falling. If you walk straight, that will protect you from falling; if you don't walk straight, you will fall down. Gravity has no interest in either seeing you fall down or in saving you from falling down. The laws of the universe are neutral.

Dharma is the name for this neutrality of the universe. The Hindus call it *rit*: it is the supreme law. It shows no favouritism either in making one person fall or in lifting someone else up—nothing of the sort. When you walk correctly, the law protects you. If you want to fall down, it will help you fall down; the law applies in all conditions. You can use it however you like, it is always open and available to you, its doors are never closed. If you want to hit your head against a closed door, it will not stop you. If you want to push the door open and walk through, it will let you. The law itself is neutral.

Endeavour is bhairava . . . Great effort is needed. Udyama means an intense effort. When your effort is total it is called udyama, endeavour. Then it will not be long before you reach the goal.

The fifth sutra:

The world ceases to be for one whose circle of energy is complete.

If you have made the right effort, if you have put your total energy into your search for truth, for being, then your circle of energy will be complete. Right now it is not whole: it is fragmented, divided.

Scientists say that even the most intelligent person in the world uses not more than 15 per cent of his intelligence—the remaining 85 per cent goes to rot! This is about the intelligent ones: what to say about the fools? Perhaps the fool never uses his intelligence at all. We don't use more than 5 per cent of our physical energy. So if you live an apathetic, lifeless life, if you live in a lukewarm way, whose fault is it? You just never live totally, as if you are afraid to live in case the flame of life starts flaring up in you. You live in fear; you live, trembling; so your circle of energy never becomes whole, complete.

Your life is like a car that moves in jerks because it has been filled with dirty gas that makes it hiccup. This is how you live, hesitating and halting, like a car with hiccups. Your energy moves in fits and starts, bit by bit; it is never an integrated whole.

If you put your total energy into whatsoever you are doing . . . For example, if you are a painter, if you put your total energy into painting without holding anything back, right then and there you will be free because the moment the endeavour is total, it becomes bhairava. If you are a sculptor and you pour your total energy into sculpting so totally that you disappear and only the sculpture remains, then the circle of energy becomes complete. When you put your total energy into whatever you are doing, it becomes meditation. Then bhairava is close by, the temple is nearby.

The fifth sutra says: *The world ceases to be for one whose circle of energy is complete.* Whenever your circle of energy becomes complete, total, unbroken, whole, in that very moment the world ceases to exist for you. Then for you there is no world, you have entered existence. You have become bhairava. You are free. Then there is no longer any bondage for you, no further need for a body, no more need for any world.

Remember to bring your total energy into this meditation camp. If you put your total energy into the meditations and don't just do them superficially, you will experience that in the moment your energy becomes total; in that very same instant, suddenly, the world as you now know it will disappear. You will be facing the ultimate. Your totality will become the transformation of your life. Then you will be facing the absolute and the world is left behind.

One glimpse of this experience and you will never again be the same. One glimpse is enough to bring your whole life to this journey.

So remember while you are here, to throw yourself totally into it; only then is something possible. If you hold yourself back even a little, all your effort will be useless. Unless your effort becomes total, you will not experience the original source.

Enough for today.

2

The Art of Dis-identification

When one has known the waking, dream and deep-sleep states without identification, the fourth state is known.

The waking state is presence of perception.

The dream state is shifting imagination.

The deep-sleep state is the absence of perception and self-awareness.

One who knows the three states is the Lord of Warriors, Shiva.

When one has known the waking, dream and deep-sleep states without identification, the fourth state is known.

TURIYA IS THE fourth state. The state of turiya means the ultimate knowing. To be in the state of turiya means that there is no darkness of any kind within, that all is illuminated; not even a tiny patch of the inner world is left in darkness. There is nothing within you of which you are not aware. The light of wakefulness has spread all around, everywhere, within and without.

As we are now, we are either *superficially awake, or dreaming, or in deep sleep.* We have no idea whatsoever of a fourth state. When we are awake we see the outside world, but the inner being is in darkness. We see objects, but we have no awareness of our own selves. The world is seen, but there is no awareness of the being. It is a state of semi-waking, of half-wakefulness. In the morning, when we come out of sleep, what we think of as being awake is just this half-awake state. This is not really of any value because it is the non-essential that is seen, and the essential remains hidden. We see the rubbish, but the diamonds remain in the darkness. We can see the whole world, but we do not see who we are.

The second state is the state of dreaming. In the dream state, not only do we *not* see ourselves, but the outside world also disappears. All we see are images floating in the mind, reflections of the outside world. We see these reflections the way we might see the moon or the stars mirrored in a lake. In our so-called waking state we see objects directly; in the dream state not even objects are seen—we see only their reflections.

The third state that we are acquainted with is the state of deep sleep. In this state, not only is the external world, the world of objects, lost to us, but even their reflections, the dreams, disappear, and we are left in deep darkness. This is known as deep sleep. In this state we have no perception either of the outer world or of the inner world.

In the waking state we perceive the outer world. In the dream state, which is between waking and deep sleep, we perceive the reflections of outer objects that float in our minds, but not the objects themselves.

The fourth state is known as turiya. This is the state of enlightenment, fulfilment. The whole search and effort is for this state. All meditations, all disciplines of yoga, are efforts to reach this fourth state. The fourth state is the perception of both the inner and the outer, it is total awakening. There is no darkness left, either within or without. This state has been called 'buddhahood'. Mahavira has called it *jinahood*, the state of being a *jina*, one who is victorious over oneself. The light has spread everywhere, within and without, and in this light we know objects and we also know ourselves.

These sutras are about how to reach this fourth state.

The first sutra says:

When one has known the waking, dream and deep-sleep states without identification, the fourth state is known.

As we are now, we know, but not in a dis-identified way. When we dream we are not aware that we are dreaming; we become completely identified with the dream. It is only when we wake up in the morning that we realize we were dreaming, but by the time we realize this, the state has long since disappeared. While we are in the dream state we are not aware of it as separate; we are identified with the dream. It feels as though we *are* the dream. In the morning, by the time we realize it was a dream we are already identified with the waking state. You say, 'Now I am awake,' but have you ever thought about the fact that by the time night comes you will again fall asleep and forget your identification with the waking state? Again a dream will come and you will become identified with the dream.

You become identified with whatever comes in front of you, although the truth is that you are separate from all these states. It is as if the rainy season comes and you start feeling that you are the rain, or summer comes and you start feeling that you are the heat of the summer, or winter comes and you start feeling that you are the cold of the winter. But the actuality is that the three seasons are around you, you are totally separate from them.

In childhood you thought you were a child; in your adolescence you think you are young, when old age comes you will think that you have become old, but you are beyond all three. If this were not so, how could the child become a young man? There is something within you that could leave childhood behind and continue on into youth. That something is separate from childhood and youth both.

You become lost in your dream, and when you wake up, you again know it was a dream. There is an element of consciousness within you that is a traveller—the waking, dream and deep-sleep states are just stops along the way, but you are not them. As soon as you understand the fact that you are separate—apart—the birth of the fourth state will begin in you. This separateness, this apartness, *is* the fourth state.

Mahavira has coined a beautiful word for this state. He calls it the 'art of discrimination'. He says that the whole science of spirituality consists in making careful discriminations. And this is also what the Shiva Sutra aims at: you should realize that each of the three states is separate from you. As soon as this realization happens you will know your separate reality. You will have learned the art of discriminating. Right now, the state of your mind is such that you become identified with whatever appears before you.

Someone abuses you and you become angry. In that moment you become one with anger. You completely forget that a moment before there was no anger but you existed, and in another moment the anger will pass away, but you will still be. So anger is the smoke that momentarily surrounds you, and no matter how strongly it surrounds you, it is not your true nature.

When you are anxious, clouds of worry cover your consciousness, and you forget completely that you are separate from it. Happiness comes and you start dancing with joy; sorrow comes and you start crying—whatever happens, you become one with it. You are not aware of your separateness.

By and by, you will have to learn to separate yourself. You will have to learn to separate yourself in every situation. While eating, you must be aware that it is the body that feels the hunger, not you, and it is the body that is eating, not you. You are only the observer. Consciousness feels no hunger. When you feel hot and you perspire, remember that it is the body which perspires. This does not mean that you should go on sitting in the sun and let your body perspire, no. Move away, make things comfortable for the body, but remember the comfort is being created for the body, you are just the observer.

Slowly, slowly go on standing apart from everything that overpowers you. It is difficult to separate yourself. The gap is very small, and the boundaries are not clear at all, because, for millions of lives, you have learned only to identify. You have never learned dis-identification. You learned to always identify with every situation. You have totally forgotten the art of dis-identification. And the identification that you have developed is called unconsciousness.

One morning Mulla Nasruddin was sitting at the bedside of his friend who was in the hospital. The friend opened his eyes and said, 'What happened, Nasruddin? I can't remember what happened.'

'Last night you just had a little too much to drink,' said the Mulla. 'Then you stood at the window and said you could fly. And you did fly out of the window. We were on the third floor of the house, and the result is clear: you have multiple fractures!'

The friend was shocked. He said, 'But you were with me, Mulla! Why did you allow this to happen? What kind of a friend are you?'

'Let's not talk about that,' said Nasruddin. 'At that time I was also convinced that you could fly. In fact, if the string of my pyjamas had not been loose I would have come with you. But my only thought was how I will keep my pyjamas in place while flying! That held me back and I am safe. You weren't the only one who was drunk.'

Unconsciousness means becoming identified with whatever comes into your mind. If the drunk's mind got the idea that he could fly, he could not discriminate. There was no space for discrimination in him. There was no room for awareness; he had become one with the thought.

Your life is exactly the same as this drunkard's. You don't fly out of the window and break your bones and land in the hospital, but if you look closely you will find that you *are* in hospital with all your bones broken. Your whole life is one long illness, which gives you nothing but pain and suffering. You have fallen down at every step, you have hurt yourself at every step. And there is only one reason for all this devastation: your unconsciousness. You have not created any distance between you and what is happening to you.

Just create a little distance, step by step. It is an arduous journey, because what you have built over millions of lifetimes cannot be destroyed so easily. But it can be done, because that is your true nature and whatever you have created is false. This is why Hindus call it maya. 'Maya' means the world that you live in is false. It does not mean that the sun and the stars, the mountains and the trees outside are false; it only means that your identification with them is false. And you live in this identification; that is your world.

How to break this identification? First, start from your waking state, because only in your waking state is there a small ray of consciousness. How can you start with your dream state? It would be very difficult. And you don't know the deep-sleep state at all, because all consciousness is lost there. Begin with the waking state—that is where your spiritual path begins, that is the first step. The second step is the dream state, and the third is the deep-sleep state. The day you are aware in all three states you will naturally have moved into the fourth, turiya, the state of the awakened one.

Begin with the waking state, that is the path. This is why it is called the waking state, although it is not wakefulness at all. What kind of wakefulness is it when you are lost in objects and you have no awareness of your own self? How to call it a waking state? It is a waking state only in name, but it has been called the waking state. The reality is that only the buddhas, the enlightened ones, are awake. But yours is an awake state in the sense that in this state there is *some* possibility of becoming awake.

Start with the waking state. When hungry, eat, but always keep a remembrance that it is the body that becomes hungry, not you. If you hurt your leg, take care of the wound, apply some medicine, but always keep a remembrance inside that it is the body that is hurt, not you. You will find that with just this much remembrance, 99 per cent of the pain has vanished. Even this small awareness will remove your pain instantly. Only 1 per cent is bound to remain, because your awareness is not yet total. The day your awareness is total, suffering will disappear completely.

Buddha has said that an awakened person ceases to suffer. You cannot make him suffer. You can cut off his limbs, you can throw him in the fire, you can kill him, but you cannot make him suffer because he remains separate, each moment, from everything that is happening.

So start with the waking state. Walking, remember that it is not you who is walking, it is the body that is walking. *You* have never walked. How can you? Being has no feet to walk with. Being has no stomach to feel hungry. Being has no desires, all desires belong to the body. The being is desire-less, hence it can never walk. It is only your body that walks. Try to keep this awareness as much as possible. By and by, you will have a unique and thrilling experience: walking on the road, one day, suddenly, you will feel that the body is walking and not you. You will have become divided into two parts: one part, which is walking, and the other part, which is not walking; or one part that is eating and the other that is not eating.

The Upanishads say that two birds are sitting on the same tree, and the one on the upper branch is calm. It does not move or fly, it neither becomes sad nor happy, it neither comes nor goes, it just sits serenely. The one on the lower branch is very restless: it jumps from one branch to another branch, it jumps from one fruit to another. It weaves many dreams, it is very busy. Both of these birds are inside you—and it is you who are that tree. The bird that is calm, unmoving, simply sitting there watching, is called the witness.

Jesus says that you sleep in a bed, but there are two of you: one is dead, and the other is forever alive. One has always been dead, and the other will always be alive. You, yourself, are that bed. When you sleep at night, there is one in you that is dead and one that is eternally conscious. But to discriminate between the two, to maintain a distance between the two, an intense endeavour is needed.

Start with the daytime. With the first ray of consciousness, as you wake up in the morning, start the experiment. After a thousand attempts, perhaps, you will succeed, but even if one attempt is successful you will realize that the thousands of attempts have been worthwhile. If, even for a moment, you come to experience that the one who moves is not you, you are the one who is unmoving; the one who is full of desires is not you, the one who is forever desireless is you; the one who is mortal is not you, the one who is immortal is you; if you become aware of this, even for a moment—if you become a Mahavira or a Buddha or if you reach the state of a Shiva, even for a moment—you will have opened the doors of the ultimate treasure. After this, the journey becomes easy. After tasting it once, the journey is very easy. All the difficulty is before you have tasted.

Start with the daytime, and gradually you will be able to carry this awareness into your dream state.

Gurdjieff, one of the great masters of this century, used to teach his disciples to first practise awareness during the day, and then he would ask them to keep awareness in dreaming. And the process was that just before falling asleep they must try to remain aware of only one thing: that this is a dream. While still awake and when they were not yet dreaming, they had to keep reminding themselves of the thread: 'Everything I am seeing is a dream.'

Look around the room and let this feeling sink in deeply: that what you are seeing is a dream. Touch the bed and let the feeling deepen—'Whatever I am touching is a dream.' Touch one hand with the other and experience—'What I am touching is a dream.' Let sleep overcome you as you go on deepening these feelings. This continuous stream of feelings will remain within you.

After a few days you will find that in the middle of a dream you have suddenly become aware that it is a dream. And the moment you become aware that you are dreaming, the dream shatters, because for a dream to continue, the absence of awareness is a must; no dream can continue without the absence of awareness. In the middle of the dream you will become aware that it is a dream, and the dream will break, and you will be filled with such bliss as you have never known before. Your sleep will be broken, the dream will disappear, and a profound light will surround you.

An enlightened one does not dream, because even while he sleeps he is able to keep the awareness that it is a dream.

In India they have experimented deeply with the idea that the world is maya—illusion. Shankara's Vedanta philosophy is nothing but an experiment in this. The seeker has to continuously remember, around the clock, that whatever is happening is a dream. While awake, walking on the road, in the middle of the marketplace, he has to remember that all is a dream. Why? Because this is a method, a process, a technique. If you have kept this remembrance throughout the day, it will have penetrated so deeply in you that even in the middle of a dream in the night you will be able to keep the remembrance that it is a dream. Right now you cannot do this.

If understood rightly, you will see you are doing it even now, but in the reverse order: while you are awake you feel and think that everything you are seeing is real. It is because of this perception that even when you see a dream in the night, you take it to be real.

What can be falser than dreams? How many times have you realized when you woke up in the morning that your dream was false, meaningless? Yet, every night you make the same mistake again. Why? There must be a very deep reason behind this folly. The reason is that everything you see when you are awake, you take to be real. And when you take everything you see to be real, then how can you know that the dream that you see at night is not real? You take the dream also to be real.

The experiment of maya, illusion, is just the opposite. In it, the whole time you go on remembering that whatever you come across is unreal. You will forget again and again, but again and again keep remembering that it is unreal.

Remind yourself that everything that you see all around you is nothing but a vast drama in which you are only a spectator. You are not an actor, not the doer, but only a witness.

If you nourish this awareness, it will become a constant flow within you. Finally, your dreams begin to break in the middle in the night, and this will be a great attainment. When dreams break, you are ready to take the third step. If your dreams are shattered, you will be able to take the third step of remaining aware in deep sleep. But right now this will be difficult for you. It is not possible to do it all at once; you have to proceed step by step.

When a dream breaks, there is nothing to see. In the daytime, when your eyes are open, objects are very visible. No matter how much you believe that it is maya, illusion, objects will go on being there. No matter how much Shankara says that the world is an illusion, even he must use a door to go out, even he can't walk through the wall. Although everything is an illusion, you will eat food and not pebbles. No matter how much he goes on saying that all is illusion, he will speak only if there is a listener, he won't speak if no one is there.

So in the outer world, no matter how deeply you go into the feeling that the world is an illusion, the world of objects is going to remain. If someone hits your head with a stone, you will bleed. You may not feel anguish, you may not suffer for it, you may say that it is all illusion; you may succeed in remaining dis-identified, but in any case the incident will have happened.

However, there is one unique thing about dreams. Because they are totally illusory, an extraordinary experiment becomes possible in the realm of dreams: the moment you come to know that the dream is an illusion, it disappears; there is nothing left to be seen, there is no object. And only when the object is completely gone can the vision turn back to the seer. As long as there is something to see, you will look outside, because the scene attracts you. When the scene is no longer there, when the screen is empty, when even the screen is no longer there, you are left alone. This is why a meditator meditates with closed eyes, because to call this world maya, an illusion, is a technique, a method.

The world is real. Its existence does not depend on what you think about it. Even if it is a dream, it is a dream of existence—and not yours. But there are personal dreams, and they arise when you sleep. Hence, the most revolutionary thing happens when you break your dreaming: the sky becomes completely empty, there is nothing to see. The play is over and it is time to go home. Now what will you do just sitting there? This is the moment when your eyes suddenly turn in, because there is nothing left on the outside to see, to be sought, to be thought. No object remains, so the energy that had been flowing towards objects now turns towards itself, the observer.

Meditation is energy turning towards yourself. And the moment energy turns towards yourself, you can be aware even in *sushupti*—in deep sleep—because in deep sleep you exist, but the world does not exist, the dreams don't exist. You are caught looking towards the world and your dreams, so you remain unconscious in the deep-sleep state. Now this entanglement is uprooted. Now you have no connection with what is seen, now you can be without it. Now the lamp simply burns; it has no concern with whether or not someone passes under its light. Now your consciousness will turn inward. Then you will be awake, even in deep sleep.

What you have to do after your dream is broken is not to open your eyes yet, because once you open your eyes, the world of objects is there once again. The seen will come back. So as your dream breaks, don't open your eyes, just go on looking at the emptiness. The dream has vanished, nothing is there in its place—just go on observing that emptiness. In doing this, you will find that your consciousness has turned inward. Then you are awake even in deep sleep.

This is what Krishna means when he says in the Gita, that the yogi, the meditator, is awake even when everyone else sleeps. What sleep is to others is not sleep to the meditator: he is awake even in deep sleep.

When you have known each of these three states separately, you become the fourth. The word 'turiya' means 'the fourth', simply 'the fourth'. There is no other meaning to it, and there is no need to give it any other meaning. It is enough just to call it 'the fourth' because all definitions will confine it, all words will confine it. Just an indication is enough, because it is boundless, infinite.

As soon as you step out of the first three states, you are existence itself. You have become narrow because you entered into them. It is as if from being under the open sky you enter a tunnel, and the tunnel becomes narrower and narrower. By the time you reach the point of having five senses, you have become very narrow. Now you will have to go in reverse. As you move farther and farther back, your spaciousness will increase. The day you find yourself outside the first three states, you have become as vast as the sky, you have become existence itself.

Take another example: you look at the sky through a telescope, and through the tiny lens of the telescope your whole attention becomes narrow and focused on some outside object. When you take your eyes away from the telescope, then you realize that you are not the telescope.

In the same way, you are not your eyes, but you have looked through them for many lives. You are not your ears, but you have been listening through them for many, many lives. You are not your hands, but you are so used to touching with them for many lives. You have become attached to your telescope! You are like a scientist who has become so accustomed to his telescope that he goes around with it fixed to his eyes. No matter how much you tell him, 'Put away that telescope. You are not it!' he can see only through the telescope and he has forgotten that there is any other way to see. This is forgetfulness.

The process of destroying this forgetfulness starts in the waking state and culminates in the deep-sleep state.

When one has known the waking, dream and deep-sleep states without identification, the fourth state is known. Begin, and move on from one to the other. On the day you become totally conscious in deep sleep, you will know that, now, there is no difference between you and a Mahavira or a Buddha or a Shiva.

But you are doing just the opposite: even when you are awake, you are not fully awake, so how can you be awake in deep sleep? Even here you are asleep—your waking state is in name only. You have the illusion that you are awake because you manage to carry out your day-to-day activities. You ride your bicycle or drive your car and think that you are awake. But have you ever realized how automatic all this has become? A cyclist doesn't even have to think that now he has to turn left, now right. He can be completely wrapped up in his thoughts and the bicycle will turn right and turn left automatically. Out of sheer habit, he will arrive home. There is no need to be conscious while you ride your bicycle: everything has become so mechanical, such a habit, yet, you are bound to arrive home. The driver of a car goes on driving automatically; it is not necessary for him to be alert and conscious.

Our lives start moving in a routine, in a well-trodden rut. We start functioning like an ox at the oil mill. We start walking around the same track, day in and day out. At the most, the track may be a little wider for one and a little narrower for another, ugly for one and a little beautiful for another, but it is a track all the same.

Your life goes around in circles, like a bullock at an oil mill. You get up in the morning and start on the track and at night you go to sleep, completing the circle. Again you get up in the morning . . . and the same routine. The repetition is so habitual that you no longer have any need to be conscious in your activities. Everything happens as if in a trance. At a certain moment you feel hungry, at a fixed time you feel sleepy, you get up and go about your business at the appointed time. You are spending your whole life in this way, as if asleep, moving in a circle.

When will you wake up? When will you shake yourself out of this sleep? When will you get out of the rut? When will you declare that you are not ready to be an ox at an oil mill? The day you consider getting out of it, you will have started the journey towards godliness.

Going to temples does not make you religious. That also is a part of the same rut. You go because you have always gone, because your parents have always gone, and their parents have also always gone. You go on reading a scripture because this is how it has always been. It is the same old rut. Have you ever gone to a temple in full awareness? If you can do this, there will be no further need to go to a temple, because where there is awareness, there you will find the temple.

Awareness is the temple. But the Christian is hurrying to the church, the Sikh is rushing to the gurdwara, the Hindu to the temple: they are all stuck in their rut. No one else can break this state of slumber except you.

So the first thing for you to understand is that even your waking state is in a stupor, whereas even the deep sleep of a meditator is an awake state. You are an upside-down meditator. On the day you reverse what you are today, the ultimate in life will be available to you. When you know the three states separately, and the knower has become separate from the three states, you will be pure knowing, nothing else. You are pure consciousness—but only when you go beyond the three states.

I was reading about a Sufi master, Junnaid . . .

If someone abused him or called him names, he would say, 'I will answer you tomorrow.' Then the next day he would say, 'Now there is no need for any answer.'

The man who had abused him asked, 'I called you names yesterday, so why did you not answer yesterday? You are a unique person. People don't wait for even a second if you abuse them. People react immediately.'

Junnaid said, 'My master taught me that if you rush something, you are bound to become unconscious. Give it a little time. If someone insults you and you react to it immediately, the reaction will be in unconsciousness because the insult may still be surrounding you, the heat of the incident may still be gripping you, its smoke may still be clouding your vision. Let the clouds pass. Allow twenty-four hours to pass before replying.'

Junnaid added, 'Now I realize how tricky my master was, because I have not been able to react to anyone ever since.'

Do you think it is possible for someone to react with anger after a twenty-four-hour wait? Being angry becomes impossible even if you can wait for just twenty-four minutes or twenty-four seconds. The truth is that even if you can wait and watch for one second, the anger will disappear.

But you don't wait even for a split second. A person calls you names and your reaction is as instantaneous as if someone has pushed a button and a machine goes into action. There is not even the slightest gap between the two, no distance. And you think you are very conscious! You are not even a master of yourself. How can an unconscious person be a master of himself? Anybody can push his button and manipulate him. Someone flatters you and you are full of ecstasy, choking with emotion, taken over by it. Someone insults you and you are full of tears.

Are you your own master or can just anyone manipulate you? And the people who are manipulating you are also not their own masters. You are the slave of slaves. And the irony is that all are experts in manipulating each other, and no one is conscious. What greater insult can there be to your being than the fact that anyone can manipulate you?

Mulla Nasruddin was working in an office. Everyone was upset about his work because there wasn't enough work for him in the first place. Most of the time he was either dozing or fast asleep. Everybody in the office was fed up with him. People even started taunting him about it. The boss called him in and scolded him for his behaviour, but nothing changed. Finally, because of all this trouble and humiliation, the Mulla resigned. It was easier to resign than to change his ways.

Many people who escape the world to become sannyasin are in fact resigning from the world for the same reason. Change is difficult, resignation is easier.

Everyone in the office was relieved to hear the news. But because Mulla had worked there for a long time and was leaving of his own free will, they decided to give him a farewell party. They had been so troubled by him, but they could not get rid of him; he had become a burden. So they were really happy. They made elaborate arrangements complete with sweets and refreshments. Nasruddin was amazed. Each colleague spoke a few words in praise of the Mulla. After all, he was leaving.

The Mulla was so overcome with emotion that tears came to his eyes. When it was his turn to speak, he got up and said, 'Friends, I am indeed touched by your love and affection. I didn't know how much you care for me. I can't leave you, ever, for the rest of my life. I withdraw my resignation.'

We are being manipulated. This happens all the time, everywhere—everybody is manipulating everybody else. And the flavour of this manipulation is different all the time because there are many different kinds of people all around you. Because of this you are in a deep confusion and delusion. It is bound to be so, because you are not influenced by just one person. Only someone who is awake within is influenced by just one. There is clarity in the life of such a person, an uncloudedness. There is cleanliness, a decisiveness in his life; there is direction in his life.

There is no direction in your life, there cannot be. You behave like a man in a crowd who is being pushed around, and you call it walking. You are not really walking, you are being pushed around so much that you can't stand still. Someone pushes you to the right, you go to the right; someone pushes you to the left and you go left. Your whole life is like this, decided by the crowd. If you look carefully into this you will see: somebody says something and you do what he says; then somebody else says something else and you do that. In this way you are filled with so many contradictions.

One of my acquaintances fell from a rickshaw and was injured. It was a minor injury. Then he was released from the hospital. Six months passed, he was completely well, but he still used the crutches. I asked him when he was going to stop using the crutches.

'You see,' he said, 'I also want to drop them. My doctor says I no longer need them, but my lawyer says it is better to keep them, at least until the case has been decided in court. So you see my dilemma?'

Your lawyer says one thing and your doctor says something else; the wife says one thing and the husband says something else; the son says one thing, the father another—there are millions of masters all around, manipulating you—and you are alone. You listen to everybody. You listen to whoever can dominate you. Then your inner world becomes fragmented and your personality becomes schizophrenic. Until you begin to listen to the inner voice, you cannot be an integrated whole.

I call a person a sannyasin when he has begun to listen to his own inner voice and is ready to risk everything for it.

But you cannot recognize your inner voice unless you are conscious. Until then, whatever you may take to be your inner voice will not be your inner voice; it will still be a voice from the outside. An unconscious man knows nothing of the inner voice. All the politicians in Delhi talk about this inner voice: Prime Minister Indira Gandhi, President V.V. Giri, they all talk about 'the voice of the innermost soul'. How can a sleeping person know it? How can you know which voice is the inner voice? The voice that seems to satisfy your desires, the voice of your innermost desires, is what you call 'the voice of your innermost soul'.

Only an awakened person has an inner voice. Once this voice comes within range of your hearing, all that is dark, all that is impure and dirty in your life, all those insane voices and the mess within you . . . You have become a crowd, not an individual. You are like a marketplace where everything is going on all at the same time; you have become like the Bombay Stock Exchange, where all kinds of nonsense is going on and you cannot hear a single thing. A person who meets you for the first time cannot even guess who you actually are. There are all kinds of voices shouting loudly and, in all this noise, your own voice is completely lost.

The fourth state means that you have recognized your being. Only when you have gone beyond the first three states can you recognize your being.

Begin with very small experiments. When anger arises, stop. What is the hurry? When you feel hatred, wait. Give it a little gap. Respond only when you are back in your senses, not before that. You will find that everything that is wrong in your life has started to fall away from you, everything that is wrong has begun to melt away. You will suddenly discover that there is no need for you to react to anger. It is even possible that you might go and thank the person who has insulted you because he has done you a favour: he has given you an opportunity to wake up.

Kabir has said:

Always keep a critic in your life.
Keep a cottage for him in your backyard.

Look after him, take care of him, let the person who abuses you be near you, because he gives you the opportunity to wake up.

All the situations which throw you into unconsciousness can be used as stepping stones to awareness. It is up to you. Life can be compared to a huge boulder lying in the middle of the road. Unintelligent people see the stone as a barrier and turn back. For them, the road is closed. The intelligent ones climb over the stone and use it as a stepping stone.

And the moment they make it a stepping stone, the way to greater heights becomes available to them.

A seeker has to remember only one thing: in each moment, to use every occasion and situation to become more aware. Then whether it is hunger or anger or lust or greed, every state can be used to grow in awareness. If you go on accumulating awareness in this way, bit by bit, eventually, you will have enough fuel stored in you. In the fire that is created from this fuel, you will find that you are neither the waking state, nor the dream state, nor the deep-sleep state—you are beyond and separate from all three.

The waking state is presence of perception.

Presence is the ability to perceive everything around you, the waking state.

The dream state is shifting imagination.

The spider's web of thoughts and the expansion of fantasies in your mind is the dream state.

The deep-sleep state is the absence of perception and self-awareness.

These are the three states that we pass through, but while we are passing through each of them we become one with it. When we reach the second state, we become one with it, when we reach the third, we become one with that—hence, we fail to see the three separately. To see them separately, a little distance is needed, a perspective is needed. To see something as separate, a little space is needed, a gap between the seer and the seen. If you stand very close to a mirror, you will not be able to see your own reflection: a little distance is needed. But you stand so close to the waking, dream and sleep states that, in fact, you become one with them. You become coloured by them. And this habit of drowning in others' colours has become so ingrained in you that you don't even notice it.

This habit allows you to be exploited. If you are a Hindu and you are told to set fire to a mosque, you will think a thousand times about whether it is right or not. You will think that the mosque is also dedicated to the same God. It may look different, the colour of its stairs may be different, the details of the path may be different, but the goal is the same. But if a mob of Hindus is about to set fire to a mosque and you are part of the mob, then you don't stop to think because you are drowned in the colour of the crowd. Then you can easily burn the mosque. If later on someone asks you how you could do such a terrible thing, you also will wonder how you could bring yourself to do it. Alone, you never would have done it, but in a crowd you are drowned. Why? Because you are in the habit of being drowned.

No Mohammedan is as bad, as evil alone as he is when he is in a mob; no Hindu is as bad or evil alone as he is in a mob. No individual has ever done the harm that has been committed by a crowd. Why? Because a crowd colours you, you become one with the colour of the crowd. If the mob is angry, you will feel anger arising in you. If the crowd is weeping and wailing, you will begin to weep also. If the crowd is happy, you forget all your troubles and become happy with the crowd.

Just look at what happens if you go to a house where someone has died. If many people are crying, suddenly, you will find that you also feel like crying. Perhaps you might think you are a very compassionate person, full of kindness and love, or you might think that the tears are coming because of sympathy. It is not so. You heard the news when you were at home, and nothing like this happened to you there because you were alone. You may have thought it is okay: birth and death happen all the time. It is more likely that rather than feeling sad about the death, you might have felt it as a disturbance: 'Now I am expected to go there and offer my condolences. As if I have nothing better to do! And why did he have to die today when I'm so busy?'

This is what you would have thought. But when you get to his house and find yourself among the crowd of mourners, you will find that your feelings have changed. You also will feel the same way the crowd does, but this feeling is not worth much. In fact, it is dangerous because it is the crowd that is colouring you. Beware of this feeling of sympathy that you absorb from the crowd—that does not come from your heart.

You must have noticed that people who are normally unhappy and burdened with sorrow start to look so happy around the noisy crowds of Holi, the festival of colour and celebration. They also start dancing and singing, throwing colours and being joyous. What happens to these people who normally don't know joy? These same people normally move about like zombies, and now they have started dancing! What has come over them? Once again, it is the crowd that has coloured them.

The seeker has to beware of the crowd. He has to search for his own voice, his own expression. The crowd has always been prodding you and pushing you around. With the crowd, you become what it wants you to become. Why does this happen? It happens because you do not know your separateness, and you lose it immediately at any opportunity. You are always ready to lose it. When you go to sleep, you lose it in sleep; when you wake up, you lose it in waking; when you dream, you lose it in dreams. If people look happy, you become happy; if people look sad, you become sad. Are you there, or are you just someone who is always influenced? Do you have an existence, a centre of your own, or not? It is that centre which is your being.

Awaken your own being. Stop being drowned! This is why all religions are against alcohol. There is nothing particularly wrong with alcohol, but all the religions are against it. The whole reason is that alcohol is a way of losing yourself, whereas religions want to wake you up. The person who drinks alcohol loses himself in unconsciousness. All these things drown you in unconsciousness, all these things make you more unconscious. You are already unconscious enough—you have very little consciousness and you are ready to lose even that on the slightest pretext.

And it is very surprising that you are happy only when you manage to lose even that too. It is impossible to find a bigger fool than you are. You lose consciousness and only then you say, 'I am happy!' Why is this so?—because even your small ray of consciousness enables you to see the problems of life. It makes you conscious of your life and fills you with anxieties. It makes you aware of the fact that you are unaware. And this small ray of consciousness reveals the darkness within you, which is deep. You want to smother this ray so that you are not reminded of the darkness. It is like the proverb, 'If you get rid of the bamboos, you won't have to worry about playing the bamboo flute.' So you drink alcohol or take drugs or you get into politics or some other crowd activity—you lose yourself anywhere, in anything— to forget yourself.

In the West, psychologists advise people to forget themselves if they want to stay healthy. In the East, the spiritual masters tell you that you can be healthy only if you are awake. These are two very contrary statements, but both are meaningful. The Western psychologist accepts your present state. He only makes sure that you can live in your present, normal state, that you can somehow get through your life. So he is right, he is saying, 'Somehow, forget yourself. More awareness is dangerous, because as you begin to see everything, you will be filled with anxiety. And nothing is right in this life, everything is in chaos, so the best thing is to close your eyes to it and be happy. What need is there to look at your problems?'

But the Eastern masters don't accept your present state. They say, 'You are ill. You are insane. You don't need peace as the first goal. At first, even if your anxieties grow and you become more disturbed, it does not matter, because it is through this that you will be transformed, that a revolution will happen in your life.'

It is like when a man suffers from cancer and there is no cure, so he is given morphine to help him forget the pain. But the Eastern masters say that morphine cannot bring transformation to life. Help the person to wake up. Transformation is possible, but as he is, he is not living his ultimate potential. It is not even the first stage of the journey. He is simply standing off the path. He is standing outside the gate he has not entered yet. There is the possibility of ultimate bliss, but not in the state of sleep in which you are now.

Understand the difference between happiness and bliss. Happiness is when even the small ray of consciousness that is already awake in you is also put to sleep. Then you are not aware of your own suffering. 'Ananda', bliss, is when the small ray of your consciousness becomes like a great sun, and the darkness disappears completely. Happiness is negative, it is insensitivity to suffering: you have a headache, you take an aspirin. That is a state of happiness, not of bliss. The aspirin only makes you insensitive to the pain, it gives you some unconsciousness of it.

You are ill, you are in distress, life is filled with problems, so you get drunk and everything seems to be all right. A bum walks into a pub, and when he leaves there is a song on his lips. You buy happiness at the cost of losing the small ray of consciousness that you have. But these things will never bring bliss to you, because happiness is nothing but the forgetting of sorrow, whereas bliss is the remembrance of your being. It is not the forgetting of something, it is a total remembrance of something. It is not a forgetting, it is a total remembrance. Kabir calls it *surati*, total remembrance.

These sutras will lead you towards total remembrance. So be aware: stay away from anything that makes you more insensitive or unconscious. And there are so many easy ways of becoming unconscious that you are not even aware of them. You are so completely under their spell that you have no idea of them at all.

One person is mad after eating, he goes on eating. It may not have occurred to you, but he is using food in the same way as another uses alcohol. Too much food makes you sleepy. The more you eat, the more sleepy you will be. If you fast in the day, you will not be able to sleep well that night. Food brings on drowsiness, so a person who eats all day is seeking forgetfulness through food.

Another person is on a trip of ambition. He says he will not rest until he has accumulated ten million dollars. Until then he is like a madman. Day or night, dawn or dusk, it doesn't matter, there is only one thing on his mind: ten million! He is dedicated only to that one number, nothing else concerns him. His eyes are focused on the millions, and he will begin to worry only on the day he succeeds in amassing the millions. Then suddenly he realizes that it was all in vain. He has acquired his millions—what next?

I have heard:

Three men were locked in the same cell in a lunatic asylum. They had been friends before and they all became insane at about the same time. They probably helped each other. A psychologist went to study them. He asked the doctor in charge what was the trouble with the first one. He was told that the man was trying to undo a knot in a rope. He couldn't manage to do it and he lost his mind in the process.

'What about the second man?'

'He succeeded in untying the knot, and that is how he went mad.'

'And the third?' the psychologist asked, a bit puzzled.

'He is the one who had tied the knot.'

Someone is busy tying the knot, someone is busy untying it, someone succeeds, someone fails, but it makes no difference—they all go mad.

But why are people involved in such useless activities like tying or untying knots? It is to avoid encountering themselves. These are tricks to avoid yourself, otherwise, you will have to face yourself. If you are not ambitious, if you don't want to win the elections and reach the capital, if you do not want to play politics, if you are not mad after money, how will you manage to avoid meeting yourself? At some point you will have to encounter yourself. Everyone is afraid of this encounter: this fear makes people tremble.

You hear so much about knowing your self, your being. But if you understand what you are doing, you will see that you do everything to avoid knowing yourself. The buddhas say: When you know yourself, supreme bliss—the ultimate nectar—showers upon you. Kabir says that clouds of nectar thunder, and nectar showers on you. But this happens at the very end. In the beginning you will have to pass through much pain and suffering because you will have to destroy all the lies you have created in your life, through many lifetimes. And the destruction of each lie causes pain. The shattering of each deception hurts, because deceptions have given you an illusion of sweetness, a comfortable drowsiness, a kind of unconsciousness—and now to destroy them all? But without destroying them you will never be able to reach the state where clouds fill with nectar and bliss rains on you.

This middle part of the journey is what is called tapascharya, ascetic discipline. Begin your ascetic discipline in the waking state, then carry your discipline into the dream state and then into the deep-sleep state.

The dream state is shifting imagination. The dream state is when the mind is filled with imaginary possibilities. Don't think that you only dream at night; you also dream in the daytime. Sitting here and listening to me does not necessarily imply that you are hearing what I am saying. You may be listening and weaving dreams inside at the same time. A continuous stream of dreams is flowing within you, around the clock. Even when you are awake, dreams go on moving within you. Close your eyes and look inside, and you will always find something going on.

It is just like at night we see the stars and they disappear in the daytime—but it is only the light of the sun that is hiding them. Don't think that they really disappear during the day. They are very much there. Where can they go? If you go down into a deep well and look up, you will be able to see them during the day. Darkness is needed to see the stars. They are not visible because of the sunlight.

The same is the case with dreams. It is not that dreams are only there at night. What is needed to see them is the darkness of the night, so when your eyes are closed they become visible. In the daytime your eyes are open because there are so many other things to do. Although the dreams are present and moving inside you, they are not seen. If you sit down in an easy chair with your eyes closed, you will start seeing them—you will immediately start daydreaming. They were already there, moving inside you—there is a constant thread of dreams inside you.

This undercurrent has to be broken, because only if you succeed in breaking it in the daytime will you be able to break it in the night. If you cannot break it in the daytime, how will you be able to break it in the night?

Mantras are devices to break this undercurrent. For example, a master gives a mantra to a person. He tells the person to go on doing his work, to stay in the marketplace, tending to his business of buying and selling, but to allow an inner chanting of 'Rama, Rama, Rama' to continue. What does this mean? It means that if he continues to keep chanting 'Rama' while doing his routine work, then the energy that was flowing in the current of dreams will flow into the current of chanting 'Rama'. It is the same energy that was the dream.

Now he has created his own personalized dream within himself: 'Rama, Rama, Rama . . .' On the outside he goes on doing his daily work, but inside he keeps a constant remembrance of Rama. The unused energy in him that was going into dreaming will go into the remembrance of Rama, of the divine. This does not mean that the divine will come running to him, but it will help him to break his dreaming. The day you find that there are no dreams any more even when you sleep at night and instead there is a constant flow of 'Rama, Rama . . .' you will understand that your daydreaming has also disappeared.

The success of a mantra can only be seen during sleep at night, not when you are awake in the day. How will you know? If you repeat the mantra throughout the day, you will not dream at night; instead, a current of the chant will keep on flowing while you sleep. You can't even imagine how intense this current can become.

Swami Ram used to repeat this mantra, 'Rama, Rama'. Once he was a guest of his friend Sardar Puran Singh. They were alone in a small cottage high up in the Himalayas. There was not a soul around for miles and miles.

One night Sardar Puran Singh could not sleep well because of the heat and the mosquitoes. He was amazed to hear the sound of 'Rama, Rama' in the cottage. He knew that Swami Ram was asleep. He got up to see what was happening. He felt a little frightened, too, because it seemed there was a third person there. He took the lamp and looked around, but there was no one there either inside or outside. He went back into the room and, to his surprise, discovered that the sound was louder inside the room than outside. As he approached Swami Ram's bed, the sound was even louder. He raised the lamp to look closely: could it be that Ram was awake and chanting 'Rama, Rama'?

But he found Ram fast asleep. In fact, he was snoring. He was even more puzzled, so he sat down near the bed and put his ear closer to Swami Ram. He found that each pore of his body was vibrating with the sound of 'Rama, Rama'.

This happens when your remembrance goes very deep. Normally, a great deal of energy is being used up in dreams. You don't have them without a price. Dreams have no value in themselves, but the price you pay is immense because you are dreaming the whole night. Recently, in the West, there has been much research done on dreams. Scientists say that a normal, healthy person dreams eight dreams each night, and each dream lasts around fifteen minutes. This means that every night, at least two hours are spent dreaming. But this is in the case of a completely healthy person who has no mental disorders. Such healthy people are not easy to find. Generally, people dream for six out of the eight hours they sleep. The constant flow of dreams uses up a large amount of your energy. It is not for free! You buy them at the cost of your life energy.

A mantra crystallizes this energy around words like 'Rama', 'Krishna', 'Christ', 'om'; any other word will also do. It is not necessary that it be the name of God. Your own name will do just as well.

The English poet, Tennyson, has written in his memoirs that he stumbled upon a method in his childhood. If he could not sleep at night, he would repeat over and over to himself, 'Tennyson, Tennyson, Tennyson . . .' and he could fall asleep. This is how he discovered the technique; later in his life, whenever he was restless, he would repeat to himself, 'Tennyson, Tennyson, Tennyson . . .' and the restlessness would disappear. He used his own name as a mantra.

Your own name can bring the same result, but it won't, because you don't have that much faith in your name. Otherwise, there is no difference. It makes no difference whether you chant 'Rama' or 'Rahim'. It is not a question of names, all words are the same. All names are the name of God, including your own name. Any word repeated will create harmonious music, a harmonious vibration inside you and the dream energy will dissolve into it.

Mantras are a method to dissolve dreams. No one will attain godliness by repeating a mantra, but dissolving dreams is a great step towards experiencing it. A mantra is a technique, a process, a tool, a hammer that shatters dreams. And what are dreams? They too are only words, and that is why a hammer of words can shatter them. There is no need to use an actual hammer. Dreams are unreal, so an unreal hammer will do the trick. A genuine medicine is dangerous for a pseudo ailment; only an imaginary medicine will help cure an imaginary disease.

What are dreams? They are shifting imaginations. And what is a mantra? It is something definite. It too is a form of shifting imagination, but dreams are momentary, changing, whereas the mantra is continuous and uniform. Gradually, the energy of all the dreaming is absorbed in the mantra. The night you find that there are no more dreams and only the mantra is continuing throughout your sleep, know that you have conquered your dreaming. Your dream is now broken and reality has begun. After that you can enter the deep-sleep state.

But you are doing just the opposite—you give energy to your dreams. Meaningless thoughts move inside you and you cooperate with them. You are sitting still and you start thinking about how to fight in the coming elections. The dream has begun! You will not be satisfied unless you become the President. In your dream you have become the President and the people are congratulating you and you are enjoying it all immensely. You never stop to think what kind of stupidity is this and what are you doing. You are just giving energy to a worthless fantasy. Your mind is filled with meaningless fantasies.

If we look at people's lives closely, we will find that 99 per cent of their lives are wasted in empty dreams: dreams of wealth, dreams of power, dreams of conquering the world. Even if you achieve all this, what will you gain?

There was a great American President, Calvin Coolidge. He was a very serene person by nature. He must have become the President just accidentally, through some coincidence, because a peaceful person can never reach such a turbulent seat of power. It is a totally mad race to get there. There, the greater madman defeats the lesser madman and makes it to the top. How Coolidge got there is a miracle. He was so quiet by nature that he hardly spoke at all. It is said that there were days when he would not utter more than five or ten words.

At the end of his term his friends asked him to run for office again. Everyone wanted to have him as President again. He refused. People asked, 'Why? All the citizens are in favour of it.'

He said, 'No more. It is enough that I made the mistake once. What have I gained from it all? I will not waste another four years of my life. And there is nothing beyond being the President. I have experienced this position and there is no place higher to go. If there was something more, perhaps the dream would have continued.'

You may not be aware that it is difficult to find a greater failure than the person who has realized his dreams, because at the peak of success, such a person will find that all he has struggled for, competed for, all that he has worked so hard for had nothing to give him once he got there. But just to hide his stupidity, he will go on smiling, waving and giving victory signs to the people who are still behind him in the rat race. He feels defeated and he goes on showing victory signs to the other fools who are still in the race! If every successful person in the world were to be honest and say that they did not get anything out of their success, many of these mad races that come from dreams would end. But it goes against the ego to say this. They go on pretending that they have attained the ultimate happiness. Someone whose tail has been cut off goes on making arrangements for others to lose their tails too, otherwise he will be ashamed of himself because he is the only one without a tail, so let everyone else be without a tail.

Whenever the current of dreams happens in you, just become alert and watch, 'What am I doing?' All the stories about Sheikh Chilli in the children's books apply to you. The mind is a Sheikh Chilli, and as long as you keep dreaming you will remain a Sheikh Chilli. Sheikh Chilli was always dreaming and taking it all for real. God forbid that these dreams should ever come true! They need tremendous energy to be fulfilled, and you discover in the end that you have nothing in your hands. Only ashes are left in your hands—always.

All the successes of this world turn to ashes. And by the time you have only ashes in your hands, your life has passed by and there is no way to return. And then all that is left for you is to hide this reality from others and show that your life has not been lived in vain, that you are fulfilled, that your life has been fruitful.

The dream state is shifting imagination. Don't give energy to dreams. Whenever you start dreaming, give yourself a shake and wake up! Break the dreaming as fast as you can. Mantras can be useful to break dreaming. Later we will discuss in detail how mantras can be effective. Mantras definitely can shatter dreams.

The dream state is shifting imagination. In deep sleep, everything disappears. There is no perception, no awareness either of the inside or of the outside. You are like a rock, fast asleep.

Just see what a mess your life must be in: it is only when you are fast asleep that you are able to say you had a very pleasant rest when you wake up in the morning. Just think about it: what a hell your life must be that you find happiness only in the oblivion of sleep, only when you are unconscious. The rest of your life must be filled with pain and misery.

You only feel at ease and satisfied after a good sleep, and sleep means nothing but unconsciousness. But you are right—for you it is enough, because your whole life is nothing but one long tale of worry, tension, anxiety and turmoil. If, in this situation, you are able to find a little rest, you feel that you have found everything. But, in fact, it is nothing. Sleep means where there is nothing, neither the inner world nor the outer world, where all disappears into darkness.

Yes, certainly you feel rested, but what use is this rest if the next morning you fall again into the same rut? The energy you have gained from the night's rest will be used to create new tensions, new anxieties. You rest every night and you create new tensions every day.

If you could just realize this small fact: that you get so much pleasure out of an unconscious slumber. Why? Because there is no tension there, there is no anxiety there. You forget all your problems when you slip into this unconscious state. Then imagine how much joy you will experience when you are fully aware *and* all your problems and tensions have disappeared.

This is what we have called moksha; this is nirvana, this is *brahmananda*, the ultimate bliss. When you get so much pleasure from your sleep just because your problems disappear, imagine the kingdom of bliss you will experience when this peaceful state is yours around the clock, when the problems are actually dissolved, the tensions actually gone and you are in total relaxation, for twenty-four hours a day. This is a state you touch briefly, sometimes in deep sleep.

Samadhi, superconsciousness, is similar to the state of deep sleep with only one difference: there is awareness in it. Turiya, the fourth state, is similar to the deep-sleep state with only one difference: in deep sleep there is darkness, while in the fourth state there is light.

For example, imagine you are brought to this garden in an unconscious state, on a stretcher: the rays of the sun will still touch you because they are not unconscious, it is you who are unconscious; the breeze will still pass over you, caress you, because the breeze is not unconscious, it is you who are unconscious; the flowers will still spread their fragrance to your nose, because they are not unconscious, it is you who are unconscious; the freshness of the early morning dewdrops will still touch you because they are not unconscious, it is you who are unconscious—all this will happen, but you will not be aware of it. When you return to consciousness you will say, 'I feel so rested!' This rest is because of all these factors also—the sunrays, the fragrance of the flowers, the cool breeze and the dewdrops—but you have no awareness of it at all. You were unconscious, and yet when you are conscious, again you say, 'What a restful sleep!'

Look at it another way. You are sitting in a garden in total awareness. The morning sunrays bring their cosy warmth, the flowers fill the air with breathtaking perfumes, the cool breeze creates music in the leaves of the trees as it rustles through them, the dew glitters on the petals giving freshness and newness to everything around, and you are sitting there, aware—can you imagine the bliss?

In the deep-sleep state you touch exactly where Buddha, Mahavira and Shiva touch in their fully awakened state. Even from sleep, you bring back a little news in the morning: how blissful, how rested you feel. Although you can't explain the experience of bliss clearly, what it was like, how it was— you can't define it because you were in deep sleep—yet, in the morning you come out of it fresh and cheerful. On the face of a person waking up in the morning, who might have slept deeply in the night, there is a small reflection of buddhahood. This is especially so on the faces of little children who sleep very deeply. As your worries grow, deep sleep becomes more difficult. Watch little children as they wake up in the morning, just before they are actually out of sleep, and you will see there is the freshness of a buddha reflected there. Something blissful is happening within the child, although he is unaware of it.

All tensions fade in the deep-sleep state, but there is no awareness there. In samadhi, the state of turiya, all tensions fade, and awareness is also there. Awareness plus deep sleep equals samadhi.

One who knows the three states is the Lord of Warriors, Shiva.

The experiencer of all three states—waking, dreaming and deep sleep—the one who is apart and separate from the three states, the one who passes through the three states, but does not identify with them, the one who goes beyond the three states and knows himself to be separate and apart is *veeresh*, the lord of warriors, Shiva.

'Veeresh' means 'the warrior of warriors', the great warrior. Veeresh is one of the names of Shiva. Mahavira also means 'the great warrior'. We have only named those who have attained samadhi as *mahavira*. We don't call a person a great warrior just because he has scaled the Everest or reached the moon. It is okay, it is a courageous act, but these are not the ultimate heights to be scaled or the ultimate destinations to be reached. We call someone veeresh or mahavira if he has reached to his being and to the universal being. What Everest can be higher than the universal soul? What destination can be farther than the universal soul? We call someone mahavira, a great warrior, who has reached the ultimate. We don't settle for less than that. So what if you have reached the moon? It has only opened more vistas for exploration: Mars, and so on and so forth. And so what if you have reached Mars? The universe is infinite.

We call one who has reached the ultimate, where there is no further to go, a great warrior. And why do we call him a great warrior? Because there is no greater act of courage than this: there is nothing more courageous than the act of attaining your own being. There is no greater adventure and exploration than this, because there is no path more arduous. There is no other place that requires a more intense effort to reach.

The journey to being is the most arduous journey. It is like walking on a razor's edge. Perhaps this is why you are escaping from yourself and trying to get entangled here, there and everywhere. And perhaps this is why, although self-awakening attracts your heart, you do not gather courage. Fear grips you. It is arduous. You will have to walk it alone. The biggest difficulty is this: you can go everywhere in the world together with someone else, but this is the only place where you will have to go alone. No wife, no brother, no friend can go there with you. Not even the master can go there with you. At best, the master can point the way.

Buddha has said, 'A master, an awakened one, only points the way. It is you who will have to travel.'

We are afraid to be alone. And there are so many people around us, so many dreams. Some of the dreams are very pleasant, very sweet. You have great interest in them. Only a few rare individuals set out on this journey of breaking all these dreams, dropping the complex web of all these dreams. Of these, many turn back halfway. One in a million starts on this journey, because it is arduous, difficult. Out of millions who start, perhaps one person reaches. This is why we have called such a person veeresh, a warrior of warriors.

The fourth, which is beyond the three and lies hidden within you, is the Everest. That is where you have to reach, and the way to reach there is to be more awake in your waking state. Right now you are lukewarm. Become a burning flame of awareness so that this flame can penetrate your dream state. Then be awake to your dreams also, so that your dreams shatter. Be so aware in the dream state that a ray of your awareness pierces into the state of deep sleep. When you have entered the deep-sleep state with this lamp of awareness with you, you have opened the doors to becoming a veeresh. You have knocked on the temple door for the first time.

Bliss is infinite, but you will have to travel the path. You must pay the price. The more bliss you aspire to, the higher the price. There can be no cheap deals.

Many try to make cheap deals. They seek shortcuts, and they end up finding gurus who exploit them. The gurus tell them, 'Put this amulet on and it will take care of everything,' or 'Just have faith in me,' or 'Do this charity, that charity, get a temple built.' These are cheap tricks: they solve nothing, they only deceive you. You will have to make the journey.

There are some people who try even cheaper methods. They smoke marijuana or hashish and believe they are in samadhi. They take bhang, marijuana that is eaten, and believe they have become awake. There are thousands of sadhus and ascetics who take drugs like opium and bhang. This has become even more prevalent in the West, because they have discovered even better drugs: LSD, better-quality marijuana. They have discovered even more scientific chemicals: you take an injection and you are deep in enlightenment. You take a tablet and you are enlightened. Like instant coffee, they have now produced instant samadhi.

If only it were so cheap! If only it were possible for someone to reach enlightenment by taking drugs—the whole world would have become enlightened long ago. No, it is not that cheap. But the mind searches for the cheap. The mind wants somehow to do away with the journey in between and enter ultimate liberation directly. The journey in between cannot be done away with, because it is in going through the journey that your liberation comes. This journey is not merely a journey, it is your evolution. So this is the trouble.

Such a thing is possible in the outer world. A plane takes off in London and you can get off directly in Mumbai, and everything else in between has been skipped. But the person who arrives in Mumbai is the same person who boarded in London. It is not a different person who gets off in Mumbai; he has not evolved during the journey. This is how it is with the outer journey.

But there cannot be an airplane journey which takes you into ultimate liberation from where you are. And those who say there can be are simply deceiving you. This journey is not from one place to another place. It is from one state of consciousness into another state of consciousness. You will have to pass through the journey that lies in between because it is in this passage that you will be refined; your impurities will be burned and you will be transformed. It is through the pain of the process of the journey that you will grow. This pain is indispensable. No one can reach without passing through this pain. If you try to find shortcuts, you are only deceiving yourself.

In the West, there is a great search for shortcuts. That is why people like Mahesh Yogi have a big influence there. The reason is that Mahesh Yogi says, 'What I am telling you to do works at jet speed. What I am asking of you is to chant this short mantra for fifteen minutes every day and you will get there straightaway. Nothing else needs to be done. Your conduct or behaviour need not change, nothing in your life needs to go through change, nothing in your outer world needs to be dropped, nothing has to be done. Just sit down, relax and repeat this mantra for fifteen minutes—this mantra is all.'

A mantra is a valuable thing, but it is not all. A mantra can dissolve your dreams, but it cannot deliver the truth. The shattering of dreams is just a small aspect of the path leading to the attainment of truth. If someone thinks that just repeating a mantra is everything, that chanting on your beads is everything, he is being childish. This person is not yet worthy to even understand the path, let alone reach the goal.

The path is arduous. You will have to pass through its arduousness. And that is why the sutra says endeavour is needed. A desire for such an immense effort is needed, such a longing is needed so that you can stake yourself totally.

Ultimate liberation can be bought, but only if you stake yourself totally. Nothing less will do. Anything else you give is not giving; it is not paying the price. Only when you give yourself totally do you pay the price and attain.

Enough for today.

3

The First Step: A Sense of Wonder

Wonder is the ground of religiousness.
  Strength means to be rooted in oneself.
  Transcendent logic or discriminating awareness leads
to self-realization.
  To rejoice in the bliss of existence is enlightenment.

TRY TO UNDERSTAND this: in the dictionary, wonder is defined as 'surprise, amazement'. But there is a basic difference between wonder and amazement. If this basic difference is not understood, you will set off on an altogether different journey. Amazement is the foundation of science; the sense of wonder is the foundation of religiousness. Amazement is extrovert, wonder is introvert. Amazement is pointed towards something else; wonder is pointed towards yourself. This is the first thing.

Something which we cannot understand, which leaves us speechless, which defies our mind's grasp, which proves to be bigger than us, which leaves us simply dumbfounded, which demolishes us—*this* gives birth to wonder.

If this state of wonder that arises from within when we are faced with the illogical, with the incomprehensible, turns towards the outer, it gives birth to science. If we start thinking about matter, contemplating about the world, if we start investigating the mystery that surrounds us, science is born. Science is amazement. Amazement means that the sense of wonder has gone on an outward journey.

There is one more difference between surprise and wonder. The thing that fills us with amazement will leave us feeling fed up, if not today, then tomorrow, because amazement creates tension. In fact, this is why there is so much effort to eliminate amazement. Science is born out of amazement, but then it proceeds to destroy that amazement with interpretations, theories, formulae, keys: it does not rest until the mystery is destroyed, until it can hold the knowledge about it in its fist. Science does not rest until it can claim to have explained the mystery.

Science is determined to eliminate the element of amazement from the world. If science succeeds in this, then there will be nothing left in the world which man cannot claim to explain. This means that no godliness will survive in the world, because godliness means that which we cannot claim to know, even when we have known it; that which always remains unknown in spite of all our knowing about it; that which can never be finally known in spite of our knowing it more and more; that about which we can never cease to wonder.

There are some things which have become known to us: we can call them known. There are some things which we don't know yet, but we will know someday: we can call them the unknown. And then there are also some things in this existence that we have not known and which we will never be able to know. We call this the unknowable. Godliness is unknowable. This is the third dimension. Science does not accept godliness because it says that there is nothing in the world which cannot be known. We may not know it yet, because up to now, maybe, we have not tried hard enough, but sooner or later, it's only a matter of time, we *will* know it. One day we will know the whole existence, nothing will remain unknown in it.

Science is born out of a sense of amazement and then it gets busy with destroying this amazement. This is why I call science matricidal: it tries to kill what gave birth to it.

Religion is just the opposite. True religion is also born out of amazement; this sutra calls it the sense of wonder. The only difference is that when a spiritual seeker is filled with amazement about something, he does not go on an outer journey, he goes on an inner pilgrimage, on a pilgrimage towards his consciousness. Whenever any kind of mystery surrounds him, he thinks of himself: 'I must know who I am.'

If the mystery becomes introspective and the search, the journey, turns inward, the arrow of the search will turn towards your consciousness, not towards an object. The energy of inquiry is channelled into first knowing your own reality—then it is wonder.

And the second point to be understood is that wonder is inexhaustible. The more we know, the more it grows. Hence, wonder is a paradox because, normally, it should decrease as we go on acquiring more knowing. But a Buddha or a Krishna, a Shiva or a Christ, don't lose their sense of wonder. When they attain the ultimate knowing, their sense of wonder also becomes ultimate. They don't say that now they have known all: they say that after having known everything, everything still remains to be known.

The Upanishads have said, 'The whole comes out of the whole, the whole still remains.' When you have known all, all still remains to be known. This is why spiritual knowing does not become a nourishment to the ego, but scientific knowledge does. In spiritual knowing, you will never become the knower, you will always remain humble. And the more you know, the more you will feel 'I don't know anything.' At the ultimate peak of knowing, you will be able to say, 'I know nothing.' At the moment of ultimate knowing the whole existence is transformed into a vast wonder.

If science succeeds, the whole universe will become known; if religion succeeds the whole universe will become unknown. If science succeeds, you, the knower, will be full of ego and the whole universe will become just ordinary, because where there is no sense of wonder, everything becomes jaded. Where there is no sense of wonder, there is no soul. Where there is no possibility of a deeper mystery, the journey ahead will come to a dead end. The quest and, with it, curiosity, will die.

If science has its way, the world will be filled with a boredom such as it has never experienced before. If Westerners today are more bored, the root cause lies in science, because people's capacity to feel wonder is disappearing. People are not amazed by anything; they have simply forgotten how to be amazed. If you give them a problem which seems unsolvable, they will say, 'Oh! It can be solved!'—because, essentially, in the eyes of science, nothing can remain unsolved forever. Science says, 'We will unveil it.'

But the religious journey is just the opposite: the more veils you remove, the more you will find that the mystery goes on deepening. The closer you come, the more you realize the difficulty of ever knowing it. And the day we penetrate to the very core of existence, everything becomes so mysterious. For a buddha, stones and pebbles lying on the ground are as mysterious as the stars twinkling high in the sky. It is not only the vast that is mysterious to him, but the tiniest phenomenon has become mysterious to him. A seed sprouting in the soil is as mysterious as the creation of the whole universe.

So as your sense of wonder deepens, your eyes will become like those of a small child. A child is wonderstruck by everything. Watch a child walking on the street: everything strikes him with awe. To him a coloured pebble looks like a diamond. You laugh at him because you are a knower—you know that it is only a coloured stone. You say to him, 'Don't be crazy, this is not a diamond,' but that small child wants to put it in his pocket. You will say, 'Don't carry such a burden. After all, it's a dirty stone lying in the mud. Throw it away!' But the child will grip it harder. You cannot understand the child—it is a wonder for the child. This coloured stone is in no way less valuable to the child than the diamond. The value comes from the sense of wonder because stones in themselves are of no value. A tiny butterfly can mesmerize a child more than you would be mesmerized by the divine itself, if it were to come face-to-face with you. The child will start chasing the butterfly . . .

In the highest state of wonder, of buddhahood, you are in the clear, innocent state of a small child. This is why Jesus said, 'Only those who are like small children will be able to enter the kingdom of my Lord.' Jesus is saying the same thing Shiva has said in this sutra: Wonder is the ground of meditation. Wonder is the first step to religiousness.

It will be good to understand many points about this.

The more knowledgeable you are, the more difficult it will be for you to access the ground of meditation. The more you boast of your knowledge, the fewer are your chances of becoming religious. The more burdened your mind is with scriptures, the more your sense of wonder will be destroyed. You ask a scholar about God and he will start answering— as if God is a thing that can be answered, as if God can be explained. You ask a scholar and he has all the ready-made answers. No sooner do you ask than the answer is already there. Not even God makes him speechless. All the aphorisms are in place and he explains them immediately.

But if you go to Buddha and ask about God, Buddha will remain silent. Perhaps you will leave, thinking, 'This man remained silent because he does not know.' Many scholars went away from him thinking exactly this. But the real reason Buddha remained silent is that wonder is the doorway to existence. Had you been a little wiser you would have remained with this man who did not answer, and tried to understand him. You would have looked into his eyes. You would have lived in his company, near him, because he has experienced something and the experience is so immense that words cannot express it. He has seen something that cannot be put into words.

Questions and answers are okay for schoolchildren. But the question itself is absurd: you cannot ask a question about God. How can you ask a question about the infinite? In front of the infinite, both the question and the answer drop by themselves. Your question is petty there. This is why Buddha remained silent. But you would also have left thinking, 'If this man knew, he would have answered. If he does not answer, that means he does not know.' You recognize a scholar because your head is also full of words. You will not be able to understand a sage because a sage is full of wonder, and your sense of wonder is dead.

The biggest misfortune in this world is when your sense of wonder is destroyed. When your sense of wonder is destroyed, the possibility of your liberation becomes extremely difficult. When your sense of wonder is destroyed, your childlike heart dies, becomes lifeless. You have become old.

Do you still feel awe? Is life a question mark to you? Are you thrilled by the chirping of the birds, the sound of the running streams, the winds rustling through the trees?

Do you feel joy in all this? Does the life all around make you feel speechless? No, because you know it all: this is just the birds making sounds; this is just the wind making a rustling noise through the trees. You have the answer to every question and these answers have killed you. You have become a 'knower' before wisdom has happened to you.

Wonder is the ground of religiousness.

Wonder is a door for anyone who wants to enter into meditation. Bring your childhood to life again, start inquiring again. Reawaken your curiosity, your questioning, and the roots of life that have dried up in you will start to become green again. All the rocks that block you will be cleared away and the stream will start flowing again. Open your eyes afresh and look all around you again. All your answers are false, because all your answers are borrowed. You have not known anything for yourself, but you are stuffed with so much borrowed knowledge that you feel you have known.

Awaken your sense of wonder. Nothing is going to happen through your yoga postures and your breathing exercises unless you awaken your sense of wonder. All yogic and breathing exercises belong to the body. It's okay—they will purify your body, they will make your body healthy—but the purification and health of the body will not help you to know truth.

Wonder is a purification of the mind. A sense of wonder means that the mind has become free of all answers. A sense of wonder means that you have left all the rubbish of your answers, your questioning and your curiosity, and have again become new and fresh. You have realized your ignorance.

Wonder means, 'I don't know,' knowledge means, 'I know.' But the more you know, the more you will be wrong. When you say, with simplicity, 'I don't know, this whole world is unknown. Whatsoever I know is only functional, and I have not known anything as such,'—when this realization penetrates deep into your heart, you have taken the first step into meditation and religiousness. After this, the other steps are easy. But if you take a wrong step from the very beginning, you can go on travelling endlessly and it will be of no use. Someone who takes a wrong first step cannot reach the destination. Someone whose first step is right, half of his journey is over—and a sense of wonder is the first step.

Look at it closely: do you possess knowledge? If you look deeply you will realize that you have no knowledge; what you have is all rubbish collected from scriptures, teachers, saints. And you have cherished it like a priceless possession! It has not given you anything, it has only killed your sense of wonder. Your sense of wonder is writhing, lying there, almost dead: now you are not even surprised. Nothing surprises you any more.

There was a Christian mystic, Eckhart. He has made a unique statement, 'A saint is someone who is surprised by everything. Everything, even the smallest of things, surprises him. A pebble falls in the water, creates a sound, ripples start spreading and the saint is amazed. It is so wondrous! It is so mysterious! He breathes, he lives and even this is amazing to him.'

Every morning when he prayed to God, Eckhart used to say, 'It is another day! The sun has risen again. Your play is fathomless. What would we do if the sun didn't rise? We could do nothing. A human being is helpless.'

Eckhart used to say, 'Today, I am breathing; tomorrow, I may not. What can I do?'

You cannot force the breath to go on if it stops. It is not in your control. Your breath is so close to you, and yet you are not its master. If it goes out and does not come back, it will simply not come back. We are not even the master of something that is so close to us, and yet we believe that we know everything.

This idea of knowing everything has killed you. Get rid of this rubbish and be unburdened. When your vision is no longer full of knowledge, it will immediately become full of mystery.

The inner journey into this mystery is called wonder, the outward journey is called surprise. If you focus this feeling of mystery towards objects, you will become a scientist, and if you are able to focus it towards your own being, you will become a great mystic. The outcome of these two directions will be very different, because surprise is aggressive, and a sense of wonder is non-aggressive. Whenever you are surprised by something, you start analysing it and taking it apart, because surprise is restlessness. Wonder is soothing.

Try to understand this difference. It is not written in the dictionary; it cannot be, because the compiler of the dictionary has no idea what wonder is.

Surprise is violent, aggressive. When you are full of surprise about something, you are tense. You will have to resolve that tension. A certain restlessness will hang over you until your curiosity about it is satisfied, and you know it. A scientist is absorbed in his laboratory for eighteen hours a day. Why? There is a restlessness in him, as if he is possessed by a ghost, and he will remain absorbed until he has solved it.

But wonder is not aggressive and wonder is not restless. On the contrary, wonder is restfulness. Whenever you are filled with wonder, you are filled with relaxation. You are not to destroy your sense of wonder: you have to taste it, you have to delight in it. You have to merge into wonder; you have to become one with it. Surprise starts destroying, wonder starts living. Wonder is a way of life. Surprise is an aggressive aspect of man's mind.

This is why science thinks in terms of conquering—dissecting, taking apart. Religion thinks in terms of surrendering, dissolving in yourself. When wonder enters you, it will dissolve in you the way salt dissolves in water and the water becomes salty. In the same way, when you become filled with wonder, each fibre of your being will be filled with wonder. You will stand in wonder, you will sit in wonder—you will always be in a state of wonder. Everything will become mysterious to you. The smallest particle will be part of the infinite, because when the sense of wonder touches the small, it will become the vast. Then nothing is as you have known it and you are surrounded everywhere by mystery. Then each moment is new, is a new invitation.

Mulla Nasruddin was contesting the elections. On his door-to-door campaign he went to the local priest. He was drunk.

The priest was a gentleman; saying something directly would have been impolite, so he said, 'I want to ask you something. If I am satisfied with your answer, my vote is all yours. Do you ever drink?'

There was no need to ask because he was drunk right there. Mulla was taken aback. He said, 'Before I answer your question, I would like to ask you something, is this a question or an invitation?'

Surprise is a question, wonder is an invitation. Wonder is an inner call, and the more you move within, the more you will go on drowning in it. The day will also come when you will be no more, only the wonder will be. That day, enlightenment has happened. If you follow the path of surprise, a day will come when only you will remain and surprise will have vanished completely. This is the culmination of science: your ego will be left and surprise will vanish. If you go on the journey of wonder, you will disappear and only wonder will remain; your every pore will be filled with the taste of it. Your very existence will have become a wonder.

Shiva has called it the foundation of religiousness. Remove your knowledge and fill yourself with wonder. In the beginning it will seem to be very difficult because you think you know everything.

There was a great thinker, a very valuable, important one, D.H. Lawrence. He was roaming in the garden with a small child. The child asked him, 'Why are the trees green?'

Only a child can ask such a question—so fresh! You cannot even think of such questions. You will say, 'The trees are green! What is there to ask about it? What kind of question is this? This child is stupid.' But think again—why are the trees green? Do you really know the answer? Perhaps someone here who is studying science can answer, 'It is chlorophyll that makes the trees green,' but this does not resolve the child's question. The child will again ask, 'Why is there chlorophyll in the tree? Why is it there in the tree? And why is it not in a person? And how does the chlorophyll find the trees exclusively?' The answer 'chlorophyll' does not solve any question.

All the answers found by science are of the same kind. Those answers only push the question one step back, that's all. If you are a little intelligent, you can raise the question again. Science does not have any answer to the 'why'. This is another reason why science cannot destroy wonder; it only creates an illusion of destroying it.

But D.H. Lawrence was not a scientist. He was a poet, a novelist. He had a sensitivity for aesthetics. He stopped right then and there and started thinking. He said to the child, 'Give me some time. I don't know myself.'

Your child also must have asked the same kinds of questions many times. Have you ever said, 'I don't know?' It will hurt your ego. Every father thinks that he knows: the child asks and the father gives an answer. And it is because of these answers that the child loses respect for the father later on, because one day the child will realize that you knew nothing. You were unnecessarily giving answers, but you were as ignorant as the child. You were a little older, so your ignorance was older, that's all. You give answers to the small child and the small child trusts you, so he accepts your answers, believing that it must be so—but for how long will he believe it?

D.H. Lawrence stood there. He said, 'I will think it over. But if you insist, I can only say that the trees are green because they are green. There is no other answer. I myself am overwhelmed by this mystery.'

If you were to remove the curtain of knowledge, you would find mystery all around. The trees are green—this too is a mystery; red flowers come to green trees—this too is a mystery. And such a giant tree is hidden in the womb of a tiny seed—this too is a mystery. You can preserve a seed and plant it after a hundred or a thousand years, and a tree will materialize. Life seems to be eternal. Every moment is throbbing with mystery.

It is as if you have closed your eyes. You have become complacent, but this complacency is your lifelessness. You don't even hesitate to answer. There are reasons for this: it keeps your ego reassured that you know. If you know, you feel secure. If you don't know, all your security disappears. In fact, you don't know anything. But this idea that you know nothing hurts, so you cling to anything. A drowning man clings to a straw and tries to remain afloat. What you are clinging on to is not even a straw. Perhaps a straw can save someone from drowning sometime, but what you are clinging on to is not even a straw. It is just the stuff dreams are made of—empty words.

Someone has a firm belief that he knows there is a God. It is absurd to say, 'I definitely know for sure.' *Definitely* means that you have unravelled the mystery of God. *Definitely* means you have seen God through and through; you have measured God's ins and outs; you have weighed God on a weighing scale; you have examined God in the laboratory—what else can the term 'definitely' mean?

Then there is some other person who *definitely* knows that God does not exist. Both are stupid, and both are suffering from the same disease. One calls himself a theist, the other calls himself an atheist, and there is not an iota of difference between the two. Deep down both are suffering from the same disease: both of them believe that they know, and both get into arguments.

Knowledge creates argument, wonder creates dialogue. When you are filled with wonder, your life will have a dialogue. If a theist goes to Mahavira and says, 'God exists,' he will say, 'Yes. God exists.' If an atheist goes and says, 'God does not exist,' Mahavira will say, 'No, God does not exist.' And if some agnostic, a non-believer from both standpoints, goes to him, Mahavira will say, 'God may be and may not be.' Now, it is a very difficult matter. We want him to give a straight and clear answer. The answer may be wrong, but at least it will be definite.

And remember, this existence is so complex that definite answers can only be wrong. Here, an answer that is not contradictory is bound to be wrong. Here, an answer can be right only if it also contains its opposite, because existence contains all opposites.

Here, there is life as well as death. Here, the path is not clear-cut. Here, there is darkness as well as light. Here, good and evil exist together. The saint and the sinner are not separate, both live together, simultaneously. Both are two sides of the same coin. Existence contains both polarities in it. Existence is infinite, it is not divided according to some touchstone of logic. It is beyond logic. Here, all dualities are merged into each other.

One night Junnaid prayed to God, 'I want to know who the greatest sinner in this village is because by studying him, by understanding him, I will try to avoid sin. I will have a criterion that here is the greatest sinner, so I have to avoid this kind of life.'

A voice said, 'Your neighbour.'

Junnaid was surprised. He had never imagined that his neighbour could be the greatest sinner. He was an ordinary man, a working man, running his own small shop. Junnaid had never thought that he could be the greatest sinner. His idea was that the greatest sinner would be someone like the demon king, Ravana; the greatest sinner would be someone devilish, a Satan. This man was running a shop, raising his children. Junnaid was puzzled—this was a common man, nobody could call him a sinner.

The next day while he was praying, he said, 'Okay, I accept what you say. Now I want one more criterion: I want to know who is the greatest saint, the most virtuous man in the village.'

The voice said, 'The same man, your neighbour.'

Junnaid said, 'You are confusing me, and there is already great confusion in me. Yesterday I was watching the man all day—I didn't notice anything that could hint that he is a great sinner. Now this only adds to the confusion: he is also the virtuous man!'

The voice said, 'In my existence, opposites are complementary.'

It is the intellect that looks at things and divides them in two. Here, the greatest saint has a shadow, and the greatest sinner has light shining from his face. This is why it is possible that if a saint wants, he can become a sinner, and if a sinner wants, he can become a saint. This transformation is possible so easily only because both are hidden in the same person.

Darkness and light are not separate; day and night are interconnected. It is logic that splits and tries to make clear-cut paths. Logic is like a well-trimmed, neat and clean cultivated garden. Life is like a forest: nothing is trimmed and clear in it. There, things are entangled with each other.

If you want to understand life, you need the capacity to avoid clear-cut, ready-made answers. There is a kind of security in clinging to them, because you feel reassured, 'Yes, I know.' This gives you the courage, the reassurance to tread the path of life. This is why you are afraid to let go of knowledge. It is very painful. If someone steals your money, it doesn't matter so much, you can earn it again. And anyway, money is dirty, you already knew that. If someone takes your position away, it is no big deal; you, yourself, could have renounced it if the situation demanded it. But knowledge . . .?

I have observed a very interesting phenomenon: somebody can renounce his society, his village, his house, his family; but if he was a Jaina, he will remain a Jaina in the Himalayas too; if he was a Hindu, he will remain a Hindu; if he was a Mohammedan, he will remain a Mohammedan. It is the same society he had left behind that had given him this Mohammedan conditioning, had given him the understanding that he is a Mohammedan, and the Koran is the true scripture, that all other scriptures are false. He leaves everything behind, but saves this knowledge even in the Himalayas. Nothing has changed in this person's life because he still believes in his knowledge.

If you drop knowledge, the Himalayas will be there, wherever you are. The meaning of the Himalayas is where everything is mysterious, where there are lofty peaks that you cannot scale and where there are deep valleys that you will not be able to explore—where everything is beyond measure.

Wonder means where your intellect has failed, where your ego is impotent, where you become completely helpless. You may laugh or cry, but you cannot utter a word.

It is said that when Moses reached Mount Sinai, he cried and laughed, but he could not speak at all. When he returned, his disciples asked, 'What has happened to you? God was there before you. He said to you, "Moses, remove your shoes because this is holy ground and I am present here," and you removed your shoes. You cried, you laughed, but why didn't you say something? Why did you miss this opportunity? You could have asked anything worth asking. You could have at least asked for a key that can open all the locks.'

Moses said, 'When he was present in front of me, my mind disappeared; only the heart remained. I laughed and I cried out of sheer joy!'

This is an interesting thing in life—that joy can make you cry, and joy can also make you laugh. Don't think that people always cry out of grief. This is a logical conclusion, but life does not believe in logic. The river of life flows as if in flood, washing away all barriers and boundaries of logic. One can also cry out of joy, but then the very nature and quality of those tears will be different: then bliss will be reflected in the tears. One can also laugh with joy. These opposites can express one and the same thing. Such is the mystery of life.

So Moses said, 'Only my heart was there, my intellect was gone. It seems that I also left my mind where I left my shoes.'

Don't just remove your shoes outside the temple, drop your head there too! Only someone who leaves his head along with his shoes can enter the temple. And there is a great connection between the head and the shoes. This is why when you get angry with someone, you want to hit him on the head with your shoe! A seeker is someone who hits his own head with his own shoe. These are the two extremes, the two poles: the shoe is at one extreme, the head on the other, and you are in the middle. It is at that midpoint in you where all the opposites meet. At the point where your head and your feet meet is your heart.

So Moses said, 'I cried and I laughed because I was filled with wonder. I became speechless. Now I will not be able to sleep. I will not be able to forget what I have seen. What has happened cannot be wiped out. The Moses who was before is no more. Now I am a totally different man.'

It was a new birth. Hindus call it *dwij*, twice-born, when one is born like this a second time. All Brahmins are not dwij, as they are commonly called. It is only once in a while that some Brahmin becomes a dwij. You don't become a dwij just by wearing a sacred thread around your neck. 'Dwij' means one who is twice-born. Moses said, 'Now I am twice-born, dwij. Now I am a different man. That old man has died.'

If you pass through wonder, the old in you will die and the new will be born. And if you become rooted in the sense of wonder, if you remain permanently in the sense of wonder, then, in each moment, the new will be born and the old will die. Each moment the old will disappear and the new will appear. Then you will flow eternally, then you will never become old and stale—then you will have caught hold of the thread of eternal life.

Hence, Shiva says: Wonder is the foundation of religiousness.

The second sutra:

Strength means to be rooted in oneself.

Wonder is the foundation. Wonder means a journey within, an inner search to the question, who am I? If you move outside, there is surprise; if you move outside, there is logic; if you move outside, there is science. But if you move within, it is a sense of wonder; it is meditation, it is prayerfulness. The whole process changes there.

The sense of wonder will take you inward, because when the whole universe has become a mystery, then only one question will seem to be important: Who am I?

'Who am I?' is the basic foundation of the sense of wonder. As long as I don't know this 'I', the journey to know anything else will not be possible. How can I know these trees, how can I know you, how can I know the other, if I am not known to myself, if I am ignorant of myself— if I don't know who I am. Hence, 'Who am I?' is a great mantra.

And don't be in a hurry to answer—because you have all the ready-made answers. 'Who am I?'—and you answer, 'I am the soul.' This answer won't help. You already know it, and it has not changed your life. Knowing is fire, it will burn you. When you ask, 'Who am I?' and a voice from inside gives you the answer, it is not your inner voice. It is your mind that is talking, it is the scriptures hidden in your mind that are talking, it is your memory that is talking.

When you say, 'I am the soul,' it is worthless. It is of no value because this answer has not transformed you. It is not a fire, it is ashes.

There may have been an ember in it once. For some sage it may have been a burning ember at some time, but for you it is only ashes. The person for whom it was a burning ember is no longer in the world, and you are just carrying the ashes.

Go on asking, 'Who am I?' and don't give a borrowed answer. Whenever a borrowed answer comes, just say, 'This is not my answer. I have not known it, so how can it be mine? Only what I have known can be mine.' Only that which you earn through your own effort is your treasure. Knowing cannot be stolen or given. You cannot steal it, you cannot beg for it. There is no place for stealing here. Here, you will have to create yourself through your own efforts.

The second sutra is: *Strength means to be rooted in oneself.* As your sense of wonder arises, move within. Dive deep inside and try to be settled in yourself. As you ask, 'Who am I?' when will you arrive at the answer? If you want the answer you will have to be settled in yourself. We have called it health: to be settled in your own self. And isn't seeing possible only when you become still in yourself? If you are running, how will you be able to see?

Your situation is something like this: you are sitting in a speeding car, when you happen to see a flower through the window—you have barely had time to ask what it is before the car has zoomed past it. You are speeding fast, and no vehicle in this world is faster than desire. If you want to reach the moon, even a spacecraft will take time. But your desire doesn't need even that much time; it will arrive there this very moment. Desire has the fastest speed. It means that a person who is full of desire is never at rest, he is running, racing. And you are in such a hurry that even if you ask the question 'Who am I?' how can the answer arise? There is no room for an answer.

You will have to drop this hurry. You will have to settle inside yourself for a while. You will have to stop all desiring, all hurry and all journeying.

But even before you have fulfilled one desire, you create dozens more. You have barely finished one journey before many new avenues open up and you start running again. You simply don't know how to sit still. You have not stopped for lifetimes.

I have heard that an emperor employed a very intelligent man as his prime minister. But the prime minister was dishonest and, in no time, he had stolen millions of rupees from the empire's treasury.

When the emperor came to know about this, he called the prime minister and said, 'I don't want to say anything. What you have done is not right. I will not say much. I can only say that it is a breach of trust. Don't ever let me see your face again. Leave this kingdom and go somewhere else. And I don't want rumours to spread so I will not say anything to anyone about this and there is no need for you to say a word about it.'

The prime minister said, 'If you command me, I will leave. I have certainly embezzled millions of rupees. Nevertheless, as your prime minister, I would like to offer you one piece of advice. Now I have everything: a big palace, houses in the mountains and on the sea coast. I have everything. My children need not earn anything. If you remove me and appoint some other person, he will have to start again from scratch.'

The emperor was intelligent—he understood.

You never come to a point in your life when you can say, 'Now I have everything.' The day this happens, your hurry will cease. Otherwise, every moment you will have to start again from scratch. Each and every moment a new desire grips you, a new thief enters and comes to rob you of your treasure. And the thief is not one—there are so many desires. You are running in so many directions at the same time. You are trying to do so many things at the same time. You have never thought that many of your goals are opposed to each other and you cannot have them both—if you get one, you will lose the other; if you get the second one, the first is lost.

Mulla Nasruddin was on his deathbed. He told his son, 'Now, before I die, I will tell you two things. Remember them. There are two things: honesty and wisdom. Now you will look after the shop, take care of the work. A sign is hanging in front of our shop: "Honesty is the best policy." Always practise it. Never cheat anybody. Never break a promise. If you make a promise, keep it.'

The son said, 'Okay, what about the other one? What about wisdom?'

Nasruddin said, 'Never make a promise to anyone!'

Such is your life, divided into conflicting standpoints. You try to manage both honesty and wisdom. Honesty says keep a promise, wisdom says never make a promise. On the one hand, you want to be worshipped as a saint and, on the other hand, you want to enjoy like a sinner. A difficult proposition! On the one hand, you want your character to be praised like that of a Rama and, on the other hand, you would like to kidnap somebody's wife like a Ravana. You would like to manage the impossible. You want to live like Ravana, but be revered like Rama. You are in a difficult situation. Then you move in two opposite directions and you create infinite goals for yourself. Pursuing them, you become fragmented, torn in pieces. At the end of your life you will find that the treasure that you had brought with you has been lost.

There was a great gambler. His wife, his family and his friends tried their best to persuade him to stop, but he did not listen to their advice and, eventually, everything was lost. Finally, he came to a point where he had only one rupee left. His wife said, 'Now, wake up! Pull yourself together!'

The husband said, 'When so much is lost and only one rupee is left, give me one last chance. Who knows? This last rupee may change my luck.' A gambler always thinks this way. And he said, 'When we have lost millions and this is the last rupee left, why cry over it? And this one rupee is bound to be spent, it cannot be saved. Let me gamble it!'

His wife also thought, 'Now that everything is lost, this is the last rupee left, it is going to be spent anyway—most probably before the sun sets—so why not let him have his last wish?'

The gambler went to the casino, and he was amazed—he started winning every game! One rupee became one thousand; one thousand became ten thousand, which eventually became a hundred thousand. In the end he gambled those hundred thousand and said, 'Now, this is the last time I will wager and every problem will be solved.' And he lost it all!

He went home. His wife asked, 'What happened?'

He said, 'I lost that one last rupee!'

You can lose only what you have brought with you. Why talk about thousands? He said, 'I have lost one rupee. It doesn't matter. That wager was unfortunate,' but he did not tell her that he had won one hundred thousand. He was right: you can't lose what does not belong to you. And at the moment of death you will find that you have lost the soul that you had brought with you. Just 'one' will be lost: all the rest that you had lost or accumulated or destroyed or gained will be of no consequence. In the final account, it is of no value. The millions that you may have won will be left here when you die. Only one will be taken into account, and that one is *you*. You are a winner if you have become rooted in that one. If you have found that one, you lovingly dwell in it.

It is about this state that Shiva is saying: *Strength means to be rooted in oneself*.

You are weak, wretched and miserable, not because you don't have a house or wealth. You are wretched and miserable because you are not rooted in yourself. To be rooted in yourself is the source of all energy. The moment you are rooted in yourself, you are flooded with immense energy.

Someone asked Jesus, 'What should I do? I am very poor, sick and miserable.'

Jesus said, 'Don't do anything else: first seek the kingdom of God and all else will follow.'

Finding the one, all else is found. If you lose the one, all is lost. That one is none other than yourself, and that alone is your treasure because you have brought it with you. In the final accounting you will be asked whether you have saved what you had brought with you—or have you lost that too?

Strength means to be rooted in oneself. To settle in the self is to become immensely powerful. You already have that immense power within you, but you are like a bucket with thousands of holes. If you drop the bucket into the well, it will appear to be full. As long as the bucket is immersed in the water, it will look full, but the moment you start pulling the bucket and it starts rising above the water level, the water will start leaking through those thousands of holes. By the time the bucket reaches the top of the well, there will be no water left in it.

Your thousands of desires are your thousands of holes: your energy is dissipated through them. As long as you are dreaming, the bucket is full; as long as you desire, the bucket is full. The moment you take action, trying to do something to realize a desire, the moment you start pulling the bucket up, the moment you try to make your dreams come true, the energy starts leaking. By the time the bucket reaches you, you will have the thousand holes, but not a single drop of water. You will remain as thirsty as ever. Every time you draw the bucket, it will make a lot of noise in the well and you feel that water is certainly coming to you, but nothing will actually come into your hand. You remain empty-handed every time. But desire is a very strange phenomenon.

A passer-by asked a fisherman how many fish he had caught. The sun was about to set and his line had been in the water since morning. This passer-by had been down that road several times and each time had noticed the fisherman. At last he could not contain himself, so he asked, 'How many fish have you caught?'

The fisherman answered, 'If I catch the one I am trying to catch now, and if I am able to catch two more, the total will be three.'

He had not caught a single fish so far, but he was imagining, 'If I catch this one, plus two more, they will make three.'

You are also in the same state as this fisherman: one you are trying to catch and two more you are dreaming about, although even the first has not happened yet—but you calculate three and you are very happy.

Whenever you pull the bucket out, you will find it empty. And remember, the more you throw it into the well, the wider the holes will become. This is the reason children look so happy. Old people look very sad because their bucket has just become holes and more holes. They have put the bucket into the well and drawn it out so many times and all the holes have grown, that's all! But you keep on hoping at any cost: 'One day we will be able to draw a bucket full of water' because the bucket looks full whilst it is in the well, but later on you will see the water is leaking out.

You have the energy of the infinite, of the universal, but your mind is like a bucket full of holes.

This sutra—*Strength means to be rooted in oneself*— means that once you are no longer chasing after a desire, it will drop, and one hole will close. If all desires drop, all the holes will close. Then you don't need to put the bucket into any well, you are yourself the well. You will be filled with immense energy inside if only you can stop leaking energy.

You are born with vast energy; you don't have to do anything for it. Everything that is of worth is already within you: you just have to be careful not to lose it. It is not a question of attaining godliness; you have only to avoid losing it. You have it already. How you manage to lose it is one of the great mysteries of this world.

The third sutra:

Transcendent logic or discriminating awareness leads to self-realization.

Each sutra is like a key. The first is about wonder. The sense of wonder will make you turn within. The second is to be rooted in yourself so that you become available to immense energy. But how will you become rooted in yourself? The key to this is given in this third sutra: to go beyond logic and to use conscious discriminating wisdom are the ways to self-realization.

The words 'transcendent logic' have to be understood. We know what logic is: it is a tool of science. It is like a knife that dissects wonder. *Tarka*, logic, dissects and analyses. Logic moves outwards. *Vitarka*, transcendent logic, moves inwards. It does not dissect—it joins, it unites. Logic is analysis, transcendent logic is synthesis.

There was a Sufi mystic, Farid. One of his devotees brought him a pair of scissors made of gold. It was very valuable, studded with precious stones. The devotee said, 'It has been in my family for many generations. It is worth millions of rupees, but I have no use for it. I offer it at your feet.'

Farid said, 'Please take it back. If you want to present something to me, bring me a needle and a thread because I don't believe in dissecting, in cutting—I believe in joining together. A pair of scissors cuts. If you want to present something to me, it is better to bring a needle and thread.'

Logic is like a pair of scissors—it cuts. In Hindu mythology, Ganesh is the god of logic, and that is why he rides a rat. A rat is like a pair of scissors: it cuts; it is a living pair of scissors, it goes on cutting, and Ganesh rides on it. He is a god of logic, but Hindus have made him a laughing stock. If his appearance does not make you laugh, it would be amazing. You don't laugh because you have become used to his appearance; otherwise, he is a funny-looking figure. Take a close look at Ganesh's body and you will find that he is shapeless in every way. Even his head is not his own, it is borrowed. A logician has a borrowed head. Ganesh's head is very big, it is an elephant's head, but it is not his own. And a borrowed head, even if it is an elephant's, is useless: it will only make you look ugly. His body is bulky, and he rides on a rat. This huge body is only a showpiece because he still rides a rat. However great a scholar he may be, his vehicle is still a rat—logic, a pair of scissors.

Farid is right when he says, 'If you want to present something, bring a needle and a thread because I believe in sewing, in joining together.'

Transcendent logic is the art of synthesizing. The Sanskrit word vitarka means a special logic. Common logic, tarka, analyses; special logic, vitarka, synthesizes. Buddha, Mahavira, Shiva and Lao Tzu, they all use logic, but theirs is the special logic, a transcendent logic.

There is one more kind of logic, which is called kutarka, false logic. There are three possibilities. One, logic that dissects and analyses, but its intention is not bad. It is just that the mystery has to be solved. It is not interested in dissecting; dissection is just the process. Its aim is to discover a certain principle that will end the mystery, that will make things crystal clear. The aim of this logic is constructive.

When logic has no goal except to dissect, when the aim becomes to destroy, when it begins to enjoy just being destructive, then it is called kutarka, false logic. It is an insane logic. It becomes mad, it is bent on destroying. Then it has no other motive and destruction becomes its purpose.

Vitarka, special logic, is an inward journey. For example, you have come here from your house, but your eyes and vision, your direction, was facing me, and your back was to your house. When you go back home from here, the road will be the same—in what way will the road be different? Only your direction will have changed: you will turn your back to me and you will be facing your house.

Logic and transcendent logic walk the same path; this is why it is simply called 'special logic'. The path is the same, only the direction has changed. Before the logic was moving towards the other, towards some object; now logic is moving towards the self, towards home. And this change in direction changes the whole quality. When it was moving outwards towards the other, the only way to know the other was through dissection and analysis. If you want to know the object, it can only be done through analysing—there is no other way.

If you go to a medical college you will find the students there dissecting. They dissect the frog because they have to know what is inside. There is no other way; you can know the insides of a frog only by dissecting it. But if you want to know yourself there is no need to dissect, because you are there inside.

If you want to know the other, you will have to dissect and destroy because there is no other way to know. But if you want to know yourself, there is no question of dissecting or destroying because you are already present there. If you want to know yourself, just closing your eyes is enough. To close your eyes is meditation. When attention is withdrawn from the outside and focuses inward, tarka becomes vitarka: ordinary logic becomes transcendent logic.

Another name for vitarka is *vivek*, awareness. Vivek, awareness, is a process of synthesis: the more you go within, the more you will become integrated. You can understand it in this way: there is a circle with a wide circumference. If you choose any two points on the circumference, they will be apart, at a distance. Then if you start drawing two straight lines from those two points towards the centre of the circle, you will find that as the lines move towards the centre, they will come closer and closer to each other until at the centre they are finally one. On the other hand, if you start extending the two lines outwards, away from the centre, they will grow farther and farther away from each other until the distance between them becomes infinite like the infinite sky.

In the same way, when you move outward, away from yourself, everything starts becoming farther and farther apart; and the farther away from yourself you go, the greater the distance between them. This is why a thousand and one branches of science have developed. It is bound to be so, because the gaps go on growing. Every day there are more and more new sciences, because as we move forward, the gaps between things grow bigger and bigger.

New theories arise every day and scientists are facing a dilemma: one science cannot understand the language of the other. There is not one person on earth who can understand all the sciences, who can manage to have a synthesized understanding drawn from all the branches of science. This has become a complex situation. As it is, it is almost impossible to know even a single branch of science completely. There is much knowledge in the world, but the ability to synthesize it all has been completely lost.

Religiousness is one, no matter how many different names you give it, because as soon as you begin to move inward, the more the gaps start to narrow, until, at the very centre, everything merges into one. At the centre is the ultimate synthesis.

Transcendent logic or discriminating awareness leads to self-realization. To rejoice in the bliss of existence is enlightenment. Don't divide. Don't go outward. Don't keep your focus on the other, bring your awareness inward. Synthesize! Go on moving slowly towards your centre until you reach the very source of your being. Settle there, and an immense energy will arise within you.

The light that we see around Mahavira and Buddha, the bliss that we find in Krishna, Meera and Chaitanya, from where does this bliss arise? What does this light indicate? It indicates that these people have reached the place where the source of infinite energy is. They are no longer in misery.

They are no longer helpless and begging from anybody. Now they are emperors in their own right. This is also your potential, but you have to proceed step by step. First, move in wonder, then become rooted in yourself, then cultivate transcendent logic or aware discrimination as a way to reach to yourself.

And then the fourth sutra is:

To rejoice in the bliss of existence is enlightenment.

When you have returned to yourself and are firmly rooted in your own being, you have reached the deepest state of existence. At this point, existence is at its greatest depth because everything is created out of this. Your centre is not only your centre, it is the centre of the whole existence.

We are separate only at the circumference. 'You' and 'I' are separations only at the level of the body. As we go deeper than the body and turn in, the distance between us starts to become smaller and smaller. On the day you come to know your being, you will also know the universal being. On the day you come to know your own being, you will know the being of the whole existence, because at the centre everything is one. Differences exist only on the periphery. At the centre, there is no difference—there, we are all one existence.

Shiva says that by discovering this existence within your own self, the bliss that is enlightenment is attained.

Samadhisukham: the bliss that is enlightenment. This word needs to be understood. You have known many joys: at some time the joy of food, at some time the joy of health, at some time when you were thirsty, the joy of water quenching your thirst, at some time the joy of enjoying your physical body, the enjoyment of sex. You have known many such joys. But about these joys there is one common thing to be understood: sorrow is inevitably connected to them. If you are not thirsty, water will bring you no joy. You will be able to enjoy drinking water only if you are ready to feel the torment of thirst. The unhappiness comes first and lasts for long; the joy that follows is only momentary. As soon as the water passes down your throat the thirst will be quenched; then again the thirst, again the suffering . . . If you are not hungry, if there is no distress of hunger, then food offers you no joy.

And this is the irony of life: the people who are tormented by hunger, those who could really savour the joy of eating, have nothing to eat. And the people who don't know what hunger is have plenty to eat, but they can't enjoy their food. On the contrary, it is a source of suffering for them.

Only when you are thirsty can you have the contentment and the joy that come from drinking water. But it is possible to live a kind of life where you never feel any thirst. If you don't go out in the sun, don't do any work, stay indoors at home and relax, you will not feel any thirst. Then if you think you can drink water to your heart's content and enjoy, you will not be able to, because now there will not be any bliss in drinking water. Someone who works all day will enjoy the bliss of a good night's rest. It is ironic that if you want to enjoy the bliss of a good night's sleep, you have to work like a labourer all day. The trouble is that you want to spend your days like an emperor and have the nights of a labourer, but this is not possible.

In the outer world, happiness and suffering are intrinsically connected. Hence, the day you acquire a palace, you will lose your sleep. When you manage to sleep in a feather bed, you will find yourself tossing and turning all night. Look at the labourer: he sleeps under a tree on stones and pebbles, but he sleeps like a log. Mosquitoes bite him, it is so hot that he is soaked with perspiration, but he is oblivious to it all. It is all immaterial to him. He has gone through such intense suffering during the day that he has earned the bliss he will have in the night.

In the outer world, to earn the joy of happiness you have to pay with suffering. In the world, happiness is connected with an equal amount of suffering. And this is the dilemma: people want to have the happiness and avoid the suffering, but that is not possible. For thousands of years we have tried to eliminate the suffering and save the happiness. But this effort is futile. Suffering is certainly eliminated, but then at the same time happiness will be reduced in the same proportion. We reject suffering and desire happiness—and this is the root cause of the big mess humanity is in.

What is the meaning of 'the bliss of existence is enlightenment'? It is the state which has no misery or suffering attached to it. The bliss called enlightenment is not like quenching some thirst, it is not like the filling of an empty stomach or the bliss of a good night's sleep after a hard day's work. The bliss that is enlightenment is not connected to any misery. This is the difference between spiritual bliss and worldly bliss. The bliss that is enlightenment is the bliss of simply existing. There is no desire, no craving, no suffering connected with it at all. It is simply the bliss of being.

This is why Shiva calls it *lokanandah*—the blissfulness of existence. Just to be—that in itself is blissfulness. It has nothing to do with thirst and suffering or anything of the sort. Moreover, remember that the being has no hunger or thirst whatsoever, so the question of hunger or thirst and the bliss you feel when they are satisfied does not arise. All thirst and hunger belong to the body, and bliss at the level of the body will always be connected to suffering. So someone who desires the joys of the body should always be prepared for the suffering. And the greater the suffering they are ready to go through, the greater the happiness they will be able to have.

The bliss of the being is the purest of bliss; it is not possible for any suffering to be connected to it. But this happens only at the centre. On the periphery, you are only a body.

The body is on the periphery. It is the wall surrounding your home, it is not you. It is your outer circumference. At the centre you are the being; and it is here that a completely new kind of bliss reveals itself. This bliss is the bliss of simply being, just being. There is no peak of happiness or depth of misery here. There are no ups or downs, no gains or losses, no night or day, no toil or rest. Here, you simply are. Here there is only eternal is-ness, and the state of eternal is-ness is full of bliss. There is no interruption in this bliss; hence, the mystics have called it eternal, everlasting, perpetual. There is no pause or interval in this bliss.

Kabir says, 'Nectar ceaselessly showers there, unhindered, constant.'

In this world, also, there is rain, but heat must precede this rain. When the heat of summer reaches a peak—when there are cracks in the dry earth, when the trees start to wilt, when the heat becomes unbearable everywhere—the rains come. You may ask, why such an absurd law? Why can't there be rain without all this suffering? But you have to understand the ways of nature, the mathematics of nature. Clouds will form only when the heat becomes unbearable, because it is only then that water turns to vapour. There can be no rain if there is no evaporation. The vapour rises and forms clouds, and when the clouds are oversaturated to the point where they can't help showering, it starts raining. Thus, unbearable heat is a prerequisite for a rainy season to set in.

In the world of being there are no opposites, there is no duality. This is why we call it *non-dual*, or 'not two'. There is only the one, not two. But it will be difficult for you to understand what kind of happiness this is, because you know no happiness without suffering as its opposite.

Someone asked Sigmund Freud for a definition of insanity and how people reach that point. Freud's answer was amazing. He said, 'Success and insanity have much in common, and the path that leads to success is the same as the one that leads to insanity.' When you want to succeed, you become tense; when you want to succeed, you fight. When you want to succeed, your days and nights become filled with anxiety. When you want to succeed, each and every moment is overshadowed by fear: will you win or not? And you are not the only one trying to succeed, there are tens of thousands of competitors. Night and day you are in a state of acute tension, worry, fear and anxiety—and this is exactly the prescription for losing your sanity. If you observe the people you call successful, you will find that they live in the same state of constant restlessness and tension that mad people live in.

When Khrushchev was in power in Russia, he went to inspect an insane asylum. While he was at the asylum he remembered an important matter so he phoned his office, but the girl at the switchboard paid no attention. There was a reason why she did this, but it became clear only later on. Finally, he got fed up, and shouted, 'Young lady! Do you know who I am?'

This is common to all successful people, those who are in power and who have money. Inwardly, this thought is constantly echoing in their minds: Do you know who I am? He may not say it loudly, but inside he is repeating it over and over again: 'Do you know who I am?'—because it is for this that he has wasted his whole life: to have the status where he can ask this question.

So finally he could not contain himself and he said, 'Girl, do you know who I am? I am Khrushchev, the premier.'

The girl said, 'I don't know who you are, but I know where you are phoning from—the madhouse.'

The fact is that all the prime ministers and Presidents are speaking from the same place—there is no other place they can possibly be speaking from.

Once, Khrushchev went to London. Someone had earlier presented him with a very expensive piece of cloth. The cloth was so expensive that he wanted one of the best tailors in the world to sew it. He had asked for the best tailor in Moscow. He wanted to make a suit, complete with a vest, but the Russian tailor said there was not enough cloth for a three-piece suit. He could only make a two-piece suit. But the fabric was so expensive that Khrushchev wanted a three-piece suit to be made.

So he took the cloth with him to London. In London he was told that he could easily get a three-piece suit made, and with enough cloth left over to make something for his child too.

Khrushchev was shocked. He asked how his own Russian tailor could be so dishonest as to insist that only a two-piece suit could be made. The London tailor answered, 'Don't be angry with him. In Russia you are a very big man, so much more cloth will be needed there. Here, in London, you are nobody.'

People have to be ready to suffer for the joys of success and ambition they pursue their whole lives, to suffer in the same proportion as the amount of happiness they pursue—and those hardships and sufferings will break them completely. Long before they have experienced any success, they will have become almost a failure. Nobody ever succeeds in this world, because you have to go through so much insanity, so much madness as the price for this success, that by the time success comes it is not worth having.

The bliss of self-realization is totally different: you don't have to pay any price for it, because what you are trying to reach is already present in you, here and now. It is not somewhere in the future, that you have to go in search of it and work hard for it. It is present here, it is present now. You already have it; it is your intrinsic treasure. There is no need to go through any suffering as a price for it.

You may wonder what the taste of this bliss is. None of the bliss that you have known in the past can give any idea of this taste, because it was all intrinsically mixed with suffering. All the nectars that you have known and tasted have poison mixed in them. This is bound to be so with the body. In the body, birth and death are combined; nectar and poison are side by side. Any happiness of the body is bound to carry within itself its counterpart of suffering. But your being is pure nectar. It is deathless. It is eternal. There are no opposites there. It is life, pure life.

So if you can put aside the bitter taste of all the happiness you have had, perhaps you will be able to imagine the taste of this bliss a little. If you can put aside the sufferings that are an intrinsic part of all the happiness and joys you have ever known, perhaps you will be able to imagine a little glimpse. But even this won't be the real thing, because a glimpse only belongs to the periphery of the real thing. No matter how much you think or imagine, you won't be able to have any idea or concept of something that you have not experienced for yourself. Experience is the only way.

These sutras are very precious. Be filled with a sense of wonder, then turn your eyes inward towards yourself; be centred in yourself so that the great energy can become available to you and your life can become a supreme life. Attain enlightenment through transcendent logic and discriminating wisdom, through awakening, absolute awakening, destroying your sleep. Only then will you be able to rejoice in the bliss of existence. The bliss that is enlightenment will be yours.

A few more points about the bliss that is enlightenment are as below.

One, the happiness or bliss that you enjoy in your worldly life depends on many things. It depends on your worthiness, on your level of education, on your power and capacity, on your family, your relations—it depends on all these things. It is not just about you alone. If you are born to a poor household, it may take you a whole lifetime to find the joys that someone else who has been born in a rich family will be able to find much sooner. If you are rational, prudent, clever and calculating, you will find it earlier. If you are a little stupid, you will wander around a great deal and it is doubtful whether you will find it at all. If your body is unhealthy, it will be more difficult; if your body is healthy, you will find it sooner. It is coincidental and will depend on a thousand and one things.

The bliss that enlightenment is does not depend on anything. It is unconditional. It does not depend either on your intellect or on your body, on your worthiness or unworthiness, on your education, your family, your looks, your gender—it depends on none of these. Your caste, your nationality is irrelevant. Whether you are young or old is of no importance. This bliss is unconditional because it is your own inner treasure—you already have it. You are born with it. You have just not given any attention to it, that's all. You have only forgotten it, you have not lost it. Just turn your eyes in and meet yourself.

It is not that an intellectual person will find more enlightenment, more bliss, and that a stupid person will remain deprived—this is not the case at all. Even illiterate people become enlightened. Kabir, who was illiterate, was enlightened. Buddha, who was well educated and cultured, was enlightened. And once in the state of enlightenment, there is not an iota of difference between the two.

The bliss that is enlightenment is the intrinsic nature of life. On your periphery, whether you are fair or dark, ugly or beautiful, healthy or unhealthy; whether your mind is too filled with information and words or not, whether you have read more scriptures or less—all these things have nothing to do with it. Your being is enough. That you exist is enough.

Hence, all meditation is nothing but a quest to become pure, to reach the point where you will forget your body, forget your mind; you will begin to experience the bliss that is enlightenment—the bliss of existence. Do only this much: somehow forget your body for a while, forget your mind for a while. As soon as the body and the mind are forgotten, the remembrance of your being emerges. As long as you are identified with the body and the mind, there can be no remembrance of the being, because the body and mind are on the periphery and your being is at the centre—and you cannot look at both of them at the same time.

In this meditation camp, if you can manage only this much—that even for a moment the body and mind are forgotten—you will taste the bliss that is enlightenment. Once you have had a taste, that is enough; your life will be transformed. It is the first taste that is difficult. Once your vision has turned in, you have discovered the knack; then it is in your hands. Then whenever you turn your vision in, you will find it. It is the first turning in of your vision that requires the most effort.

Once the key is in your hands, you are the master. Then you can have the taste whenever you want. Then you can move in the world free of care because nobody can take away from you your bliss called enlightenment. You may be sitting in your shop and the bliss called enlightenment will be with you, you can be in the marketplace and the bliss called enlightenment will be with you.

But one thing will start to happen: your mad race after worldly pleasures and happiness will, by itself, start to become less and less. When ultimate bliss is yours, who cares about the bliss of the trivial? When diamonds and rubies are in your hands, then who will hold on to pebbles and seashells? They will drop of their own accord, you need not renounce them.

This is why I always say that an awakened person never renounces anything, because whatever has no value falls away on its own. It is the ignorant who renounce, because that looks very difficult to them. They don't know the precious, so they just try to renounce what is worthless. But their minds cling, and the mind says, 'You are leaving what you have, and how can you trust what you don't yet have in your hand? Besides, who knows whether it even exists?'

So I don't ask you to renounce anything; I only invite you to have a taste of the bliss that enlightenment is. That taste will become the ultimate renunciation in your life. Then you will know for yourself what is meaningless—and no one clings to anything meaningless, they simply start letting go of it.

There was a mystic saint in Bengal, Yukteshwar Giri. A very rich person once went to him and said, 'You are a great renunciate.'

Giri laughed out loud. 'Look at him!' he said to his disciples, pointing to the man. 'Look at him! He is a great renunciate himself, and he is calling me one. Don't try to trap me, my good man!'

The man was surprised and so were his disciples. They asked the master to explain this to them, because there was no doubt that he was a great renunciate.

Giri said, 'Suppose there is a pile of diamonds and a pile of pebbles. This man holds on to the pebbles rather than the diamonds, while I hold on to the diamonds. And he calls me a renunciate! Who is actually the renunciate?'

Is Mahavira a renunciate or you? Is Buddha a renunciate or you? *You* are the renunciate, because you are holding on to rubbish. You are throwing away the bliss that is enlightenment for the anxiety-ridden, futile trivia of the periphery, where nothing is pure, where everything is impure, where everything is stale and spoiled.

The worldly man is a great renunciate, but he thinks the sannyasin is the renunciate. In fact, worldly men look at sannyasin with pity: 'Poor things, they are deprived of everything, they have left everything. They have missed all of life's pleasures.' They worship sannyasin, but deep down they pity them too: 'Poor, naive things! They have renounced everything without enjoying anything. At least they should have enjoyed a little!'

But the worldly men have no idea whom they are speaking about. The sannyasin has found the ultimate enjoyment. Existence itself has invited and included him in the ultimate enjoyment.

I don't ask you to renounce. I ask you to know, to taste. This very taste will slowly displace all that is useless and trivial in your life. The useless just falls away, it need not be renounced.

Enough for today.

4

Deepening the Mantra of Meditation

Mind is mantra.
Effort is the seeker.
The master is the way.
The body is the offering.
Knowing is nourishment.
Dreams arise from an absence of knowing.

MIND IS MANTRA.

A mantra is something that creates energy by continuous repetition, whose very repetition *becomes* the energy. Whatever thought you repeat continuously will, by and by, become an action. Any thought that you repeat again and again will begin to manifest in your life. Whatever you are is the result of certain thoughts that you have repeated over and over again.

Much research has been done on hypnosis. Modern psychology has penetrated hypnosis at its deepest levels. It has found that hypnosis is based on only one principle: if you want to convert any thought into reality, repeat it as many times as possible. By repeating, a track will be created, which will gradually become a path within the mind. It is just like a river is flowing: if we create a track by digging a ditch by the river, the ditch will become a canal. In just the same way, if a track of thought is created within the mind, very soon the thought will begin to materialize.

There was a great French psychologist called Émile Coué. He cured tens of thousands of people just with the help of mantras. Thousands of patients from all over the world used to go to him, and his treatment was very simple. He used to tell the patient to repeat to himself, 'I am not sick, I am healthy. I am constantly becoming healthier.' The patient was told to repeat this while falling asleep, while waking up in the morning and as many times as he could remember during the day. This single thought was to be repeated constantly: 'I am healthy. I am becoming healthier and healthier every day . . .'

It seems like a miracle, because people with incurable diseases were cured by this repetition. People started going to Coué from far and wide. But the strategy is very simple.

When you are cured from some sickness, psychologists say that 90 per cent of the cure happens through this same psychology of repetition, and the medicine does only 10 per cent of the work. A patient takes a medicine four times or eight times a day, and each time he takes the medicine he has the idea in his mind: 'Now I am going to get better. I have found the right medicine.'

With homeopathic medicine, the pills are no remedy in themselves because there is nothing in them, but all the same people are cured just as often as with allopathic medicines. If a good doctor gives you just water you will still be cured because the question is not of medicine; it is because you have faith in the good doctor. This faith becomes the repetition: you know that a good doctor has treated you. That is why the doctor who charges more money cures more people than the one who charges less. As your pocket gets lighter, your faith becomes stronger. You feel that he must be a great doctor! And, of course, for such a sick patient as you, only a great doctor can help . . . It is simply another way of repetition.

Psychologists have done experiments with what they call placebos. The results of the experiments were surprising. If there are fifty patients with the same illness, twenty-five were given real medicine and the other twenty-five were given just plain water. No one knew who was being given water rather than medicine. The patients themselves didn't know, they still believed that they were getting their medicine. The surprising thing was that at the end of the treatment, as many people were cured in the group that were given a placebo as in the group that were given real medicine. The percentage of cures was the same.

This is the reason why more people are cured by a medicine when it first goes on the market; later, the numbers decrease. That is why no medicine is popular for more than two or three years, because when a medicine is new, people have great faith that now the right medicine has been discovered. Patients all over the world are influenced by this. Then slowly, slowly, their faith starts to ebb because sometimes a patient is not cured by it. Sometimes there is even a stubborn patient who doesn't care about the drug or the doctor. Because of these people, the faith of others also starts to disappear and, slowly, the medicine will lose all its effectiveness. So every few years new medicines have to be created.

Also, drugs are effective only if they are well advertised. A drug needs to be advertised in all media—the radio, newspapers, movies, magazines and television—all of them. This advertising is more effective than the drug itself, because it is the advertising that will hypnotize you. The repeated publicity becomes a mantra. If you open the newspaper and you see Aspro, you turn on the radio and you hear about

Aspro, you watch television and you see Aspro, billboards by the side of the road proclaim Aspro, wherever you turn you see Aspro—it becomes a bigger headache than the original headache, and in this way the first headache gets better.

Repetition creates energy. A mantra means to repeat something over and over again. This sutra says:

Mind is mantra.

It means that beyond this, no other mantra is needed. If you understand the mind, the workings of the mind itself are a constant repetition. What else has your mind been doing for so many lifetimes? Just repeating. What do you do from morning until night? Every day, you repeat the same things. What you did yesterday and the day before yesterday, you are repeating the same things today, and if you don't change you will repeat the same thing again tomorrow. And the more you repeat, the more intense the repetition will become. Finally, you will get so caught up in this mess that it will become very difficult for you to get out of it.

People come to me and say, 'I can't give up smoking.' They have repeated it so many times that smoking has become their mantra. If a person smokes two packs of cigarettes a day, that simply means that he is repeating this activity forty times a day. He has repeated it again and again, and he has been doing this for years. Now, suddenly, today, he wants to stop. But something that has become a mantra can't be suddenly dropped. You may stop smoking, but it will make no difference because your whole mind will demand a cigarette, your whole body will demand a smoke: 'I want to smoke! I want a smoke!'

This is what we call addiction. Addiction is something that you have turned into a mantra. And now you want suddenly to stop it? It cannot be done. Something that has become a mantra, an addiction, can only be broken with an opposite mantra.

In Russia, Pavlov has done much research on this subject. Perhaps he is the only person who has successfully cured people with addictions. If you were heavily addicted to smoking and wanted to give it up, Pavlov would use this method of mantra, of repetition. His mantras were a little too strong: he would give you a cigarette, and as soon as you had it in your hand you would get an electric shock that would make your whole body tremble so much that the cigarette would fall out of your hand. You would remain in his clinic this way for seven days. Every time you smoked you would get an electric shock. In seven days, the mantra would have entered more deeply in you than your habit of smoking. The very mention of the word 'cigarette' might make you tremble. Instead of enjoying smoking, a kind of repulsion would happen in you. You would develop an aversion to smoking.

Pavlov cured thousands of people through the use of this alternative mantra. And Pavlov says that unless the people trapped in certain addictions—which are nothing but repetitions, a mantra—are given an alternative addiction, an alternative mantra that is stronger than the earlier one, there is no way out.

Your life, as it is, is the result of your mind, and so you go on repeating the same things. You certainly want to get rid of your anger, yet every day you keep getting angry. And the more the repetition, the stronger the anger will become. How often have you made a vow that you will not get angry, but all your vows are broken and you again get angry? This has only complicated the problem. It would have been better not to make any vow because, now, your mantra, your repetitive habit, will become doubly strong.

Now you know that your anger is bigger than your vow, more powerful than your vow.

Vows won't help. No matter how many times you make them, they are useless because your anger is stronger. And this hypnosis will also sink into you because now, even as you make the vow, inside you know that it is not going to work. In the same moment you know, deep down, that although you are making a vow, you won't be able to keep it. Never make a vow if you can't keep it. It is better for you to remain with only one habit, only one addiction. To make a vow and then to break it is at a great cost, because you will also be creating another habit of breaking your vows. Then you will never be able to keep any vow that you take in life.

Your so-called religious teachers have made you very irreligious because they have encouraged you to make vows so cheaply. You go to the temple, to the holy man, to the monk, and he tells you, 'Take a vow!' Under his influence, with the impact of the peaceful surroundings of the temple and under the weight of your own ego, when the monk asks, then to say that you can't manage even a small vow looks pathetic. So you end up saying: 'Okay, I will stop smoking cigarettes from now on.'

I have a friend who is slightly out of his mind—but he is better off than you! He went to a Jaina monk—he is a Jaina—and the muni said, 'Take a vow!'

He said, 'Okay. I have taken it.'

The monk asked, 'What vow did you take?'

He said, 'I have taken a vow that from now on I will start smoking beedis.'

He is a little out of his mind, but he faithfully kept the vow! Until then he had not been a smoker. And I tell you: he is in a better position than a man who takes a vow not to smoke and then starts smoking, because on top of everything else he has even broken his vow and now he is filled with self-condemnation. This friend at least managed to keep his vow. He may be a little out of his mind, but he is better off than you because he could at least fulfil his vow.

Whenever you break a vow, you start condemning yourself and feeling guilty. And the more self-condemnation and guilt you feel, the more miserable you will be. Being happens to emperors, not to miserable people. The miserable go further away from their being.

If you understand the nature of the mind, you will be able to understand this sutra. The whole movement of the mind is a constant repetition. The mind is a mantra, and whatsoever you have repeated has become your addiction. Whatsoever you go on repeating will become a part of your life. If you have repeated something for many lives, then you will go on creating the same thing again and again. You become tied down to repeating the same wrongs.

So what is to be done?

The first thing is: don't be in a hurry to get rid of the wrong. It would be better if, instead of trying to destroy the wrong, you give energy to a mantra about something right. You smoke cigarettes? No problem, just try to learn meditation. Smoking is not at all an obstacle to meditation. Simply learn to meditate, just deepen the mantra of meditation. The day you succeed in learning to meditate, you will reclaim your self-dignity. And when you have reclaimed your self-dignity and learned to meditate, it will become easier to stop smoking because you will have succeeded in creating a positive mantra.

Don't focus on the negative way, otherwise you will get into trouble. You will feel guilty and lose hope. Your monks sitting in the temples are all sad. There is no laughter, no joy, no happiness, no flowering in their lives because they have focused on the negative. The negative is their only interest and they have tried to repress it.

I teach you not to be in a hurry to drop what is wrong, just hurry to cultivate what is right. When the right has settled in you it will be very easy for you to drop the wrong. Don't fight with the illness, just try to become healthy. This is what Coué is telling people. He is telling them to repeat the idea: 'I am becoming healthy.'

You can also do just the opposite. If you have a headache you can say, 'No, I have no headache.' But as often as you say this, you will also be repeating the word 'headache'. And if you have a headache, then you can repeat it as many times as you like that there is no headache, it will make no difference. Inside you will know that your repetition is a lie. No matter how much you go on saying that there is no headache, your head will still be aching. You are repeating this because Coué has said so—but your head *is* aching. And your headache will disappear only through your inner process, not because Coué has said so. No, it will not help if you go with a negative approach.

This is why I say don't try to renounce the world; rather, seek the truth. So I say, don't go in the direction of renunciation; instead, seek ultimate bliss. Don't focus on what is wrong, because even to renounce the wrong you will have to look at it again and again. The more you look at it, the more the mantra will be repeated, and you will be hypnotized by what you keep looking at.

Much research has been done on car accidents, because now even more people are dying in car accidents than in wars. The number of people in the world who die every year in car accidents is twice as high as the number of people who died in one year during the Second World War. It is a very big number. Something has to be done.

Many things have come to light. One is that car accidents happen mostly at night between midnight and three in the morning. Almost 50 per cent of accidents happen between twelve and three because that is the time to sleep and the mind is drowsy and awareness is less. During moments of unawareness, it is very easy to become hypnotized. The driver is hypnotized by the monotonous sound of the engine, with his eyes fixed on the same road for miles. The psychologists say that thousands of people die because of the white line in the middle of the road, because the driver keeps watching it and gets hypnotized. Then he is not in his senses, as if he is drunk. Between twelve and three it is already time to sleep, and then the monotonous sound of the engine creates boredom and makes you sleepy. It becomes a mantra: the same long road going on endlessly, so colourless at night because you cannot even see the trees or the hills by the side of the road, and then this straight white line in the middle . . .

Try a small experiment. Draw a straight white line on a table, and put a hen on the table and bend its head so that it can see the line. Then release it—the hen will stay there; it will not move away because it has been hypnotized. It will stay sitting there for hours in the same position. Its gaze will be fixed on the line; the line will have created a trance.

Psychologists say that the white line in the middle of the road creates a trance in the driver. So they say a road should not be made straight; there should be changes in it so that there is no monotony, and the trance can be broken. They also say that it would be better if the sound of the engine changed, because the change will help to break the trance and many accidents can be avoided.

Hundreds of accidents in your life also can be averted. First, don't fix your eyes on what is wrong, because what you see will slowly find its place inside you. You are already so accustomed to giving your attention to the wrong—you only pay attention to what is wrong in you. An angry man usually focuses on his anger, thinking how to get rid of it. Although he thinks he is paying attention so that he can get rid of anger, he doesn't know that the more he pays attention to anger, the more he will be hypnotized by the 'white line' of anger.

A sexual person keeps focusing on sex.

I have heard that Mulla Nasruddin became old. When he reached the age of one hundred, journalists went to interview him because he was the only person in the area to have reached that age. They asked him many questions. One of the questions was, 'What do you have to say about the fair sex?'

Nasruddin said, 'Don't raise such a question! I stopped thinking about women three days ago.'

A hundred-year-old man and, until three days before he was thinking only of women! Women will become an obsession because you want to get rid of them, you want to escape from them. This has become your negative mantra. And you will never be able to be free from what you want to get rid of. If you keep looking at the wrong, then you are giving your attention to the wrong.

Mahavira has talked about four forms of meditation: two right and two wrong. No one in the world except Mahavira has ever suggested that the wrong can also be a form of meditation. Psychologists will agree with him. He has said that wrong meditation too is, after all, meditation. For example, a person who is angry is also going into meditation, because in anger he becomes oblivious to the whole world. In anger the mind becomes focused. That is why in anger so much energy becomes available.

Have you ever noticed that a person who is angry can pick up and throw down someone twice as big and strong as him? If he was aware, if he was not possessed by anger, he would have thought many times before picking trouble with a person twice as strong as him. A man can move a huge rock when he is angry, something he can't even imagine doing when he is aware. In anger, a man can do anything, because in anger all your energy wakes up. What happens? The divided energy that was flowing in all directions becomes focused. Just like when the sunrays are focused at one point through a magnifying glass and fire is created, in the same way, similarly in anger, the whole mind becomes focused and a fire is created. Mahavira calls this too meditation.

Mahavira has said that there are two forms of wrong meditation: sorrow and rage. In great sorrow, a person becomes as if he is in meditation. For example, if someone has died, you weep and cry, you scream—your whole attention becomes focused just on one point.

Beware of wrong meditation—and all of you are engaged in wrong meditation. This is the cause of all the trouble in your life, the basic suffering and misery in your life: that you have focused your attention on the wrong. You think everything that is wrong has to be dropped, and you think you are doing this so that you can drop it. But in fact it is because of this wrong meditation that you are unable to get rid of the wrong.

I say unto you, leave the world aside; just focus your attention towards truth. You are an angry man? So what? Everybody is. Don't focus your attention on anger; instead, focus on compassion. Bring into your attention that which is good, that which is right. As the energy that moves with the right, with the good, grows more and more; the energy that moves with the wrong, with the bad, will vanish. Because the energy is one, it cannot move in both directions. If you have put your energy into becoming peaceful, then whenever you want to be agitated and restless, you will find you have no energy left for it because it has already moved into being peaceful. And why would someone who has had a taste of peace bother to become restless? Only someone who has not tasted peace will become restless. Only someone who has not tasted godliness will indulge and be submerged in the world.

Let this sink deeply within you: avoid the negative, avoid the 'no'. Simply don't be concerned about dropping the wrong or the bad, because you will become hypnotized by the very effort of dropping and you will never actually be able to drop it. An attachment develops with anything we want to drop.

I have heard that once a man went to a hotel. The manager said, 'We will not be able to give you a room. A very fussy person is staying underneath the only room we have vacant. He creates such a fuss at the slightest noise or anything he hears down below in his room. Because of him we have left the upper room vacant.'

'You don't have to worry,' said the traveller. 'I will be out all day, busy in the market, and won't be back until eleven or twelve at night. When I return I will go straight to bed because I have to catch a train at three in the morning. I will hardly be in the room for three hours. There is no chance of my being a disturbance to your guest. Moreover, it is good that you have told me, so I will be extra careful.'

The man returned at midnight, exhausted from the day's work. He sat down on the bed, removed a shoe and threw it carelessly on the floor. As it hit the floor he suddenly remembered that the person sleeping below might be disturbed, so he quietly placed the other shoe on the floor and went to sleep. After about fifteen minutes there was a knock on the door. He opened the door and saw a man standing there, trembling with rage.

The traveller became afraid. It was the middle of the night, darkness all around. 'What next?' he thought to himself. But he said, 'Have I done something wrong, sir? I had already gone to sleep.'

The man said, 'Wrong? What about the other shoe? The first one fell, so I thought you have returned. But then what happened to the other one? I can't fall asleep. The other shoe is hanging over my head. I thought I'd better ask and get rid of it.'

Everyone has the other shoe waiting to drop, the shoe of negation: this has to be dropped, that has to be dropped, this is bad, that is bad. There are so many evils that this life seems to be too short to accomplish them and you will never be able to drop them all. There is evil everywhere, in every nook and corner; the whole of life is full of it. And your saints, your holy men and priests only fill you with a sense of guilt. They tell you, 'This is wrong! That is wrong! Everything is wrong!' From them you will never get even a hint about the right, because they say, 'How can you do the right unless you first get rid of the wrong?' Their argument seems to be logical. They are saying, how can you make light as long as darkness has not disappeared—unless the darkness disappears first?'

And I say to you, if you listen to them, however logical their arguments may sound, you will go astray for lives upon lives. It is because of them that you have gone astray in the first place. The devil has not led you astray; it is your so-called saints who have done it. And their argument appears logical: as long as the wrong has not been dropped, how can you do the right?

But have you ever tried to get rid of darkness? Do you want the darkness to be removed first and then you will light the lamp? Then you will never be able to light the lamp. I say to you, first light the lamp, and don't even talk about the darkness, because no sooner is the lamp lit than the darkness will be gone. Bring the light in; don't focus on the darkness. Nobody in the world has ever succeeded in getting rid of darkness by removing it. In the same way, evil cannot be removed, but the good can be brought in. The world cannot be renounced, but the being can be attained. And as soon as the being is attained, the world will drop by itself.

We hold on to the world simply because we can see nothing better to hold on to. And how can we drop the world unless we find something better? No matter how much you want to, you cannot drop it. You will struggle, you will be in anguish, you will tire yourself out, you will destroy yourself, but you will reach nowhere. Your life will become a senseless affair that leads nowhere. Then again you will return to take another body and the same vicious circle will begin. Only the person who can avoid this, this focusing on evil, will attain the good.

The mind is mantra—you can use it in the service of good, you can use it in the service of evil. Repetition becomes energy. You often become angry, so just accept it! No matter how many times anger arises, don't repent it. Don't fight with it either. As often as you become angry, try and do some act of compassion as well. As many as the times that people are hurt and harmed by you, try to help people, to benefit them too. Just start savouring the taste of helping people too. Don't punish yourself for the wrongs; rejoice in the beauties of the good. Don't torture yourself for your wrongs, just do a little good and rejoice in it. If you have abused someone, then praise somebody else, glorify somebody's virtues too. You have enjoyed abusing people enough; now enjoy appreciating them as well.

Don't entangle yourself in the thorns—they are there—
just let your focus be on the flowers. Once you are entangled
in the thorns you will never be able to reach the flowers.
There are many thorns and, by the time you reach the
flowers, you will have got so badly bruised and bloody that
even the flowers will not give you any delight. Even the
touch of them will not thrill you. Even the flowers will hurt
you, because if you are already wounded, then even flowers
will hurt.

Don't pay attention to the thorns, pay attention to the
flowers. And if you have totally rejoiced in the flowers, you
will find, one day, that the thorns no longer exist—because
someone who is in total appreciation of the beauty of the
flower cannot feel the prick of the thorns. The real thing is
to rejoice in the beauty of the flower, to be enchanted by it.
The real thing is to drink the wine of the divine, and then the
wines of the world will not attract you any more. Otherwise
you will keep fighting with them and being defeated by them.

A person who fights with evil is defeated by it. A mind
that fights with evil makes a mantra out of evil, because
repetition is mantra, is mind. Try to understand this process
of how the mind repeats.

Have you ever watched it? For just seven days observe
your mind. Write down everything that the mind repeats.
You will find that your mind has a circular movement. If
you watch carefully, you will find that just as night follows
day, just as morning and evening move in rotation, so too
your anger, your love, your sex, your greed have a fixed
timetable in your mind. Greed catches a hold of you in a
certain time pattern, the same as hunger does. But you have
never observed this; otherwise, you would make a precise
calendar of your twenty-eight days and write down: 'Beware
of me on Monday morning.' Your wife and your children
would know that on Monday mornings, 'Keep away from

Dad!' And it can be useful, because on Monday mornings you . . .

If you can carefully observe for some days, you will be able to see those pivotal points when your mind turns. Not only does the body have a circular movement, but the mind also.

All movement in the world is circular. The moon and stars move in a circle, the earth moves in a circle—everything moves in a circle. The seasons move in a circle, the seasons of your mind also move in a circle. Just as women have a menstrual cycle which completes itself in exactly twenty-eight days, scientists now say that in men also there is a similar chemical process of twenty-eight days. Anyway, their bodies are not much different.

Have you noticed that during their menstrual period women tend to become more irritable, more quarrelsome and angry, more sad, restless and agitated? The Hindus were very clever. They used to isolate them in a room for those three to four days, because it was no use expecting much from them during this time. Such an intense chemical process is going on in their bodies during this time that it will be very difficult for them to remain aware. They are bound to become unaware.

But every twenty-eight days the same happens to men. Men also have a menstrual period. There is no outward flow of blood, but there is an internal release of hormones, from certain glands, that is not visible. Every twenty-eight days men also get depressed, restless, agitated and bad-tempered.

If you observe a little, then you will find that your mind has a cycle that completes itself in twenty-eight days. And if you observe more intensely, you will discover the exact times when certain things happen. You will be amazed because you will find that you don't become angry because of somebody else. You become angry because of your own inner causes; the other is just an excuse. Seeing that, you will no longer throw the responsibility on the other. Then when you lose your temper, you will ask the other for forgiveness. You will say, 'Forgive me: I am not in my right state. It is only a coincidence that you crossed paths with me. The same would have happened with somebody else.'

By observing yourself, you will easily see that the mind is moving in a circle. Mind is a mantra, and if you fail to understand this, you will just go on revolving in that circle. This is why the Hindus have called the world 'sansara'—a wheel that turns round and round. You are repeating the same thing over and over again. So don't think that you are doing something unique. Everyone else is also doing the same.

When you fall in love for the first time, you think that perhaps such a unique thing has never happened before in the world. But this is happening every day; everybody is doing the same. The animals and the birds are doing the same, plants are doing the same, humans are doing the same. It is not that love has happened only to you: it has happened in the same way to everybody. Anger has also happened the same way to everyone.

There is only one thing that is outside this circle and which does not happen on its own, and that is meditation. Everything else happens on its own, you don't have to do anything for it. You just keep sitting on the wheel that is revolving on its own, and since you are also tied to it, you will go on revolving. There is only one phenomenon which is outside of this wheel and which can help you jump off of this wheel, and that is meditation. It doesn't happen on its own. It happens only once in a while, to a buddha.

The great Western historian Arnold Toynbee has calculated that up till now, only six people in the whole history of mankind have managed to get out of this circle. Even if it is sixty and not just six, still the number is not very big. It is almost a miracle for it to happen. Love, anger, greed are ordinary phenomena; they are happening to everybody, even to animals. They don't make you a human being. The beginning of being human happens in your life only on the day when you get out of this mantra called mind, the vicious circle called mind. When this circle of the mind is broken and you come out of it—that is meditation.

Meditation is not a cycle. Meditation is a state. Mind is a movement. Meditation is the name of a stopping, mind is the name of wandering—and not even wandering to new places but to the same old places over and over again. You are moving like an ox on a treadmill. If you continue to observe this phenomenon consciously, you will understand it. It is not a theory, it is a fact. It is not a doctrine of philosophy—this circular movement of your mind, your mind being like a mantra—it is a fact of your life.

Those who have tried to understand life have discovered this fact. It is not a mental hypothesis, it is a fact discovered through experience. You can also come to the same conclusion through experience. There is no need to believe it just because I say so or just because Shiva says so. You have eyes. If you watch your mind with closed eyes for a few days, you will be amazed at what you discover. You will discover that you are chained to this wheel; the whole creation is chained to this wheel. There is no declaration of your humanness in this. Your dignity is not in it; your dignity is in your slipping out of it—that very moment you attain your buddhahood, your shivahood.

Mind is mantra. Repetition is the very nature of the mind. Hence, nothing new ever happens in the realm of the mind. Nothing original ever happens in the mind: everything is old and stale there, just leftovers. And you keep chewing on the same cud! Have you ever observed a buffalo chewing cud? First, the buffalo takes the food in and then regurgitates it in the mouth and goes on chewing it. The mind chews in the same way. Whatever you take into your mind as food, the mind keeps chewing on it. You read a book and it keeps on revolving in your mind. You will leave here after listening to me, and it will keep on moving in your mind the whole day: a circular movement has started. The mind will chew it again, digest it and repeat it.

But nothing new ever happens in the mind; nothing original ever happens in the mind. The being is original, and godliness is the ultimate originality; it is eternally new, there is nothing more fresh. But you will not be able to know it through the mind. The mantra that is the mind will have to be broken. So try to understand this sutra very deeply: *Mind is mantra.*

The second sutra:
   Effort is the seeker.
Here, effort means the attempt to get out of the vicious circle of the mind. Someone who has managed to get out of this circle is a siddha, the fulfilled one. Someone who is still trying to get out of the circle is a *sadhaka*, a seeker. Your effort must be immense, only then will you be able to get out of it. You will have to work as hard as you have done to create the mind. But the difficulty is that because you see everything through the mind itself, whatever you see will be coloured by it. This is the greatest difficulty.

I am talking to you and you are listening, but you are not really listening—your mind stands in between. Whatsoever I say, the mind will give its own colour to it, changing it to its own shade. The whole meaning of what I am saying will be changed.

A drunk Mulla Nasruddin boarded a bus. There was an old woman on the bus, all her hair had turned white. She felt pity for Mulla. His mouth smelled strongly of liquor, so the old woman said to him, 'Son, are you in your senses or not? You are on a journey heading straight to hell.'

Mulla, startled, jumped up and called the conductor, 'Stop the bus, brother! I have boarded the wrong bus!'

This mind, if it is unconscious, will colour everything in its own way. Mulla thought that the bus was heading towards hell!

Your mind is doing the same thing for twenty-four hours a day. So the most difficult thing is the effort to put the mind aside and then to listen. The one who is able to do this is a *shravaka*, a right listener. And this is what right listening is: to put the mind aside and listen directly.

Effort is the seeker. You will have to make the effort: you will have to make *great* effort. Laziness will not help you to get out of this circle. How can you get out of this circle by just lying down? That way the circle will keep on turning, and because of your fear of falling, you will keep holding on to it even tighter.

If you have ever observed a hunter catching parrots in the woods, you will find that they use a very simple trick. Your mind uses the same trick to catch you. The hunter ties a string across two branches or poles and the parrots land on the string, but because of their weight they turn upside down. It is not possible to sit on a string. Hanging upside down, the parrot becomes afraid and holds on even more tightly to the string so that he doesn't fall. Now he is in trouble. He feels that if he lets go of the string, he will fall. There is no need to catch him, he catches himself. The hunter just comes and takes him away.

The parrot has completely forgotten that he has wings, that there is no reason for him to fall, that there is no need to be scared. But once you are upside down on a string, a similar fear catches a hold of you too: 'What would happen if I jump out of the wheel? I will get lost, I will go astray!'

One of the characters in a novel written by Hemingway says, 'I would rather choose suffering than nothingness. I will not choose nothingness. It will be better to choose even suffering.' You would not like emptiness. Even hell is okay— at least you are filled with something. This is the same as the parrot hanging, afraid that he will lose everything. He feels trapped, but still, being trapped seems better than falling to the ground.

And it is you, yourself, who is holding on to this wheel, the wheel is not holding on to you. The mind has not chained you. If that were so, then a Buddha or a Mahavira would not be possible, because it would also have chained them. What would have happened if they had escaped? The mind would have continued to torment them, the mind would have still chased after them. No, the mind is not holding you; it is you who are holding on to the mind. Out of fear, you are grasping it so tightly. Yet, you go to your saints and monks to ask how to be free of the mind.

There is no need to ask anyone else to free you from the mind. Only this much needs to be understood: that *you* are holding on to it. Except you, no one else is responsible for your life being what it is. But now clinging has become your habit because you have always done it. You have become accustomed to it. And no extra effort is needed to cling; but to drop it, effort will be needed.

If you have kept your fist closed for many lifetimes, then it will be very difficult to open it. The fingers will have become stiff and frozen with your fist tightly clenched for so long. This is what has happened. Just a little effort is needed so that the muscles can become alive again, so the blood can start flowing in the hand and fingers again, and you will be able to open your fist. Anything that has been closed can be opened, this much is certain. Otherwise, how could you have closed it? The fist can be closed because it can be opened. It must have been open once, this is why it can close now. It can open again. But if it has remained closed for a long time, then it becomes difficult to open it. The whole difficulty is only this. It is because of this that effort is needed.

'Effort' means you will have to endeavour to drop the mind. And the mind will try to persuade you again and again: 'What are you doing? What madness are you up to?'—because your dropping it is its death.

Effort is the seeker. Unless you are a seeker you will not make the effort. You do make some effort, but it is always half-hearted—and a half-hearted effort won't help. It is as if you hold on to the wheel with one hand and let go of it with the other, then you hold with the other hand and let go with your first hand—this will not solve the problem. No, a lukewarm effort is futile.

One evening, a businessman told his wife that he was going to the Taj Mahal Hotel to entertain a very important client who was going to place an order worth millions of rupees.

He went, and when he returned home that night stuffed with food and drink, his wife asked, 'Did your client place the order?'

'Fifty-fifty,' he answered.

The wife said, 'At least something happened.' But then she thought, 'What does it mean, fifty-fifty?'

So as they were getting ready to go to sleep, she asked, 'What do you mean by "fifty-fifty"?'

The husband replied, 'I went to the hotel, but the client didn't.'

Whenever you are half-hearted, it is something like this—nothing will happen because the other half isn't there. You are always fragmented, you are never total. Whenever you are total, a revolution starts to happen in your life. It is only then that you reach the boiling point; then, at a hundred degrees, you evaporate. The water has turned into steam. Then you no longer flow downwards like water; then you only rise upwards like vapour. Then your direction is no longer downwards, it is upwards.

Effort is the seeker. You have to drop the laziness.

People come to me and say that the morning meditation is difficult, that it is difficult to come in at six o'clock in the morning. You don't understand what you are saying. If you are finding it difficult just to get up for meditation at six in the morning, you will have great difficulty in awakening out of the mind. If getting up at six in the morning is so difficult, how will you jump out of the wheel of birth and death? Just because of a small habit of not getting up at six o'clock in the morning . . . You may feel laziness for a day or two, but you are allowing your laziness to win, and you are ready to lose meditation for the sake of laziness. That shows that meditation has no value for you whatsoever. If you gave it some value, you would never have raised this question.

Somebody comes and says that four meditations during the meditation camp are too tiring: 'What if I drop two of them?' You can drop all four! If four meditations tire you, two will tire you half as much, but nevertheless they will tire you. And I know that if I make concessions for your mind and say that two will be okay, you will again come back tomorrow to ask if you can do only one. Because it is the same mind—you will get tired doing two meditations also.

If you follow your mind, then tomorrow, if not today, you will be drowning yourself in laziness, because doing anything will be too much of an effort. Remember, life means effort; death means rest. So if you want to be dead, you need not do anything. If you want to live, then you will have to do something. And if you want the ultimate life, you will have to make the ultimate effort. If you want to attain godliness, then such small efforts will not do. Your whole life should become one total effort. You have to stake all that you have. If you hold anything back, you will miss out. Here, the risk will have to be total, only then can anything happen. This is why so few attain: the reason is nothing but laziness.

Even when you do the meditations, you are so cautious because your feet might get hurt, or someone might push you: 'I'll do it this way so that I don't get tired.' Why do it at all? Who has asked you to do it? But you are not clear either. You live in such a haze, where everything is foggy and dark. You are not even sure why you have come here, what has brought you here. Somebody else was coming, so you just came along with that person, or you thought, 'Let's go and see what others are doing there.'

You have been pushed and pulled like this for infinite lives—but no one can reach the destination in this way. It is not by coincidence that you will reach a destination, somehow. A destination implies a goal-oriented journey. To reach a destination implies an effort to move in a particular direction, with your total life-energy. Destination implies determination. And as soon as you are totally determined, your mind will fall in one stream and your energy will accumulate.

The energy in you is infinite. If you think that you have so little energy and that you will get tired so easily, you are mistaken.

There are three levels of energy in the human body. The outer layer is for day-to-day activities. It is like the small change that you carry in your pocket: it is not all the money you have; it is just pocket money that you use for minor expenses, a few rupees.

Once, Mulla Nasruddin was passing through a village. It was dark, and four men jumped on him. Mulla fought them so ferociously that he almost defeated them. Only with great difficulty were those four people able to overpower him. But when they searched his pockets they found only seven paise!

One of them said, 'This is too much, Nasruddin! You have risked your life for just seven paise.'

Nasruddin said, 'I didn't understand that you were fighting for these seven paise in my pocket. I have five hundred rupees hidden in my left shoe!'

By then the thieves didn't dare to take his left shoe, because if he could fight so ferociously for only seven paise . . .

They said, 'Goodbye! Maybe next time . . .'

The energy for your day-to-day use is not more than those seven paise. It is for your daily activities—for sitting, standing, walking, eating, digesting, sleeping, working. This is your superficial energy, the small change in your pocket. When you start meditating, this energy is exhausted almost immediately because you are not accustomed to using it for meditation. This is a new level of activity that has begun. Now, if you listen to this tiredness and stop meditating, you will never be able to totally enter meditation. Don't listen to it. If you go on with the meditation, then you will soon find that the second level of energy has become available to you.

You have experienced this phenomenon many times. You were about to go to bed at night, you were overcome with exhaustion, so sleepy that you could barely keep your eyes open, and you discover that suddenly your house is on fire! Do you think you can sleep after that? Do you say, 'I am too sleepy?' No, your sleepiness will totally disappear. Where has all this new energy come from? You were just dozing off, and if someone had asked you to read the

Gita for them, you would have said, 'No friends, it is too difficult.' You can leave the Gita, but now that your house is on fire, you are running around to put the fire out. And even when the fire is out, you will not sleep that night. Now you will stay awake; you will not be able to sleep, however hard you try.

What has happened? The second layer of energy, the reserve layer, which is not the layer you use for your daily routine, has been tapped. It is because of this that you are filled with so much energy that all sleep has disappeared.

If you persist with your meditation experiments without giving up, then, very soon, a second source of energy will become available to you. Once this energy becomes available, then no matter how many meditations you do, nothing in you is going to be tired; nothing inside is going to be exhausted. But this too is only the second layer.

There is also a third layer of energy. The second layer of energy is your treasure. This too can be exhausted, although not as easily as the first. If you go on making an effort, this source of energy will also dry up—and that is when the third layer is tapped. This third layer does not belong to you: it belongs to existence and it can never dry up.

However, if you are lazy, you will not even touch the second level, let alone the third. Existence is the ultimate energy, and it is hidden within you.

The first layer of energy is of the mind, the second is of your being, the third is of existence. Exhaust the mind and you will reach the energy of your being. Exhaust the being and you attain the energy of the divine, the universal being, which is eternal, inexhaustible. Then you are one with the whole.

Hence, Shiva says: *Effort is the seeker.* Continuous effort, deeper and deeper, is the seeker. You have to keep on trying until the third layer of energy is tapped and you reach that ultimate source of energy. Then you are a siddha, one who has come home. Then you can relax. To relax before this will be suicidal.

The third sutra is:

The master is the way.

This quest for life cannot be done alone, because on your own you are already trapped in your own cycle. You can't see anything outside it. You don't even have any idea that there is something outside it. You live in a cocoon, and you think that this is the whole of life. Someone who has known a vaster life will have to give you the news from the outside. You are a prisoner inside your own house. You don't have even the least idea that there are stars and a moon, and the open sky is there outside your house. Someone from outside who has seen the moon and the stars will have to come and knock at your door and tell you to come out from behind your closed doors.

But at first you are bound to be filled with doubt: 'Does a thing such as the outside even exist?' This is what people are saying when they ask, 'Does God exist? Does the soul exist?' And you would like someone to prove the existence of the sky for you while you remain sitting inside the house. How can someone prove it? If you go on sitting inside the house, how can it be proved that the sky exists? You will have to step outside. You will have to take a few steps outside with someone who claims that the sky exists.

The sky can only be shown, it cannot be proved; there is no way to prove it. And if somebody tries to prove that the sky exists while sitting inside the house, you can even defeat him because you can say, 'What nonsense! There is only the roof and the walls. I don't see anything else. What proof is there that something is outside? You bring a little bit of sky inside and show me.' Now, the sky is not a thing that can be brought inside. We can't bring a small piece of the sky inside as a sample and show it to you and then you will come out. No, truth cannot be broken into pieces to be brought in and shown to you. You will have to go outside yourself.

This is why this sutra says: *The master is the way.* The master is someone who has experienced, who has known and who is free of the prison. Only he can make you aware that you are in a prison, only he can tell you that it is possible to be free, and only he can show you the way by saying, 'Come, follow me.'

There are doors in this prison where you can get out. There are doors in this prison where the guards are asleep. There are also doors in this prison where the guards are very alert, and if you try to escape through those doors you will find yourself in even more trouble. Now at least you are a little free inside your prison-house, but if you try to escape through the main entrance, where the guards are alert, you will be caught and thrown into a dark dungeon. Then your prison will become even smaller.

Remember, if you try to get out through denial, you will fall into that dark dungeon. If you fight with darkness, you will be thrown into a deeper darkness. There is the main door, but no one can ever go out through that door. No one ever has. The reason for this is that the main door has to be well guarded and has to remain well protected. But in this prison there are also secret doors where there are no guards, because no prisoner ever pays any attention to those areas. The attention of the prisoners also goes only to the main door.

I have heard that in France, during the French Revolution, the inmates of a prison rebelled. It is better if prisoners don't rebel. There were some two thousand prisoners and only twenty guards. They could have freed themselves at any time. What could twenty guards have done? The prisoners had never rebelled because prisoners never unite. Prisoners are enemies to each other too because they don't even have the simplicity to stick together. There is no way for them to make friends. They were inimical to each other so twenty guards were enough. But then they became united and rebelled.

When they rebelled, the head jailer was in trouble. He thought, 'What to do now?' The first thing he did was to tell the guards, 'Don't worry about the main door. Go and protect the small windows and the back doors.'

Even the guards said, 'This is a wrong decision.'

But the main jailer said, 'Don't worry. Leave the main door unguarded.'

So the main door was left unguarded; there was not a single guard. But no prisoner could escape because the smaller doors were guarded. All the guards went where there had never been any guards. And the place which had always been well guarded was left unguarded. If the prisoners had seen this, they would have all escaped.

Later on, the guards asked the head jailer about it because they didn't understand how the trick had worked.

The head jailer said, 'The rebellion means that some outsider has got inside. Some free man from the outside has got in among the prisoners. He knows and, because of this, he will try to free them through the back doors. Only someone who doesn't know will try to get them out through the main door. So until yesterday we were guarding the main door because those who were inside were ignorant, but now it seems that some master is among them.'

In life, to fight the darkness to get free seems to be the main door. Your mind tells you, 'First, destroy darkness, and only then you will find the light. First, drop the wrong, and only then will the path to the right be paved. First, throw away the world from within you to make the throne of godliness unoccupied.' But this is the main door.

A master will never tell you to go out through that door, because no one has ever been able to go out from there. That door is well guarded, and whoever tries to escape through there will be thrown into deeper dungeons.

As I see it, all your so-called saints and monks are locked in worse prisons than yours. You don't have the eyes to see, so you can't see this. The worldly man is in great trouble, but your so-called saints are in even worse trouble. At least you have a small courtyard in your house where you can feel a little bit of open space, but they have lost even the courtyards. Not only are they inside the prison, but they don't have even the normal amount of freedom that an average prisoner has. They are locked in their dark dungeons for twenty-four hours a day.

Your monks and saints come to me—their minds are utterly sick, insane.

A Jaina monk said to me, 'I am sixty years old. I have been a monk for forty years now, but one single doubt constantly haunts me: could it be that I made a mistake in becoming a monk? Could it be that an ordinary, worldly man is enjoying life and I am unnecessarily creating troubles?'

It is natural for this doubt to arise in any intelligent person. This man is not a fool, this man is intelligent. It is natural that this doubt occurs to him because he can see that he has attained nothing. He has wasted forty years in fighting anger, sex and greed, but nothing has really been attained. It is not that his anger has dissolved; it has simply become hidden, gone underground. You can hide the fact from others, but how will you hide it from yourself? You know deep down that you have suppressed them, that you are sitting on top of them. You appear to be a good man, you don't commit any crime, but the criminal is hiding inside you and can appear at any moment. Given the opportunity, you can commit a crime at any moment. All that has happened is that your prison has become smaller. Even the small amount of freedom that he had to move around has also been lost and he is in a dark dungeon.

Whosoever tries to escape through the main door will become even more trapped. But there are secret doors, and only a master can show you those secret doors. There are keys that can open the secret doors, but only one who has already escaped can lead you out.

Scriptures can become companions that you can go on reading inside the prison, but they cannot lead you out of the prison. Who will interpret the scriptures? You! Who will understand the scriptures? You! And you will only understand according to yourself. If you had the understanding, there would be no need of scriptures. You have no understanding, this much is certain. And when a person without understanding interprets scriptures, he finds himself in more trouble.

No, you need a living scripture. A master is a living scripture. Search for a living master who can show you the way.

Shiva says: *The master is the way.* There is no other way. If you try to untangle the problem on your own, it is more likely that you will only become even more entangled, because the mind is very subtle. The mind often thinks of solving problems on its own. It often happens: your watch has stopped, and your first impulse is to open it and fix it. It happens to almost everybody. The more ignorant you are, the stronger will be this impulse. A small child will simply sit down and open it immediately because he feels that there is no problem at all. It was working, now it isn't—why not open it and see?

A watch is not such a complex mechanism, but if you try to repair it yourself you will find yourself in the same situation as Mulla Nasruddin.

One day Mulla Nasruddin went to a watch-repair shop. He placed his watch, which was just a pile of little wheels and pieces, on the counter. Shocked, the watchmaker looked first at the watch and then at Mulla.

Nasruddin said, 'It fell out of my hands.'

'Why did you bother to pick it up at all?' said the watchmaker. 'Now, nothing can be done. And it has not come to this fate just because it fell out of your hands.'

Nasruddin said, 'I tried to repair it a little.'

The watchmaker said, 'Take it away. Now it is beyond repair.'

A watch is a very simple mechanism, it is not that complex. The mind is a very complex mechanism. You have no idea of the complexity of the mind. There is nothing on earth as complex as the mind. There are about seventy million cells in your brain, and each cell is capable of storing at least ten million pieces of information. Scientists say that all the libraries in the world can be stored in one man's brain. Each cell can store ten million bits of information, and there are seventy million of these cells.

All the knowledge on earth can be stored inside your little skull. It is such a small brain, hardly weighing 1.5 kilograms, and there are seventy million cells which are invisible to the naked eye. The cells are microscopic. This is why brain surgery was not tried until very recently. Only recently it has started, but it is still risky: you try to cut something, and thousands of other cells are cut and destroyed. Everything is so delicate. After all, surgical instruments will have to be used, will have to operate inside the brain, and just during this process hundreds of thousands of neurons can be destroyed.

Never mind doing brain surgery—just try standing on your head for half an hour every day and your brain will be damaged. You will never find people doing *shirshasana*, the headstand posture, to be intelligent, because there is such a flow of blood to the brain that it destroys the delicate cells. It is as if a flood has come.

Man's brain has developed as it has because at some stage in his evolution he stood upright, on his hind legs, and because of this, the flow of blood to his brain was reduced. The brains of animals did not develop any further because their brains and their bodies are on the same level. Their nerve fibres remained thicker, they are not as fine as a human's. The whole dignity and uniqueness of man rests in the fact that he stood upright. By standing on two legs the gravitational force has a downward pull on his blood flow, so his heart has to pump harder, and only then can the blood reach the brain. A very limited quantity of blood reaches the brain, and this is why delicate nerves and cells could evolve. In a flood, even the big trees are washed away, what to say about the small plants? In the brain, the cells are so delicate that the slightest increase in blood flow will destroy them.

So in this complexity of seventy million cells, if you sit down to sort things out on your own, it is impossible to imagine that it will do some good, the harm is certain. Yet this is what many people do: they try to open their own minds. They start doing some kind of meditation on their own, they sit in some yoga postures on their own. They have taken some clues from books, or they have heard something. They catch things out of the air and then they start doing something on their own. This cannot do anything but harm.

A Buddhist monk was brought to me. He had not been able to sleep for three years. He had been given extensive treatment, but to no avail. His insomnia had defied all tranquilizers and no treatment seemed to work on him. You can imagine his state: a man who has not slept in three years will be almost insane.

I asked him something which no doctor had yet asked. The doctors all did the usual tests: they checked his blood pressure, checked the condition of his heart. They did a general examination of all his major body organs and just started to treat him, but this was not his trouble at all.

This man was practising a particular meditation technique used by the Buddhists: vipassana. He had read about this meditation in the scriptures and began to practise it. A master takes each individual disciple into account, or if he does give a collective method, he takes the group as a whole into account. But the scriptures cannot do that, because they have no idea who will be reading them. Anyone can read them because they have been around for thousands of years.

Vipassana is a very old meditation technique. He read about it and started practising it. Then he started to enjoy it because the technique is beautiful; Buddha himself practised it. Once he started enjoying it, he didn't know when to stop. Even too much enjoyment turns into a poison. So this man started enjoying the meditation so much that he began to practise it internally, twenty-four hours a day.

If you practise something for twenty-four hours a day, your sleep is bound to be disturbed. If so much effort is going on inside you, then there will be no possibility of sleep. Now, this man had practised this technique for so many years that the brain cells that help you sleep had been damaged. Now there was no chance of sleep. And a doctor can help only if the brain cells are intact: tranquilizers can relax them and you will be able to sleep. But if the cells are destroyed, then what can the doctor do?

I suggested to him that he stop all meditations completely for a whole year and practise being lazy as much as possible. He shouldn't even think of the meditation, he should not read any scriptures, and he should sleep as much as he could. He should lie down, relax, eat, drink and enjoy. For a whole year he should become an utterly worldly man.

He said, 'I never expected this from you. What are you saying? You are corrupting me!'

I told him, 'If you think I am corrupting you, that's okay. But practise what I am saying for a year and then come back to me.'

After exactly three months he was cured. Then I gave him a new meditation technique.

A technique has to be given carefully, according to how much you will be able to do. The length of time should be increased gradually. It is important to take into consideration the state of the meditator's whole mind.

Hence Shiva says: *The master is the way*. Don't become a way unto yourself, otherwise you will spoil everything. First of all, search for a living master. It is difficult, because to accept a living person as a master is disturbing; it hurts your ego. So people take more interest in the scriptures because scriptures cannot hurt your ego. You can throw the scripture away and it can't object. Wherever you put it, it will remain; it can't do anything on its own. You can't do this with a living master. You will have to drop your ego; you will have to bow down.

You bow down to the scriptures, but it still remains your choice—you remain the master. Any time your mind wants, you can change and tell the scripture to get lost, and the scriptures won't be able to do anything about it. But the master is a living phenomenon: there you will have to bow down, and your ego will be hurt surrendering to a living person. This is why people seek first in books. When they are tired of books, only then do they look for a master. It often happens that by that time they have been so corrupted by the books, their vision so distorted by the words, that they are unable to recognize the master.

Even if you go to a master, you carry your ideas from the books with you. You have read in the books how a master should be, but no book can ever tell you how a master should be. A book can only tell you about a particular master. If someone has written a book about Kabir, it can only tell about Kabir, that he was this type of master. But Kabir is not going to be repeated again; the things described are about Kabir, not about any other master. If you are a follower of Kabir and have become totally filled with his words, you will look for the same qualities in any other master. But you will never find such a master, because a Kabir will never be repeated again.

The Digambar Jainas don't accept anybody as a master unless he is standing naked. It was Mahavira's joy to always remain naked, but that may not be another person's joy. Now, this man is searching for a Mahavira who no longer exists. It is very interesting because when Mahavira existed, in all likelihood, this same man would have felt troubled because of Mahavira's nakedness. The scriptures popular at that time did not mention nakedness. All Jaina *tirthankaras*, the Jaina masters before Mahavira, wore clothes, so even the Jainas were not ready to accept Mahavira, because to be naked was considered obscene. The scriptures of that time said that it is indecent for a master to be naked. They denied Mahavira. When Mahavira died and his life became a scripture, then they started following Mahavira. Now, even if these people were to come across a Parshvanatha in clothes, they would not accept that he is their own tirthankara.

Remember, your scriptures are talking about a particular master and that master will not be repeated again. Masters are always unique. If your eyes are filled with scriptures, you will never be able to recognize a living master because the scriptures are describing masters who were in the past and will never be repeated again. If the followers of Mahavira go to Buddha, they will deny him. They will say, 'At the most, he may be a great soul, but he is not a tirthankara because he is wearing clothes.'

There is a man I know, a Jaina. He has written a book. He is a good man, but being a good man does not give someone understanding. There are bad, ignorant people and there are good, ignorant people too. The ignorance may be so deeply rooted that goodness will make no difference. He is a good man, so he maintains a kind of goodwill towards all religions. So he has written a book, *Bhagwan Mahavira and Mahatma Buddha*—'Mahavira the God and the Great Soul, Buddha'. He is a writer and the people in Pune know about him. He is the one who brought me to Pune for the first time. He is an old devotee of Gandhi, from whom he learned this idea that all religions are one.

He wrote this book, but inside him was the Jaina mind. I was staying with him and I asked him, 'I understand everything else, but why do you keep this difference— *Bhagwan* Mahavira and *Mahatma* Buddha?'

He said, 'You see, Mahavira is indeed Bhagwan. I can accept Buddha, at the most, as a mahatma, but not as a

Bhagwan, because he wears clothes. A Bhagwan is always naked.'

This is the difficulty, and it is not only Jainas who have this difficulty. The same problem appears with everybody. Hence, a Jaina cannot accept Rama as a god because he is with Sita, and this causes difficulty. A Jaina can't imagine a woman with a god. A Bhagwan would have renounced everything—if he is liberated, then why is this woman with him? So even a precious woman like Sita is lost to the Jaina mind. The Jaina mind can't understand it.

As for Krishna, they throw him into hell because he has not one, but sixteen thousand women around him. No one is more eligible for hell than Krishna! So the Jainas put Krishna into hell, but for fear of the Hindus they also played a trick. Jainas are all traders by caste, and a minority, so they are afraid some trouble may start with the Hindus. Perhaps this is also the reason why Jainas believe in non-violence.

Usually, only cowards believe in non-violence, because to believe in violence, at least a little courage to quarrel and fight is needed. Cowards believe in not killing and in not being killed. As a principle, it's fine—don't kill anybody, live and let live. But it is simply the need to survive; they are not concerned with others at all. And because of their fear they have played another trick: first they have put Krishna in hell, because it is necessary to place him in hell—he does not fit anywhere in their doctrine. But because they have to live among the Hindus, they have also said that he will be their first tirthankara in the coming eon.

A compromise was struck: this is the businessman's mentality, calculating. Now, the Hindus can't be angry because there is no real harm to them. Their doctrine has remained intact and the conflict was also avoided.

If you seek the master through scriptures, you will never be able to find him, because by the time the scripture is written, the person around whom it was written will have already gone. Every master is different and unique. You will not find another like him. You will not find a Mahavira again, nor a Krishna, nor a Buddha. But you go on searching for them, and this is also why you go on wandering. When they were alive you were looking for someone else, from before. You simply go on missing.

If you want to find a master, first put all the scriptures aside. If you want to find a master, try to be in the presence of an enlightened person, sit near him and don't bring your concepts along with you. Don't carry your systems of judgement with you. Let your heart meet his heart directly; don't allow your intellect to get in the way. If you allow your intellect to get in the way, there will not be a communion of hearts and you will not be able to recognize the master.

The master is recognized through the heart, not through the intellect. Whenever you set your intellect aside and see with your heart, instantly something happens. If there is a possibility of communion with this master, it will happen instantly, without a moment's delay. You will find that you have merged into him and he has merged into you. From that day on, you will be an inseparable part of him. From that day on, you will follow him as a shadow. The master can be sought through the heart, and there is no other way but the master.

The body is the offering.

And, remember, you have taken your body to be your whole being, but it is no more than an offering. Just as an offering is made in the sacrificial fire rites, you have to slowly let go of your body in the process of meditation. All other offerings are meaningless. Putting refined butter and wheat into the sacred fire is not a true offering. You will have to offer yourself, and only then will the fire of your life be lit. You will have to stake your body completely. If you try to save it, your fire will simply not ignite, the sacred fire will not be lit. Put all at stake.

> *The body is the offering.*
> *Knowing is nourishment.*

You live on food. Food enters your body, it is necessary for your body. But consciousness, knowing, meditation, awareness—these are the food for the soul. Until now you have fed only your body and have starved your soul. For lives after lives, your body has been well nourished but your soul is starving.

Knowing is the food for the being. And the more aware you become, the more knowing you become—and knowing does not mean knowledge, knowing simply means consciousness. The more you become aware, the more turiya, the fourth state of consciousness, crystallizes in you; the more alert and aware you become, the more life energy will flow through your being. Your being is almost dried up; you have denied it all nourishment. You have almost forgotten that it needs any nourishment. Your body consumes food while your being is fasting.

This is why many religions have used fasting on the body level as a technique: let the body fast for a while and give food to the being; reverse the process for a while. But it is not necessary for you to starve your body. Give the body what it needs, but don't let all your effort be exhausted just in feeding the body. Let the major part of your life's effort be in the service of awakening, knowing, because that alone is the food for your being.

Knowing is nourishment.
Dreams arise from absence of knowing.

If knowing, awareness, has not penetrated you and your inner flame did not get its fuel, then dreams will arise in your life, then desires will be born in your life. Then your life will be a wandering in darkness. Then you will live in imagination. Then you will live in the thirst of desires and you will go on thinking about their fulfilment.

I asked Mulla Nasruddin, 'Mulla, where do you intend to go for your vacation this year?'

He often goes on a vacation.

'I only go on vacation every three years,' he replied.

'What do you do in the other two years?' I asked.

He replied, 'I spend one year musing over the previous vacation and reliving it in my mind, and I spend one year planning the next vacation.'

At least Nasruddin goes on a trip every three years—you don't even go once. Half your life you spend thinking of the past and the other half thinking about the future. The journey never begins. Either you roam around the byways of your memory with your dead dreams, or you wander in your imagination, which is a dream of the future that has not happened yet. You are divided between these two. In the middle is the present, and that is where *life* is—but you go on missing it!

Knowing will awaken you to the here and now, to this very moment. Knowing will bring you into the present. The past will disappear: in fact, it has already disappeared and you are unnecessarily carrying its ashes. The future has not come yet, and you cannot bring it—it will come when it will come. But the present is now, and that which is present is truth. To dream means to wander in that which is not present.

Keep this sutra in your heart: *Dreams arise from absence of knowing.* When knowing is absent—when the being is not awake—you are lost in dreams. The past and the future become everything for you, and the present is just nothing. But it is the present which is really everything. As you continue to wake up, the past and future will keep diminishing and the present will go on expanding. On the day you will be fully awake, only the present will remain. On that day there will be neither the future nor the past. And when there is no past and no future, all diseases of the mind, all its repetitions and cycles, are destroyed. Then you are here, in the present—pure, unblemished, innocent and fresh like the morning dew. Then you are present, like the lotus flower. If you can be totally present in this moment, then you are godliness.

You are not at all present in this moment, and this is why you are the body, you are the mind, but you are not the being. Meditation is an effort to pull you out of the past and future into the present. You neither go backwards into the past, nor do you go forward into the future—you remain only here.

To be here and now, totally calm and alert in this moment, is meditation. Through this, wisdom is born. Through this, you reach the highest peak of life, to the highest enlightenment and bliss.

The one who loses this, loses all. The one who attains this, attains all.

Enough for today.

5

Conquering Your Attachments

Being itself is mind.

Maya, illusion, is unawareness of the doer.

The seeker who remains attached to veils of illusion can gain supernatural powers, but will not know enlightenment.

When illusion is forever vanquished, one attains spontaneous wisdom.

The awakened one knows that this universe is an emanation of his own energy.

Being itself is mind.

THIS IS A very significant sutra. You see a wave in the ocean, but the wave is also the ocean. However much on the surface, however agitated the wave may be, it is a part of the boundless and fathomless ocean. The small also carries the vast in it. Even in one particle, the whole universe is hidden.

No matter how insane you are, no matter how distressed your mind is, no matter how many disturbances and diseases surround you, still you are divine. It makes no difference that you are asleep, unconscious, because in your unconsciousness too, it is the divine that is unconscious within you. Even in your sleep, it is the divine that is asleep within you. It does not matter that you have done much wrong or thought about doing wrong, because it is the divine that is thinking that also. Those wrongs also have been committed through the medium of the divine.

Being itself is mind means that your mind is a form of your very being. It is very important to understand this, otherwise you will start fighting with your mind—and whoever fights with their mind will be defeated. The way to victory is to accept the mind: that it too belongs to the existence. The afflictions of the mind begin to fade away not with conflict, not with the futile state of duality and struggle, but with the realization that the wave too is nothing other than the ocean.

When you are able to understand that the infinite is also hidden in the finite, the finite will no longer remain finite. It is you who has given it a boundary. Even the tiniest particle has no boundaries because it is a part of the boundless. You see boundaries because of your vision. The moment you are able to see that even in the finite the infinite is hidden, all boundaries will disappear.

This is the most profound experience of life, when you begin also to see godliness in your own mind. When you begin to see it even in your wrong actions, when you can see its footprints even in all your going astray, that is the day all straying ceases. To go astray means that you believed yourself to be separate from existence. All your wrongdoing, all your afflictions, are based on this belief in your separateness. You believed yourself to be separate: this alone is ego.

And it is very surprising that as far as the ego is concerned, there is not an iota of difference between a saint and a sinner. The sinner is as filled with ego as your so-called man of virtue. Their actions may be different, but their feeling is the same: both believe themselves to be separate from existence. One thinks he is evil, the other thinks he is good, but both consider themselves to be separate from existence. And as long as you believe yourself to be separate, you will be separate. You are not separate, just your belief has made you narrow and isolated. Only your belief has imprisoned you. You are imprisoned within a cage of your own belief: otherwise there are no walls anywhere, only open sky all around. And no one has stopped you, no one has obstructed your way.

How can the ego disappear?

Being itself is mind means that you are not you, you are existence. You are one with the whole. You are not a small wave, you are the whole ocean. With the realization of your vastness, your ego will disappear. And where there is no ego, nothing will remain that can be called sin. There is only one sin, and that is to believe that you are separate. This sense of separateness is there even in people you call saints.

I have heard that a saint died, reached heaven and knocked at the door. The door opened and the guard said, 'Welcome! Please come in.'

The saint stopped there, shocked. He said, 'What kind of heaven is this where you let anyone in without even bothering to know anything about them? You have not asked who I am or where I am from or what my actions have been—good or bad . . . Nothing! I don't want to be in a place that is open to any Tom, Dick and Harry. No reservation, no inquiries; a direct welcome—no, this is not the heaven of my ideas.'

This ego is not filled with sins, it is filled with virtue. This man must have followed many spiritual practices, must have attained great siddhis, supernatural powers, but all in vain. All those siddhis have only helped to swell his ego. This man is an *asiddhi*, a failure.

George Bernard Shaw received the Nobel Prize in Literature in 1925. There is a small, very exclusive club in Europe that has only a hundred people in the whole world as its members. It is for a few chosen people, people with great fame and honour, people who have received the Nobel Prize, people with outstanding achievements—great painters, sculptors, writers—but only a hundred, because the club never allows more than that. When a member dies, only then can a new person join. People wait their whole life to be invited to become members of that club.

When Shaw got the Nobel Prize, he received an invitation from that club. The invitation said: 'We will be honoured to have you as a member of our club.'

Shaw replied, 'Any club that is honoured by my becoming a member is not good enough for me. It is a little below me. I would like to be a member of a club that is unwilling to make me a member.'

The ego always seeks the difficult, the unattainable. But life is very simple, hence, the ego always misses life. And there is nothing simpler than existence, so the ego never goes to that door. That door is already open: you are already always welcome there without any questions about who you are. If you are questioned as to who you are before being welcomed at the door of godliness, then even that door has become a door to the worldly.

You are already standing at the door of existence, and if you stand with your back to it, it is entirely your own doing. The door has not rejected you. If you are keeping your eyes closed and you cannot see the door, then you are the cause. Otherwise, the door is always open and the invitation is always there for you. 'Welcome' is always written there.

Being itself is mind means that you can't ever consider yourself to be separate, no matter how evil you may be. This does not imply that you should go on doing evil; it does not imply that you should continue to be bad. No, it will simply not be possible for you to go on being bad any more.

Psychologists say that a person becomes what he believes himself to be. Our belief slowly becomes our life. Psychologists say that even if a man is bad, don't call him bad because by calling him bad—with the constant repetition of 'You are bad, you are bad'—it becomes a mantra. And if people around you constantly repeat that you are bad, then that person will also start repeating inside himself, 'I am bad.' Not only that, but then he will even try to validate what others expect of him. By and by, evil will become his habit.

Perhaps the religious seekers became aware of this truth long ago, so they have asked you to make life's ultimate reality your mantra: *Being itself is mind.* You are divine, your being itself is your mind. This is the greatest statement that can be made about you. And if this becomes your mantra, if this permeates your life, if this starts to echo in each and every pore of you, you will gradually discover that you have started becoming what you have been thinking yourself to be. What you have repeated inside has started becoming a reality in your life.

Religiousness begins with this understanding: you are not, only existence is. True, you are in deep slumber. True, you are bad in many ways. True, you have committed many wrongs, but this makes no difference to your essential nature at all. Your essential nature is unblemished purity. No matter what wrongs and mistakes you may have done, once you remember that you are godliness, existence, all your evil will be swept away.

If you want to destroy all your evils one by one, you can try it, but you will not be able to accomplish it even in many lifetimes, because there are *so many evils*, if you try to destroy them one by one, you will never succeed. In destroying one evil you will also be creating ten more. You will destroy one evil, but ninety-nine evils will still remain in you, and they will colour even the one newly acquired virtue—they will turn it back into evil.

This is why even when you do something virtuous, it also turns out to be like a sin. Even when you touch nectar, it becomes poison, because all your other evils jump on it. Even if you build a temple, this does not create humility in you, it only nourishes your ego. And the ways of the ego are very subtle: it swells even with the most meaningless rubbish.

Mulla Nasruddin had a dog. It was a mongrel and its appearance was disgusting. It was a thin, ugly, weak creature that went about with its tail between its crooked legs, always afraid, always trembling. But Mulla never tired of praising him.

I asked him, 'Tell me something about this dog.' He had named the dog Adolf Hitler.

He said, 'There may be doubts about Hitler's breed, but he is a very precious creature. No stranger can approach even the vicinity of my house without our knowing it. Hitler lets us know immediately!'

I asked, 'What does your Hitler do?'—because to look at him, it seemed doubtful that he would be able to do anything. 'Does he bark, howl, bite—what does he do?'

Nasruddin said, 'No, but when a stranger comes, he simply rushes inside the house and hides under my bed. So not once has it happened that a stranger has come and we didn't know.'

Even this quality made him feel proud!

Your ego is like Mulla Nasruddin's dog, Hitler. Nothing is known about its breed—and do you know how your ego was born? How can something that does not exist be born? It is an illusion. There can be no information about its breed. You are born of existence, but from what is your ego born? Have you ever observed your ego closely? You may have given it big names like Adolf Hitler—everyone thinks in that way—but its feet are made of clay. It is so pathetic.

Even the biggest egos are helpless and pathetic. Why?— because even the biggest ego is impotent. It has no energy of its own; energy belongs to being. The source of energy is separate, and this is why the ego has to be supported twenty-four hours a day. It can't even stand on its own feet, we have to give it support. Sometimes we support it with position, sometimes we support it with money and power, sometimes we support it with virtue; and if there is nothing else, we support it with evil.

Go and look in the prisons: the inmates tell false stories about evil acts that they have never even committed. A man who has killed one person boasts that he has wiped out a hundred, because that is the only way to inflate your ego in a prison. There, an ordinary prisoner is just ordinary. The notorious prisoners are the ones who have committed terrible crimes—and many of them! People who have been tried for only one or two crimes have no prestige. Only people who have been tried for a number of crimes, who are presented in court every day—today for one hearing, tomorrow for another hearing—are the grand masters in the prison. Prison is the place where the inmates talk about the false, evil crimes that they have never even committed.

You try to support your ego in any way possible or impossible—through good deeds, through evil deeds, through wealth and position—and yet you cannot save it because death will destroy it. Death destroys only what is not; what *is* cannot be destroyed. You will remain—but remember, when I say that you will remain, I am speaking of the essence in you of which you are unaware. What you take to be 'you' will not remain, because it is only your ego. Your name, your form, your wealth, your prestige, your qualifications—nothing of what you have earned will remain. If you know that you are something other than these, if you have had even a glimpse of something which is beyond your qualifications, which you have not earned but were born with, which was with you even before you were born, only this will remain after your death.

Being itself is mind.

This being is worth seeking. Your mind also has a ray of your being or else it would not function. Even if you commit a wrong, who will do it? You need energy to do it, and all energy comes from this same source. You are misusing this energy, but you will not be able to change this misuse to right use because the root—the basic cause—of misuse is the ego.

There is only one sin, and that is to believe yourself to be separate from existence: all other sins follow it like a shadow. And there is only one virtue, and that is to experience yourself as one with existence. When the wave merges with the ocean, all virtues follow in its wake automatically.

Being itself is mind.
Maya, illusion, is unawareness of the doer.

What is this illusion, this maya? Why is the mind fogged in darkness if the being itself is the mind? The answer is the unawareness of the doer. You don't know who the doer is within you, the real actor within you. You are oblivious to the essence within you, and what you assume to be the doer does not even exist. You live your life holding on to something which doesn't exist, hence your misery. In spite of your lifelong efforts, your misery has not lessened; in fact, it has multiplied. In spite of working hard your whole life, you find that you have not experienced even a drop of bliss; the mountains of misery only grow bigger. Yet, people go on running after the futile until their very last breath.

Why this infatuation with the futile? Try to understand this, because the futile has a speciality all of its own.

A man bought a new bungalow, so he created a garden and planted some flower seeds. The plants started growing, but weeds also started growing alongside them. He was a little worried, so he asked his neighbour, Mulla Nasruddin, 'How am I to know which are the flower plants and which are the weeds?'

'That's simple,' Nasruddin answered, 'pull them all out! The ones that come up again are the weeds.'

This is the speciality of the futile: pull it out and it is still not destroyed. By pulling things out, the meaningful will be destroyed, but the meaningless, the futile, will grow again.

You sow seeds of the meaningful, and yet there is no certainty that you will reap the crop, because there are a thousand and one obstacles ahead. And even if you don't sow seeds of the futile, you will still have to reap their crop, because even when you uproot them a thousand times, they keep on growing. You don't have to make any effort to grow the futile, but it requires great effort to grow the meaningful. This is why you choose the futile, because it grows on its own. You don't have to make much effort to become a thief because the habit of stealing grows like weeds. Does anyone have to make an effort to become filled with sexual desire—some prayer, some spiritual discipline, some yoga? No, it grows on its own like weeds. Do you have to go somewhere, to some university, to learn how to be angry? No, that too grows like weeds.

The difficulty arises when you want to learn meditation. You come across great difficulties when you want to learn love, because attachment and infatuation grow and flourish like weeds. Love needs great effort, and if you want to bring love into your life, you will have to uproot weeds every moment. Otherwise, the weeds will destroy everything that is meaningful. The weeds will cover whatever is meaningful and significant, they will overshadow it.

The meaningless has one speciality: it demands no effort. If you keep on being lazy and lethargic, what is meaningless will flourish on its own. It will keep a tight grip on you until your last breath.

A seeker is someone who has embarked on a search for the meaningful. To find the meaningful is a journey, an uphill journey towards the mountain peak, towards the heights. Finding the meaningless is like rolling downhill, just as a stone rolls down the mountain on its own. The force of gravity will bring it down, nothing else needs to be done.

Until now you have not done anything in your life, and this is your feeling of futility. You may say, 'No, it is not so; I have worked hard. I have earned a lot of money; I have reached places of power and prestige; I have collected many titles . . .' And still I say that all this is not *your* doing. It has all grown on its own like weeds. And if you really look carefully inside yourself, you will be able to see that you have not done anything to earn money: the desire for money was there inside you like weeds that have grown. Even if you pull them out, they will grow again on their own. You have done nothing special to build a house: that desire was inside you and has grown like weeds. That desire will grip you until your last moment. But a seeker is someone who has understood the truth that whatever grows on its own must be futile, and that he will have to plant something meaningful himself.

I have heard that a woman went to a psychiatrist and said, 'I need some help. I have been postponing it, but now I will have to ask for help.'

The psychiatrist asked, 'What is the problem?'

She said, 'The problem is not mine, it is my husband's. The problem is that the love he showed in the beginning has slowly disappeared. The intensity of passion he had before has gradually become less. He used to be overwhelming, like a flood, but now he is becoming like a dried-up river.'

Inwardly, the psychiatrist wanted to laugh, but he kept a straight face—the seriousness of a professional—and asked, 'But how old are you?'

'Only seventy-two,' she answered.

'And what is your husband's age?'

'He is only eighty-six.'

Everybody thinks like this: *only* eighty, *only* ninety. They are propping this 'only' up against death: 'You call this old? It is almost just the beginning!'

Then the psychiatrist asked the lady, 'And when did you first notice that his energy, his power was declining, that his desire for sex was waning?'

The wife answered, 'Last night, and again this morning.'

Until the very last moment, people hold on to rubbish because they don't have to do anything for it, it grows on its own. People come to me and say, 'We try to meditate, but we lose track again and again. We meditate for two days, then we stop.' This doesn't happen with your desires and passions. It is not so with your anger. You don't drop your anger, even by mistake; you go on clinging to it. What is happening? Meditation falls away in spite of your persistence: you do it for a few days and then you forget, then you remember it again after a few months. You forget prayerfulness after just a few days—but is it the same with your anger, with your greed, with your sex, with your attachments and infatuations?

Try to understand this one fact: meditation has to be actively cultivated, and this is why it falls away again and again. It is a seed that has to be sown and taken care of, but all the rubbish, the weeds, grow on their own. So, whatsoever continues to grow on its own, know that it is rubbish, just futile. And as long as you go on living them, you will not accomplish anything. At the moment of death, you will find yourself empty-handed. You had come empty-handed and now you are leaving empty-handed.

This lack of awareness, this unconsciousness, this inability to discriminate between what is meaningful and what is futile, is in itself maya, illusion.

Shankara has defined wisdom as the ability to discriminate between the meaningful and the meaningless, to be able to see this in your life. In life, both are there, the flowers as well as the weeds. You will have to decide what is meaningful through your own experience of life. If your attention shifts to the meaningful, then your attention is on the ultimate reality; if it remains with the futile, then you will wander in illusion.

You don't know who you are or in which direction you are going. You have no idea from where you have come. You have simply become entangled in the rubbish by the side of the road, you have made the side of the road your home. Because of the worthless rubbish that has been growing without your doing, you are filled with worries and anxieties. But you have no business to be concerned with that.

Maya, illusion, is unawareness of the doer. A lack of awareness is the inability to discriminate, the inability to distinguish a diamond from a pebble. You will have to become the jeweller of your life, because awareness arises only when you become a jeweller of your own life. You have life—now look deeply into it. And this I call the criterion for the search: anything that happens by itself, consider it to be worthless, futile; and what refuses to happen even with your efforts, consider that to be meaningful. This is the criterion. When you find that what was so difficult to bring about in your life has begun to happen, know that the flowers are also coming. And on the day when what used to grow on its own stops growing, know that you are freed from illusion.

The seeker who remains attached to veils of illusion can gain supernatural powers, but will not know enlightenment.

The meaningless has become so important in your life that even when you try to choose the meaningful, you still end up choosing the meaningless. People come to meditate, but if you try to understand their motives, you will be very surprised. Even through meditation they desire only the meaningless. They come to me and say, 'I want to meditate to get rid of physical ailments. Can you guarantee that they will disappear through meditation?' It would be better if they had gone to a doctor, it would be better if they had found a physician. Even when they come to a physician of the soul, it is still about curing their physical ailments. They are ready to meditate, but meditation is not more than a medicine to them, just a medicine for the body.

People come to me and say: 'I have many problems in life. My finances are not in good shape. Will meditation solve all this?' The veil of your attachments is so dense and thick that even when you seek nectar, it is in the service of poison. It is really amazing! You want nectar, but only to commit suicide by drinking it. But you can't commit suicide with the nectar, because the moment you drink it, you become immortal. But even when you go in search of nectar, your goal is still suicide. You want to use even meditation to fulfil your desire for money or pleasure, the two aspects of this world.

Go to the temples and listen to people's prayers and you will find that even in the temple their demands are all worldly: someone's son is not getting a girl's hand in marriage, another person's son needs a job, someone has trouble at home. You ask for worldly things even in the temple. It is as if your temples are supermarkets where these things are also sold, where everything is available. You have no understanding of what a real temple is. And the priests who are sitting in your temples are no more than shopkeepers, because the people who go there are just customers for worldly goods. You will always avoid the real temple.

Once I was a guest in the house of a friend who is a dentist. One day while I was sitting in his drawing room, a small boy entered, looking very afraid. He looked around cautiously and asked me almost in a whisper, 'Could you tell me if the doctor is in?'

I told him that he had just gone out. The child's eyes lit up with joy: 'My mother has sent me to have my teeth checked,' he said. 'May I ask when the doctor will be out again?'

This is your condition: if you come across a genuine temple, you will avoid it. You can face the toothache, but you are not ready to face the pain that the dentist gives you. You are like small children. You can bear all the pain that your desires inflict on you, but you are not ready to go through the slightest pain for the state of religiousness. And the process of religiousness is bound to cause you pain. In fact, it is not the religiousness that causes the pain: the teeth of your desires have decayed so much that there is bound to be pain when you extract them.

Religiousness causes no pain. Religiousness is the ultimate bliss. But you have always lived in misery, you have accumulated only misery. All your teeth are full of pain and it will hurt you to pull them out. You are so afraid of getting them pulled out that you are even willing to live with the pain and the poison. The poison is spreading all over your body, your whole life is full of decay—but at least you are familiar with this pain.

People are ready to suffer the familiar. They are even afraid of happiness if it is unfamiliar. These teeth are yours, their pain is yours, and you have known them for many lives. But you are unaware of the fact that if these rotten teeth are removed and the pain disappears, then the door to bliss will open for the first time in your life.

Even when you go to the temple it is only to ask the priest, 'When will God come again so that I can come back then?' You go, and yet you don't want to go. It is very difficult to comprehend the games you play with yourself.

Constantly observing you and your problems, I have come to the conclusion that your problem is only one: you don't know exactly what you want to do. Do you want to meditate? You are not so sure. Then if you don't fall easily into meditation, you are upset. Now, if your mind is not entirely made up, you will not meditate with totality. Whatever you do will be half-hearted—and nothing in life is ever attained through a half-hearted approach. The meaningless needs no effort: you don't have to invest anything in it, it will continue on its own momentum—but about the meaningful? You will have to pour your life into it, you will have to put your life at stake for it.

This sutra says: *The seeker who remains attached to veils of illusion can gain supernatural powers, but will not know enlightenment.* The curtain of your ignorance is so thick that even if you move towards religiousness, you look for miracles there too. Even if you find Buddha standing before you, you will not recognize him: you will recognize Satya Sai Baba. If Buddha and Satya Sai Baba are both standing there, you will definitely go towards Satya Sai Baba and not towards Buddha, because Buddha will not do such stupid things like give you an amulet and produce ashes from his hands. Buddha is not a street magician. But you are in search of street magicians; you are impressed by miracles, because your deepest ambition, your deepest desire is for the world, not for the ultimate reality.

Wherever you see a miracle-maker, you think that you have found some master. You feel hopeful that your desires will be fulfilled: 'A master who can produce an amulet out of nowhere can surely produce the Koh-i-noor diamond if he wants. Now I just have to be at his feet and serve him. If not today, then tomorrow, I will get the diamond. What difference will it make to the master? If he can produce an amulet, he can produce a diamond too.' And your desire is for the diamond. For diamonds, not only a common man, but even great men are ready to become thieves. But you think, 'If a man from whose hands holy ash is produced out of nowhere wants, he can grant me immortality. It is only a matter of serving him properly.'

No, you will miss the Buddha because no miracles happen around him. Where all desires have been dissolved, the question of satisfying any of your desires simply does not arise. Although what happens near Buddha is the greatest miracle, the ultimate miracle—there is the light of desirelessness there—your desire-filled eyes will not be able to see that. You will be able to see Buddha, you will be able to understand him, you will be able to bow down at his feet only when the meaninglessness of the world has really dawned on you and your curtain of illusions has really fallen away.

Infatuation is intoxication. You have been walking through life like a drunkard—staggering, not even certain about where you are going, in unconsciousness. And no matter how hard you try to watch your steps, it will make no difference. All drunkards try to keep their balance. You can deceive yourself, but not others. All drunkards try to show that they are not drunk, but the more they try, the more obvious it becomes. Your infatuation is your intoxication.

And when I say that infatuation is intoxication, I am also saying this in chemical terms. In the state of infatuation your whole body is filled with intoxicating chemicals, even in the scientific sense. When you fall in love with a woman, the blood in your whole body is filled with certain hormones and chemical substances. These chemicals are the same as those found in LSD, hashish and marijuana. This is why the woman you have fallen in love with begins to look like such a sublime beauty! She doesn't look like she belongs to this earth. She looks other-worldly. And the man you fall in love with does not seem to be of this world—but when the intoxication fades, he seems not to be worth a penny! But while you are intoxicated . . .

This is why none of your love affairs can be permanent, because you are in a state of intoxication. It is a form of infatuation. It has not happened consciously, it has happened in a state of unconsciousness. This is why we say that love is blind. Actually, love is not blind, it is the infatuation that is blind. We mistake infatuation for love. Love is the 'eye'. There is no greater eye than the eye of love. It is the eye of love that sees the godliness hidden in this creation.

Infatuation is blind: it sees things where there is nothing. Infatuation is a dream. And the people we call seekers are also suffering from infatuation. They acquire certain supernatural powers . . . It is not difficult to acquire powers. Only a small effort is needed to read others' thoughts. Only a small practice is needed to influence others' thoughts. A person comes and you can tell what he is thinking: only a little practice is needed. It is a science, and religion has nothing to do with it.

There is a science of reading the mind just as there is a science of reading a book. An illiterate person will be amazed to see you reading a book—as if some miracle is taking place. Where he is unable to see anything but a few black marks and dots, you are getting such great pleasure out of a poem, out of an Upanishad, out of the Vedas; you are enchanted! An illiterate man is amazed to see this.

Mulla Nasruddin was the only one in his village who could read and write—and when there is only one literate person in the village it is difficult to judge whether he is really literate, because who will know? Whenever someone in the village wanted to get a letter written, they would go to Nasruddin and he would write the letter.

One day, an old woman went to him and said, 'Write a letter for me, Nasruddin.'

'I will not be able to write it,' said Nasruddin. 'My foot is hurting.'

The old woman said, 'This is too much! What does the pain in your foot have to do with writing a letter?'

Nasruddin answered, 'Don't go into details. But I say that I have pain in my foot and I will not write the letter.'

But the woman was also stubborn. She said, 'I will not budge until I know the truth. I may be illiterate, but I have never heard that a pain in the foot has anything to do with writing a letter.'

'If you insist, then I will tell you,' said Nasruddin. 'Who will go to the next village to read the letter? It is always I who has to go because only I can read a letter written by me. Now I have a pain in my foot so I am not going to write it!'

An uneducated person is struck with wonder to see someone lost in a book. But anyone can learn how to read, there is a method to it. Thoughts are going on in your mind: you can see your thoughts, the other person can also see them— there is a technique for doing it. But this technique of seeing thoughts has nothing to do with religion. Neither the art of reading a book nor the art of reading another person's thoughts has anything to do with religiousness. But these conjurors learn to do exactly that. They are not enlightened.

But you will be very impressed. You go to a holy man and he calls you by your name. He says, 'You come from such and such a village and there is a neem tree adjacent to your house'—you go crazy for him! But what does a holy man have to do with a neem tree, your village, or your name? A holy man is one who has realized that no one has a name or a form and no one belongs to a village. The villages, names and forms are all of the world. You are a worldly person, and the so-called holy man impresses you because he is even more worldly. He has learned a greater art: he speaks about you without you having given any information to him. He wants to impress you.

Remember, as long as you want to impress anyone, you are possessed by the ego. Being never wants to impress anybody—what is the point, what is the sense in it? It is like drawing lines on water. What difference would it make in you whether ten thousand people are impressed by you or twenty million? What would this actually do to you?

What would you gain by impressing them? The desire to impress a crowd of ignorant people only shows your own ignorance. When a politician tries to impress people it is understandable, but why should a religious person be interested in impressing others?

And whenever you want to impress others, know one thing for sure: you are not rooted in your own being. When you try to impress others it means you are rooted in your ego. Ego lives on influencing others, it works like food for the ego. The more people recognize you, the bigger your ego will be. If the whole world recognizes you, then your ego will be at its peak. If nobody recognizes you—you pass through your village, you walk on the road and nobody looks at you, nobody takes note of you; just no recognition, no flicker of recognition in anybody's eyes, as if you simply don't exist—this is exactly where your ego gets hurt.

The ego desires attention from others. Now this is very interesting: the ego does not want to give attention, it wants everyone else to pay attention to it, for the whole world to look towards it so that it becomes the centre of attention. A religious person is not interested in others looking towards him. His concern is that he look towards himself, because it is this self that will ultimately remain with him.

The ego is childish! Children feel happy when their elders praise them. When they come home with certificates and prizes, they come jumping and dancing with joy. But if you are demanding certificates even in your old age, then you have missed your life completely.

The desire for supernatural powers is to impress others. This is not the desire of a religious person at all; this is the way of a worldly man.

This sutra says: *The seeker who remains attached to veils of illusion can gain supernatural powers, but will not know enlightenment.* However great the supernatural powers someone may acquire—that their touch can raise the dead, their touch can cure illness, they can turn water into medicine—enlightenment has nothing to do with all of that. In fact, the situation is just the opposite: the more supernatural power a person acquires, the further he will drift away from enlightenment—because the more the ego is nourished, the emptier the being becomes. The emptier the ego becomes, the more the being will be nourished. You will not be able to strengthen both of them simultaneously.

Let go of the desire to impress others, otherwise your meditation will be corrupted. Then even if you practise meditation, it will be politics and not religion. And politics is a kind of trap: then the person wants to influence others by any means. Then he doesn't mind using right or wrong methods to do it. But the only reason you want to impress others is because you want to exploit them.

I have heard:

National elections were being held, and by the evening three people were arrested. It was quite dark inside the jail and the three introduced themselves to one another in the darkness.

One of them said, 'I am Sardar Sant Singh. I was working for Sardar Sirfod Singh.'

The second said, 'That's strange! I am Sardar Shaitan Singh and I was working against Sardar Sirfod Singh.'

The third said, 'Amazing! I am Sardar Sirfod Singh!'

The leaders and the followers of the ruling party or of the opposition are all fit only for jails. That is the right place for them; that is where they belong.

The roots of all evil lie in the desire to dominate others, because the ego cares neither for good nor bad, all it cares about is to nourish itself. How that is accomplished is secondary. The ego's only desire is to nourish itself and grow bigger and bigger. But since the very nature of ego is hollowness, it always remains empty in spite of all its tricks. As life passes by your ego becomes more and more insane because you realize that it has not yet been satisfied; that time is passing by and the journey of the ego is incomplete.

This is why old people become irritable. Their irritability is not about others, the irritability is over the failure of their own lives. They have failed to fill up what they were trying to fill up. And the irritability of an old man becomes even more intense because he feels that as he has grown older, people have stopped giving attention to him. In fact, they are simply waiting for his departure.

Mulla Nasruddin was a hundred years old. I asked him if he could tell me one reason why existence had granted him such a long life. Without batting an eyelash, the Mulla replied, 'Just to test the patience of my relatives.'

All old people are testing the patience of their families. They are noticing all the time that their relatives are paying less and less attention to them. Death will eventually get rid of them later, but people are already getting rid of them much earlier by turning their backs on them; hence the irritability.

You cannot imagine how irritable Richard Nixon must be these days—all the people who were paying attention to him have turned their backs on him. The people who were close to him have now become strangers. Friends have become enemies. Those who supported him have withdrawn their support. All the attention has moved away from him. Nixon is sick, restless, agitated. The first question he asks of whoever goes to meet him is, 'Wasn't what I did right? What are people saying about me?'

Just a while ago this man was at the peak, and now he is
lying in the ditch. What is this peak and this ditch made of?
The man himself is the same man he was yesterday, the one
who was in power; the man himself has not changed. The
only difference is that before the ego was at the peak and
now it is in the ditch; but his being has not changed places.
If only this man could remember that which has no peaks,
no ditches, and which knows no victory, no defeat, which
is perfectly okay whether people pay attention or not, and
which knows no change, which is forever the same.

You will experience this unchanging one only when you
stop looking to others for attention. Drop this beggar-like
attitude. What will you attain with supernatural powers?
People will call you a miracle-maker and hundreds of
thousands may gather around you. But what does hundreds
of thousands of idiots gathering around you prove? Only
that you are the focus of attention of hundreds of thousands
of idiots, that you are a super-idiot!

What will you gain from the praise of the ignorant? In
what way will seeking the praise of the ignorant be of any
help to you? At the most, you can become the leader of
those who are themselves wandering in ignorance. What
value does this praise have?

I have heard:

There was a Sufi mystic, Farid. If people clapped when
he addressed a gathering, he would start crying.

One day his disciples asked him, 'This is strange. When
people clap, why do you cry?'

Farid said, 'When they clap, I know that I must have
made some mistake. Otherwise how can they clap? So
many ignorant people clapping! Only when they don't clap
or understand, do I know that I must be saying the right
thing.'

After all, of what value is the applause of the ignorant? Are you trying to prove you are a siddha, the possessor of supernatural powers? If you want to prove to the world that you are a siddha, you are asking for recognition from the ignorant. Then you are also still ignorant. And if you are trying to prove to existence that you are a siddha, then you are an even greater fool because what is needed with existence is humility. With existence, the ego will not do. You will receive recognition from existence only if you have completely annihilated the ego. If you go there with your arrogance, your very arrogance will become an obstacle.

This is why your so-called siddhas never reach the ultimate reality. They acquire great supernatural powers, but they miss the real power. The real power is self-realization, enlightenment. Why do they miss self-realization? Because supernatural power also is focused on the other, not on yourself. Would you want supernatural powers if there was nobody else in the world, if you were all alone? Would you want your touch to turn water into medicine? Would you want your touch to heal the sick? Would you want your touch to bring the dead back to life? If there was no one else in the world, would you still want to have these supernatural powers? You would say, 'What is the use of these powers if there are no spectators?' You want these supernatural powers only because of the spectators.

As long as your attention is focused on others, you cannot turn it towards yourself—and self-realization happens only to those who turn their eyes back from others to their own selves.

When illusion is forever vanquished, one attains spontaneous wisdom.

Illusion is to be vanquished. What is the meaning of 'illusion'? Illusion is the feeling that 'I will not be able to live without the other. The other is the centre of my life.'

You must have read children's stories where there is a king whose life energy has been concealed in a bird, maybe a parrot or a mynah bird. You can't kill the king directly because the bullet will pass through his body, but the king will remain alive. The arrow can pierce his heart, but the king will not die. You can give him poison and it will have no effect, the king will remain alive. You will have to find the parrot or the mynah bird where his life energy has been hidden. Kill the bird, and the king will die.

These children's stories are very meaningful. Older people would also do well to understand them.

Illusion or infatuation means that you don't live in yourself, that your life is dependent on something outside of you. Understand it in this way: if someone's infatuation is with his wealth, you can wring his neck and he will not die, but steal his treasure and he is dead. This man's life was in his wealth, so if his bank balance is lost, he will die. You can kill him but he will not die, you can try to poison him and he will remain alive.

Infatuation means that you have placed your centre somewhere else, outside of you. Somebody has placed it in his son, someone else has placed it in his wife, another in his wealth or his position—but always somewhere else. Your centre is not where it belongs. Your life energy is not pulsating within you, it is centred somewhere else. Then you will remain in misery.

This infatuation is sansara, the world, because you will become a slave to the very people or things that you have centred your life energy in. The king whose life is in the parrot will become a slave to that parrot. His very life will depend on that parrot. If the parrot dies, he dies, so he will have to protect the parrot with his life.

I have heard that once a king was very displeased with his astrologer. The astrologer had predicted that the prime minister would die the next day, and he died the next day.

The king became very worried. He started to suspect that maybe his prime minister had died because of this prediction—that the astrologer's prediction might have had such a deep effect on him that he died. His words might have influenced him so deeply that he died. 'Now this man is dangerous,' the king thought. 'If he says something like this about me, then it will be very difficult to survive because it will have the same effect on me as well.'

He had the astrologer thrown into prison. When the astrologer asked the king why he was being imprisoned, the king said, 'You are a dangerous man. I don't think that the prime minister died a natural death; I think he died because of your prediction; what you said influenced him so deeply that he became hypnotized by the idea and died. You are dangerous!'

The astrologer said, 'Before you throw me in prison, hear what I have to say about your future. I have figured that out too.' The king tried his best not to listen to his prediction, but the astrologer blurted it out. The king asked him to shut up, but the astrologer blurted, 'There is no way to shut up! You will die three days after my death.'

Now the king was really in a dilemma: he had to keep that astrologer in the palace, under great care and service. The king personally took care of the astrologer's body because the day he dies, three days later . . .

Whatsoever you put your life energy into, you will become its servant. Watch people as they go to their bank vaults, with folded hands, as if they are going to the temple. They have written all sorts of holy inscriptions on the safe: *Shubh Labh*—'Good Fortune'; *Shri Ganeshaya Namah*—'I bow down to Lord Ganesh, the god of good fortune'. The safe is their God, they worship it. On Diwali, the festival of lights, you should see these insane people worshipping their bank vaults. Their whole life energy is kept in it. Their adoration and worship is worth watching. Every year on this day, every shopkeeper starts a new accounts book. On the first page he draws a swastika symbol and writes 'Shubh Labh', or 'Shri Ganeshaya Namah'.

Do you know why he worships Ganesh so much? Ganesh is an old troublemaker.

An ancient story tells us that Ganesh is the lord of all obstacles. He even looks like a mischief-maker! First of all, he doesn't have a head of his own, and anyone who doesn't have a head of his own is really crazy! He can do anything—possible, impossible. Look at his physical body and appearance. Everything about him arouses suspicion. He rides a rat. The rat is the symbol of logic because its teeth cut like sharp scissors. Logic is never trustworthy: wherever it arrives it creates trouble. If your life is invaded by logic, there will be troubles in your life. There will be chaos, all peace will be gone. So Ganesh is the ancient god of obstacles. Wherever something good is happening, he arrives on the scene. People started to fear him. Because of this fear, they stand with folded hands and beg him not to create trouble: 'Please, spare us of your mischief! We will manage all the rest.' And by and by, the situation took a new turn: people began to look upon Ganesh, who was the god of mischief, as the god of good fortune and good beginnings. They had forgotten the real story. They were right to fold their hands and beg him to spare them.

Watch with what great adoration the devotee of wealth worships his safe.

The veils of illusion means that your being is imprisoned outside of you. It may be imprisoned in your wife, it may be imprisoned in your wealth or in some position or anywhere else, it makes no difference, but your being is not in yourself. That is the meaning of infatuation.

Illusion is forever vanquished means that you have dissolved all dependence on others. Now you don't live your life in dependence on anyone else, your life is self-dependent. You are settled in your own self. You have made your own existence your very centre. Now if your wife dies or your wealth disappears, it does not matter. These are just waves on the surface and you will not be disturbed. Whether success or failure comes, whether happiness or misery comes, it will make no difference to you. They only made a difference because you were dependent on them.

Victory over infatuation, illusion, means to become totally independent. A realization that 'I am not dependent on anything,' a contentment that 'I am complete in myself, my being is complete in itself'—such a state is victory over infatuations. As long as your being depends on someone else's existence, infatuation, illusion, will hold you captive. Until then, you will cling tightly to the other for fear that you may lose that person, and then how will you live without that person?

Mulla Nasruddin's wife died and he was pretending to cry. But one of his friends was crying very loudly—he was beating his chest and his eyes were full of flowing tears. Mulla could not contain it any more, so he said, 'There's no need to make so much fuss, my brother. I will marry again. Don't grieve so much.'

The friend had been a lover of Mulla's wife! Mulla's heart was not in her, but his friend's heart was. Mulla was right to say that there was no need to make such a fuss, that he would marry again.

What things make you cry? That is where your infatuation is. What do you miss when it is not there? That is where your infatuation is. Ponder over it: what is there that if you lose it, will make you feel miserable and pathetic? That is the object of your infatuation. Before you lose it, you, yourself, should let go of your attachment to it—because you are bound to lose it.

Nothing is permanent in this world, neither love nor friendship—nothing is permanent. Here, everything is changing. The nature of the world is change in every moment. It is a flow; it is flowing like a river. Nothing here is stable. No matter how much you try, you cannot make anything here stable. It is because of this trying that you are in misery. You want to stop something that is always moving. You want to stop and freeze something that is always flowing. It is not possible; it is not in its very nature.

Change is the other name for the world, and you want to find some permanent support in it. This cannot be! And this is why every moment of your life is filled with misery, because every moment you are losing those supports.

Try to discover what things would disturb you if they were lost. Then before they are lost, drop your attachment to them. This is the method for conquering your infatuations. There is bound to be pain, but this pain is worth bearing; this is your discipline of self-purification. It is not necessary to renounce anything. It is not that you should leave your wife and escape to the Himalayas. Remain where you are, but gradually go on dropping your dependence on her. This does not mean that you have to cause pain to your wife: your wife should not even know about it. There is no need for anyone to know about it.

Jesus has said, 'When even your right hand does not know what your left hand is doing, only then are you a true seeker.' The desire to let others know about you is again a desire of the ego. You want others to know: 'Look! I have left my wife and I am going to the Himalayas. I have done such a great thing!' It is not at all great. There is nothing great in it at all. Ask any husband: they all want to escape to the Himalayas! That they are unable to escape is a different matter.

One day Mulla Nasruddin went to the local lunatic asylum and knocked at the door. The superintendent opened the door and asked him what he wanted.

Mulla said, 'Has any lunatic escaped from your asylum?'

The superintendent said, 'Why do you ask? Have you seen someone wandering around?'

'No, but someone has run off with my wife,' said the Mulla. 'So I thought there must be some crazy man who has escaped from here, because I have been wanting to get rid of her, and this man has got himself trapped on his own!'

Ask any husband . . .

There is no end to the misery of whoever is living in this world. And he also can't escape because he can't see happiness anywhere else, either. Where to go? Wherever he goes, the world will go with him. Besides, he has made this place for himself with great expectations and now to let go of it will be difficult, because then his whole life will have gone to waste.

Find out your infatuations, the things you can't live without. Make an inner effort to gradually live without them. Create a state within yourself that even if all those things are lost, there won't be the slightest tremor in you. Then you have conquered the infatuations. And this can happen; this *has* happened. If it has happened to one, it can happen to all.

This sutra of Shiva says: *When illusion is forever vanquished, one attains spontaneous wisdom.* On the day you conquer your infatuations, you will find that you have begun to experience the wisdom which is not learned from others but which is natural and spontaneous. It has begun to arise within you. *This* is self-realization.

There is no way to learn self-realization from others, it sprouts from within you. As naturally as flowers grow on the trees and waterfalls flow down mountains, the knowledge that is forever flowing within you, softly murmuring, is already yours, spontaneous and natural. You don't have to get it from someone else. No master can give it to you, all masters only point towards it. When you attain it you will realize that it was already hidden within you. It is your own wealth, hence it is called 'spontaneous wisdom'.

There are two types of knowledge. The knowledge of this world has to be learned from others. It is not natural. No matter how intelligent a person is, he will have to learn worldly knowledge from others. And no matter how stupid a person may be, even then he will not need to learn the knowledge of the self from others. It is within you. The only obstacle is infatuation. With the disappearance of infatuations, the clouds disperse and the shining sun rises.

The awakened one knows that this universe is an emanation of his own energy.

On the day this natural knowledge unfolds within you, the awakening comes. What you will see is that this whole universe pulsates with your energy. Then you are the centre. You had always wanted so much to be the centre of the whole world, but this could never happen through the ego.

Each time, you were defeated. But the moment the ego dies, you become the centre.

You will have what you want to attain, but you are looking for it in the wrong direction. You are moving on a false path. What you want can be attained, but it cannot be attained with the means you have chosen. You have chosen a wrong chariot, a wrong vehicle. You can never be the centre of the universe through your ego, but the egoless person instantly becomes the centre of the universe.

As buddhahood happens under the bodhi tree, the whole world becomes the circumference; the whole universe becomes the circumference and buddhahood the centre. Then the whole universe is 'my own expansion'. Then all its manifestations are mine. All life is mine. But *this* 'mine' happens only when 'I', the ego, is no more. That is the difficulty. As long as the 'I' exists, no matter how much you expand this 'mine', no matter how great an empire you build, you will only be deceiving yourself.

You have burned your hands enough times. For lives upon lives you have wandered, and yet you have not become aware.

I have heard that Mulla Nasruddin once boarded a plane. The moment he sat down in his seat he called the stewardess and said, 'Listen: have the oil, gas, water and air all been checked properly and found normal?'

The stewardess told him, 'Just relax, sir. This is our worry, not yours.'

'Then don't ask me in the middle of the journey to get out and push!' said the Mulla.

I happened to hear about this incident, so I asked the Mulla, 'Did something like this really happen?'

He answered, 'Yes it did. A child who has been burned dreads the fire. A bad experience from my bus travels has made me apprehensive on an airplane too. Who knows? I might have to get out and push the plane.'

You have been burned many times in your life. But you have not learned to protect yourself from things that can burn you, what to say of being aware when things are at a normal temperature? The greatest calamity in life is that we fail to learn from our experiences. People say that they learn from experience, but it does not show. No one seems to learn from experience. Again and again, you go on repeating the same mistakes. If you commit new mistakes, at least there is some skill factor involved in it. At least it may bring some momentum, some maturity to your life. But you go on repeating the same mistakes again and again.

The mind is a circle and you go on revolving in it, as if you are caught in a wheel. What spins this wheel are your attachments: destroy your attachments and the wheel will stop. And as soon as the wheel comes to a halt, you will realize that you are the centre. You need not become the centre, you already are. There is no need to become divine, you already are! Hence, this knowledge is natural.

The awakened one knows that this universe is an emanation of his own energy. And this realization is the ultimate bliss, this realization is the ultimate nectar. All darkness disappears from your life the moment this realization happens to you. All suffering, pain and anguish will vanish. You will be filled with an ecstatic joy. In this drunkenness, a song arises in your life. Your every breath pulsates in delight, is filled with a fragrance that comes from some unknown source.

This is the spontaneous wisdom which no scripture or master can teach. The master can only help you to remove the obstacles.

Keep this clearly in mind: there is no way to 'learn' this supreme wisdom; you have only to learn how to remove the obstacles in its way. Meditation will not give you that ultimate treasure, it will only give you the key to its door. Meditation will only open the door for you. That ultimate treasure is already within you. Thou art that! *Tattvamasi!* You are Brahman, the ultimate reality!

All methods exist only to remove the obstacles, the rocks along the way. You are carrying the destination with you. To attain the ultimate reality is natural, spontaneous— the difficulty is only because of your infatuations and attachments. The difficulty is not that it will take time to experience the ultimate: the difficulty is that you are clinging so hard to the world that the time you take to let go of the world is the time taken to experience the ultimate. If you can let go of your attachments of the world this very moment, then in this very moment is the attainment, the meeting. If you want to postpone—and for many lives you have been postponing—you may go on postponing for many lives more.

Although it is enough! You have already postponed more than was necessary. Postponing any more is meaningless. The time is ripe; now you can drop off the tree of the world. And don't be afraid that you will no longer be if you fall off the tree. You will be no more, but only the you that is meaningless. The meaningful will be found a millionfold.

Enough for today.

6

Mastering the Mind

Being is the dancer.
> *Inner being is the stage.*
> *Essential self is realized by overcoming the mind.*
> *Upon becoming self-realized spontaneous freedom arises.*
> *Because of this freedom, which is his essential nature, the realized one can move even outside of himself; also while moving outside, he can remain within himself.*

BEFORE WE ENTER into the sutras, it will be good to understand a few things. Friedrich Nietzsche has said somewhere, 'I can only believe in a God that can dance. To believe in a sad God is the sign of a sick man.'

There is truth in this statement. You create your God in your own image. If you are sad, your God will be sad. If you are happy, your God will be happy. If you can dance, then your God also can dance. As you are, so existence appears to you. Creation is an extension of your own vision. As long as you cannot believe in a dancing God, know that you have not yet become healthy. The concept of a sad, weeping, sick God speaks of your own sick state.

The first sutra today:

Being is the dancer.

There are some things that need to be understood about dance. Dance is the only activity in which the action and the doer of the action become one. When someone draws a picture, the picture and the artist are separate. When someone writes a poem, the poem and the poet are separate. A person sculpts a statue; the sculptor and the statue are separate. Dance is the only activity in which the dancer and the dance are one; the two cannot be separated. If the dancer is gone, the dance is gone. And if the dance stops, then to call a person whose dance has stopped a dancer will have no meaning. The two are united as one.

So it is very meaningful to call existence a dancer. Creation is not separate from it. It is its dance, it is not its production. It is not a sculpted statue that it created and then walked away from. It is present within its creation in each moment. If it steps aside, the dance will stop. And remember, the moment the dance stops, the dancer also is no more. Without dance, there is no dancer. Existence is manifest in each and every flower, in each and every leaf, in every atom of existence. It is not that this creation happened in some ancient past and that was that. No, every moment it is being created. Every moment the act of creation is continuing. Hence, everything is new. Godliness is dancing both within and without.

Being is the dancer. This means that whatever you have done, whatever you are doing, whatever you will do is not separate from you. It is your own play. If you are suffering, it is your own choice. If you are blissful this also is your own choice, no one else is responsible.

I was a newly appointed professor in a college. Since the college was a good distance away from the town, the professors used to bring their lunch with them and they all sat together at one table at lunchtime. The person sitting next to me opened his lunch box, looked in and said, 'Again the same potatoes and the same chapattis!' I thought that perhaps he didn't like potatoes and chapattis, but since I was new there I didn't say anything. The next day the same thing happened. He opened his lunch box, looked in and sighed, 'Again the same potatoes and the same chapattis!'

So I said to him, 'If you don't like potatoes why don't you tell your wife to cook something else?'

'Wife?' he said. 'What wife? I prepare my lunch myself.'

So it is with your life: there is no one else there. If you laugh, *you* are laughing; if you cry, *you* are crying. No one else is responsible. It is possible that you have cried for so long that it has become a habit and you have forgotten how to laugh. It could also be that you have cried so much that now you cannot do anything else; you have practised it so much. It is also possible that you have been crying for so many lives that now you have forgotten that it was you, yourself, who had chosen to cry. But your forgetting does not make the reality untrue. Only you have chosen it, you are the master of it. Therefore, the moment you decide, this crying can stop.

To be filled with the realization that 'I am the master, I am the creator of it, only I am responsible for all my actions' brings about a revolution in your life. As long as you hold others responsible, transformation is not possible because you will remain dependent. If you think others are making you unhappy, then how can you ever become happy? It is impossible, because it is not in your hands to change others. To change your own self is the only thing in your hands.

If you think it is because of fate that you are unhappy, then again the matter is out of your hands. How will you change your fate? Fate is above you. And if you think that existence has destined for you whatever is happening in your life, then you are no more than a dependent machine. Then you are without a being.

The very meaning of being is that you are independent— no matter how great your suffering, it is the result of your own decisions. And the day you change your decision, your life will also change.

Then also, everything depends on how you look at life.

I was a guest at Mulla Nasruddin's house. One morning while I was taking a walk in the garden, I happened to see Mulla's wife throw a plate at his head. It missed his head and crashed against the wall. Nasruddin also saw that I had seen it, so he came out and said, 'Please sir, don't let this incident make you think that we are not happy. We are very happy! It is only occasionally that my wife throws things at me in this way, but this does not affect our happiness.'

I was a little surprised. I asked him, 'Mulla, would you mind explaining it a bit more to me?'

He said, 'You see, if she hits the target then she feels happy, and if she misses it I feel happy. It makes no difference to our happiness. Sometimes she hits the target, sometimes she misses it—so we are both happy.'

Everything depends on how you look at life. You, yourself, create it; you, yourself, see it and it is you who interprets it. You are absolutely alone. No one else ever enters your world—they cannot. If anyone does enter, it is because you have given your permission.

Now this creates a difficulty, and this is why you have chosen to forget it. The difficulty is that if you realize that you alone are responsible, then you cannot suffer; and if you still choose to suffer you cannot complain—and you have a great investment in both of these. You have a great investment in suffering because when you are suffering, you feel like a martyr. There is great pleasure in martyrdom. When you are unhappy you are looking for sympathy, and you have a great investment in sympathy.

This is why people magnify their suffering when they talk about it to others. What could be the reason that people go on telling their tales of suffering, even though nobody wants to listen? After all who is interested in your suffering? And listening to your tales of woe, the other person will only feel sad. It is not that flowers will blossom in his life! But you go on talking about your suffering. And the other person will listen to you only as long as he hopes that you will also listen to him; otherwise he will slip away.

You only call people 'bores' when they don't give you a chance to speak. It is a kind of agreement: 'You can bore me and I will bore you; you torture me with tales of your suffering and I will torture you with tales of my suffering— and we are both even.'

Why do people talk so much about suffering? What is the reason? They want sympathy. If someone talks about their troubles then someone will caress them and soothe them and say, 'Oh, you are suffering so much!' You are asking for love from the other person through your suffering. This is why you have such a great investment in your suffering. You have invested a great fortune in it.

Only when you are unhappy is there some hope of sympathy from others around you. Then people seem to offer you help and support, they show sympathy. You have never received love in your life, and sympathy is rubbish, but it is the nearest substitute for love. If you don't have real gold, you have to make do with false gold.

Sympathy is false love. What you really wanted was love. But love has to be earned, because only someone who is capable of giving love can get it. Getting love is an outcome of giving love. But you are incapable of giving, so you can only beg. You are a beggar, you are not an emperor. And for begging, the more miserable you look, the easier it gets.

Look at all the beggars along the road: they cover themselves with artificial wounds. Those wounds are not real, the pus has been applied from outside. But if he is really full of misery then you will find it hard to say no: you feel guilty. Your ego will be hurt if you say no to such a miserable man. If the beggar looks healthy and strong, you are bound to say, 'You look strong enough. Do something! Earn something! You can get a job.' But seeing a horribly miserable man, you are unable to say anything. You have to show sympathy, even if it is false.

You hold on to suffering because you have not received love. Someone who has received love in life is filled with joy and bliss. He will opt for bliss, not suffering. Suffering is not worth holding on to.

Also, it is convenient for you to complain. When you say that others are making you unhappy, you get rid of the burden of responsibility. And when I say to you—and all the scriptures say the same, and all the buddhas have said the same—that you alone are responsible and nobody else, then you feel a great burden. The biggest burden you feel is that now you can no longer dump the blame on someone else. Even more burdensome is the fact that you cannot ask for sympathy if you, yourself, are responsible. And another difficulty arises on a still deeper level: if only you are responsible, then a change can happen. And to bring about a change is revolution; it is going through a transformation: you have to break all your old habits.

You have an old pattern that is all wrong. The house that you have lived in up to now is truly a hell—but only you have built it. And no matter how big you may have built it, it has to be demolished completely. Your whole work from the past seems to be going to waste, so you try to avoid this truth. But the more you avoid it, the more you will go astray.

So know this first and foremost: that only you are the centre of your existence, and no one else is responsible. However heavy a burden it may seem, if you accept the truth that you alone are responsible, all misery will soon disappear. Once it becomes clear to you that you are the one who is creating your game, then how long can it take for you to destroy it? Then there will be no other to blame. But still, if you want to go on enjoying your suffering, then it is your own choice. Then there will be no excuse to complain. If you want to wander about aimlessly in the world, it is your choice. If you are determined to descend into hell, it is your own choice—but then there is no reason to complain. Then be happy in your misery.

These sutras are very valuable in this context. The first sutra is: *Being is the dancer.* Your actions and your life source are not two different things. Your actions arise from your own life source, just as dance comes out of a dancer. And if the dancer starts shouting, 'I am tired of this dance! I don't want to do it any more,' what would you say? You would say, 'Then stop! Don't dance. Who's asking you to dance? You are the one who is dancing. If it is all meaningless and you find no pleasure, no joy in it, then stop! And if it brings you pain, then stop—and the dance will disappear.'

Being is the dancer means that whatever you have done, it is you who has done it. It has come out of you. As leaves come out of the tree, in the same way, your actions come out of you. If you stop, the actions will disappear.

Another thing to understand about this sutra—*Being is the dancer*—is this: if you stop your dance of suffering, if you bring a halt to your life of misery and pain, the dance itself will not stop. Only its form will change. The dance as such cannot stop; it is a part of your life, it is your self-nature. You will dance, but then there will be no tears, there will be a smile. Your dance will have a song to it, a thrill, a pulsation of joy, bliss, an ecstasy. Right now your dance is a dance of hell. Then it will be heavenly, divine.

There was a Sufi fakir by the name of Ibrahim. He had been a king who later became a fakir and he had come to India in the course of his travels. In India he saw a sad-looking sadhu. Sadhus are usually sad, because they had known pleasure only in their family life; they have not known any other pleasure. So when they renounce the family, all their pleasure is lost. They may not be miserable, but they are certainly sad.

There is a little difference between misery and sadness. Misery means that there is intensity in the sadness, a heat, a passion, an overflowing, a flood. There are two types of overflowing: one is of happiness, one is of misery. One is when you are so filled with sadness that the tears begin to flow, and the other is when the waves of happiness fill you so much that the tears also begin to flow, but both are floods.

When someone runs away from the world because he feels it is full of misery, then the little happiness he had there will also be left behind. Then he will become sad; then there will be no flood, no overflowing either of happiness or of misery.

Go and look at your sadhus and so-called sannyasin: they are dead, like moving corpses, as if the dance has stopped. They have run away from misery, but the happiness is also gone because it was in ordinary life that they had glimpses of happiness. They were hoping that if they left misery behind, only happiness would remain. This is where they were mistaken. In the world there is misery, but that is also where there is happiness. You want to keep the happiness and get rid of the misery, so you run away from misery; but in the process the happiness is also lost.

This sadhu was sad. He must have been an ordinary sadhu, because a genuine sadhu drops happiness and misery, both. He doesn't want to save happiness; he wants to drop both happiness and misery. The moment he drops both, all sadness disappears—because sadness is just the midpoint between the two. When you drop both, then the middle point also disappears. Then a journey of an entirely new dimension begins. You may call it bliss or peace or nirvana, whatever name you want to give it.

There is no flood in bliss. Bliss is a cool ray, a cool light, there is no flood in it. Bliss is, in a sense, something like sadness. Sadness is between happiness and misery; bliss is beyond both. Sadness is a state of darkness where everything is blunt, dull; sadness is a deathlike state where everything languishes in inertia. Bliss is a luminous state of awareness, but there is neither misery nor happiness there. In this sense bliss is like sadness, where there is no happiness or misery. There is light, but the light is not that of happiness because even the light of happiness has an intensity that makes you perspire.

This is why people also get tired of happiness. You cannot remain happy for long. It will tire you, because there is intensity in it, sharpness and fever in it. If you were to win the lottery every day you would die, you would not survive. It's okay if you win it only once in a while, but if you win it every day the tension will be so great that you will not be able to sleep. Your heart will beat so fast that you will not be able to rest. The excitement will be so great that it will become your death. So happiness can only be taken in homeopathic doses. You will not be able to take an allopathic dose. It is given in very small doses—a lot of sorrow, a little bit of joy. Only that much is bearable because happiness is also tension; it has heat, excitement.

Misery is a tension, happiness is also a tension. There is excitement in both. Bliss is a non-excited state of mind; there is light there, but no heat. There is dance there, but no excitement. There is a silent, serene dance without any sound. This dance is in emptiness: it causes no fatigue, it is not of the body. Both happiness and misery belong to the body, but bliss belongs to your being; it is a different dance altogether.

This sadhu must have been an ordinary sadhu, the type you come across everywhere. So Ibrahim was surprised when he saw this sadhu looking sad, because according to his understanding a sadhu should have attained bliss.

He asked the sadhu, 'What is the characteristic of a sadhu?'

The sadhu said, 'If he gets food he accepts it; if he does not then also he remains content.'

'But this is a characteristic of a dog,' said Ibrahim. 'What is sadhu-like in this? That is what a dog does: he is happy if he gets something and he remains content if he doesn't.'

The sadhu was shocked. He asked, 'How do *you* define a sadhu?'

Ibrahim answered, 'If he gets something then he shares it, and if he doesn't, then he thanks existence with a dance for the opportunity to practise austerity.'

The definition of a religious person is this, that whatever he receives he shares—that is a true sadhu, a true religious man. If he holds on to what he gets, he is still a householder, a worldly man. If he saves it he is a worldly man, and if he shares it he is a sadhu, he is a religious man. No matter what it is—bliss, knowledge or meditation—he shares everything. Whatever he receives, he shares.

It is an interesting fact that worldly things, if shared, become less and less; hence people hold on to them. If you start sharing things from your safe, before long there will be nothing left. Because everything in the world is limited—you share it and it is gone. This is why in the world you have to hold on to things when the supply is limited. But there is no need to bring this habit to the world of being; there the treasure is boundless. There, the more you give the more it grows. The more you pour, the more new waters flow in. It is a boundless ocean.

Ibrahim is right: if the sadhu receives, he shares. He does not eat alone, he shares. If he does not get food then he dances and thanks existence. Mere contentment is not enough, because contentment still has some sadness in it.

People often say that a contented man is a happy man. They are wrong. A contented man is not happy, he just tries to believe that he is happy. Deep within he is unhappy, but there is nothing he can do about it. He is helpless, so he wears the facade of contentment. No, contentment will not do, it is a part of sadness. You bear it without complaining, without making any fuss about it, but this is the sign of a dead mind.

Ibrahim says, 'If he doesn't get anything, then he expresses his gratitude to existence with a dance for giving him an opportunity to practise austerity, to fast that day. If he receives something, then he feels gratitude because he can share it, he can spread it.' There is also gratitude when he doesn't get anything. The bliss of a sadhu, a religious man, cannot be destroyed.

On the other hand, even if your misery is destroyed in some way, at the most it changes into sadness. If you drop your misery somehow, then you just become sad. Even misery keeps you occupied, one way or another. You have not realized it, but if all your miseries were to be taken away from you, you would commit suicide, because what would you do then? There will be nothing left for you to do. The father is busy working because he has to educate his children and get them all married. Now, if all his children were to get married right now and everything were taken care of, what would the father do? Life would seem meaningless to him.

Trivial things have kept you occupied. And this makes you feel that you are doing something, that you are important, needed, that the world cannot go on without you: what will happen to your wife and your children without you? This gives support to your ego: that you are necessary, needed, that everything is happening because of you—although things will go along just as well without you. When you were not there, things were still going on; and after you have gone things will still continue. In between, for a while you dream the dream of your indispensability.

So if you drop misery, at the most you will feel contentment—but sorrow is still hidden beneath contentment. Contentment is only on the surface, and inside there is the wound of sorrow. This is just the first aid, not the treatment.

No, the true religious person is not contented; he is blissful, no matter what the situation. If he gets something, he will be blissful in sharing it; if he does not get anything, even then he will dance and be blissful for not getting it.

The nature of the being is to dance, and it can dance in two ways. It can dance in such a way that it creates a web of sorrow, of sadness filling the air, and darkness all around. Or it can dance in such a way that the rays of light dance all around and flowers bloom everywhere.

Sannyas is the dance of bliss, and the worldly life is the dance of sorrow. Hell is nowhere else; don't live in the illusion that hell is somewhere else. Hell is your wrong way of dancing—giving birth to sorrow and suffering. Heaven is also not elsewhere. Heaven is your right way of dancing—creating heaven wherever you are. Heaven is a quality of your dance; hell too is a quality of your dance.

You don't know how to dance, but you always think that the fault lies in the dance floor, with the uneven surface of the dance floor. There is nothing at all wrong with the dance floor. And for someone who knows how to dance, a faulty floor is also fine; it does not make any difference. For a person who does not know how to dance, even the most perfect and level dance floor will be useless, it will not make him a dancer.

I have heard about a man who went for an eye operation. He asked the doctor before the surgery, 'I am not able to see at all. Will I be able to see after the surgery?'

The doctor examined him and replied, 'Of course you will.'

The man asked, 'And will I also be able to read?'

'Certainly,' said the doctor.

The surgery was a success and the man could see again. But one day, very annoyed with the doctor, he went to him and said, 'You lied to me. I still cannot read.'

'How is that possible?' asked the doctor. 'You can see, so why can't you read?'

He said, 'Well, I don't know how to read.'

Your eyes may get cured, but if you don't know how to read you will not start reading. No matter how smooth the dance floor, you cannot dance unless you know how to dance. Dancing does not depend on the smoothness of the floor: you have to learn it. And remember, there is no one else who can teach you to dance. You are absolutely alone.

The enlightened ones can give you hints, but it is you alone who has to learn. Nobody can take you by the hand and teach you. The dance of life happens so deep within you that outside hands cannot reach there. No one can enter there except you. There, you are absolutely alone and all else is outside.

Being is the dancer. Happiness and misery are the two ways the being can dance. If you are unhappy then you have learned the wrong ways to dance. Change your ways! Don't blame anyone, don't complain. As long as you complain you will just go on dancing the wrong way, because you will never realize that the mistake is yours. You will go on believing that the mistake is always somebody else's.

Stop complaining! Look inside yourself whenever sorrow arises in you. Search honestly, and you will find the causes only within yourself. Drop the causes, because what is the point of going on repeating the causes that give birth to suffering? Why do you go on sowing the seeds which only grow into poisonous fruits of sorrow and pain? Why do you go on gathering the same harvest year after year? It would be better not to sow anything in the field and to allow it to lie fallow. In fact, it would be best if the field were to lie fallow for some time so that any old seeds that are left have time to die away. Then you can plant new seeds.

Why are you so afraid of lying fallow, of being empty? Meditation is the empty state in between. Meditation is like when a farmer leaves his field empty for a year or two and does not sow anything. In the same way, meditation is the state in between; it is the empty space between the seeds of hell and the seeds of heaven. Leave it alone for some time, don't sow anything. Remember one thing: rather than doing something wrong, it is better not to do anything at all. Just stop for a while and do nothing.

It is better not to do anything until you learn to do the right thing, because every action, every wrong action, creates a chain of wrong actions. This is what we call the web of karma.

You go on doing something or other. You can't just sit idly, you will have to do one thing or the other. So just be idle—and that is meditation—so that the old habits drop, and by sitting empty you become capable of seeing clearly—because you are so busy, you don't have the unoccupied state, the time and the space to see.

Meditation means only this: for one, two or three hours, whatever time you can manage, just sit silently, not doing anything. Just go on watching so that slowly, slowly your vision becomes sharp and penetrating and you begin to see that whatsoever has happened in your life, you were the cause of it. The moment this realization happens, the sowing of the meaningless will come to an end. Then a meaningful dance will be born.

Religiousness is the ultimate bliss. It is not the sadness of renunciation but the celebration of enjoying and rejoicing existence. It is to participate in the great celebration of existence, to become one with the dance of existence. Don't think of religiousness as sadness and renunciation: it is a wrong religiousness that thinks in terms of renunciation and sadness. True religiousness is always a dance. True religiousness belongs to bliss. True religiousness is always a flute playing, always a melody playing.

> *Being is the dancer.*
> *Inner being is the stage.*

And this dance is not happening anywhere outside, it is happening within you. This world is not the stage, it is your inner being that is the stage. However much you may think that you have gone outside, no one can *ever* go outside. How will you go outside? You will always be inside yourself. The whole play is going on in there. All plays go on inside you, only their outcomes are seen on the outside. It is the same as when you go to a movie theatre: the whole show is seen on the screen, but in reality it is all happening behind you, in the projector. Images are merely projected on to the screen. The screen is not the real stage, but your eyes are glued to the screen and you will forget—and you do forget—that the actual film is behind you in the projector. The whole film and the mechanism of the film is behind you, on the screen there is only the projection.

Inner being is the stage. The projector is inside you. The seeds of all games originate within; you only hear news of them on the outside, the echoes. If there is sorrow on the outside, then know that you are playing a wrong reel of film inside. And if everything you do on the outside turns out to be wrong, it only means that everything inside you is wrong.

Nothing will change by changing the screen. No matter how much you try to improve the screen by painting and repainting it, it will not make any difference. If the movie that is coming out from the inside is wrong, the screen will go on repeating that same story. And not only do you always have the same movie, you are like a broken record that goes on repeating the same lines again and again.

Have you watched your thoughts? You will find that the same things go on being repeated like a broken record. You go on repeating the same things, nothing new happens there. And whatsoever you repeat there, the echoes of it are heard all around. It is reflected on the screen of the world all around you.

One day Mulla Nasruddin went to see a movie with his wife and son. And what kind of a child could Mulla Nasruddin's son be? Not a very well-behaved child, because when everything inside is upside down, that is what is going to come out.

The child was crying, screaming, making a lot of noise. The manager had to come at least seven times to say, 'Please, either take your money back and go, or keep your child quiet.'

But how could such a child keep quiet? Again and again the manager had to come. Nasruddin would listen to him, but he would continue to sit silently watching the film and doing nothing.

When the movie was nearing the end, he asked his wife, 'So what do you think? Is the movie good or bad?'

His wife said, 'It is absolutely hopeless.'

Mulla said, 'So don't waste any more time. Give a hard pinch to the kid so we can get our money back and go home!'

You have been watching a bad film for a long time. You have been seeing for many lives that everything is wrong—when will you pinch yourself? You will have to do it yourself, there is nobody else who can do it. When will you wake up and come back home? And what is the need to go on watching this wrong movie which is filling you with such distress, which is only giving you pain and burdens, which does not give rise to anything except anguish and nightmares? You can leave this movie theatre.

You are staying in this movie theatre of your own choice. Why are you postponing getting out? Haven't you had enough yet? And if you haven't, then why do you listen to the nonsense of people like Buddha, Mahavira, Krishna, Shiva or Jesus? If you haven't had enough yet, then don't listen to them. Stay away from them, avoid them, because they are meaningful only to people who have had enough, who have seen enough of the movie and are fed up. They are meaningful only to people who are now bored with the movie and are restless in this hell, and in whom the longing for a heavenly dance has arisen. They are meaningful only to people whose only longing now is for godliness.

But the state of your mind is such that you want to get into two boats at the same time, and this creates even more suffering. You also want to enjoy this world. No matter how much suffering there is in it, some hope remains that soon there will be happiness, it is just around the corner. Hope sustains you, and yet your experience tells you that it is not going to happen because many times you have had the same hope and it has always proved futile. Experience is on the side of the buddhas and hope is against them, and you are full of both. These are your two boats.

So you go on keeping one foot in the boat of hope, thinking that 'Perhaps just a little more time . . . I could not be happy with this woman, but maybe with another woman. I could not be happy with this son, but maybe I will with the next one. I have not been successful in this business, but maybe I will in another business.' You are always changing things outside you: 'I could not be happy in this house, but I may be happy in another house. My savings are a little small; if they become a little larger then I will be happy.' You go on changing something or other around you, but this is only making changes on the screen. The story inside you remains just the same, and it is that story which gets projected on the screen.

You find misery everywhere. Your experience is of misery and your hope is for happiness—these are your two boats. If you listen to Buddha or Mahavira or Krishna, they are talking from their experience. They urge you to get off your boat of hope and get on their boat of experience. You even listen to them, because you can't refute them. And looking at them, you feel convinced that they have known something which you have not known, because all their struggle has ended. But you are not totally convinced either, because who knows, they may be only fooling you. 'Who knows?—they may not really have known, they may only be pretending. Or who knows, they might not have succeeded but I may. They may be saying that the grapes are sour just because they couldn't reach them, and I might reach them. So you can't drop hope either. Nor can you say that all their talk of experience is wrong. So you are in a dilemma, and this very dilemma is your insanity . . . these two boats are on two different journeys.

Go aboard one or the other, there is no hurry. If you want, step into the boat of the world, but do it totally. Then it will not be long before you are bored and fed up. But by also keeping one foot in the boat of the buddhas you cannot have a full experience of the world either. You go into the world, but half-heartedly, because the teachings of the buddhas hold one of your legs back. So you try to manage both, the temple as well as the shop. But in this way, neither the temple is managed nor the shop. Both cannot be taken care of simultaneously.

It will be better if you go to your shop wholeheartedly. Forget that there has ever been someone like a Mahavira or a Buddha or a Krishna or a Shiva. Forget the scriptures. Forget all that! Let the account books and ledgers in your shop be everything for you. Once you involve yourself totally in it, with all your heart, then you will come out of it very soon. Your experience itself will show you that it is all meaningless. But this does not happen, and you also are not able to board the boat of the buddhas wholeheartedly because your mind goes on saying, 'Don't be in a hurry, there is plenty of time for that; and you are still so young. After all, how old are you? All this is for old people. When you are about to die and have one foot already in the grave, then you can put your other foot in the boat of the buddhas. What's the rush?'

People think that religiousness is for old people. When they are just on their deathbed, that's when they will need the water from the holy Ganges. When they are just about to die, that's when someone should whisper the Namokar Mantra in their ears. At the moment of death, when everything is finished and you have no energy left at all, only then are you willing to go on the journey. No, like this you are bound to fall back into sansara, into the world, again. You will get back in the same boat that you have been in innumerable times.

Being is the dancer. Inner being is the stage. Remember, whatever you see on the outside is what you project from within. In life you see only what you have projected; and in your life there are many such situations.

I have heard:

Once three travellers met in a waiting room. One was an old man of sixty, another a middle-aged fellow of about forty-five, and the third was a young man of thirty. They started talking. The young man said, 'I spent last night with such a beautiful woman. No other woman in the world can be more beautiful than she is. And the pleasure that I experienced is beyond description!'

The forty-five-year-old said, 'Stop this nonsense! I have known many women in my lifetime. There is nothing indescribable about those so-called indescribable pleasures. They are not even pleasures! Last night I came to know the real meaning of pleasure. Last night I was invited to a royal feast and I have never tasted such delicious food in my life.'

'This too is nonsense,' said the old man. 'Let me tell you about the real pleasure. This morning my bowels moved so completely, my stomach was cleansed so well, that it is beyond description! I have never known such pleasure.'

All pleasures of this world are just like this. They change with age, but you keep forgetting. At the age of thirty, sex seems to give immense pleasure, and at forty-five food seems to be more pleasurable. This is why people often start to put on weight around the age of forty or forty-five. At around sixty the interest in food is gone: the only interest now is that your bowels are emptied properly, and the pleasure you get because of it is unparalleled. All three are speaking the truth, because worldly pleasures are just like this. You have wasted so many lifetimes for these pleasures, and even if you get them you still don't really have anything. What have you attained?

Inner being is the stage. You see on the outside only what you project from within. Sexual desire flows out from a young man's eyes; his whole body is filled with the hormones of sexual desire. Wherever he looks he only sees woman, and sexual desire grips him from all sides.

When Mulla Nasruddin was a young man he went to see an art exhibition with his wife. They were just married and were still going to places together. There were many masterpieces in the exhibition. The Mulla stopped before a particular painting and kept on standing there for a long time. He completely forgot that his wife was also with him. The painting was of a nude woman, a very beautiful one, her nudity covered only with a few leaves. The name of the painting was *Spring*. He was transfixed! Eventually his wife shook his arm and said, 'Are you waiting for autumn?'

Such is a man's mind. His wife guessed right. Wives are usually right.

Whatever force is more active in you becomes the whole world that surrounds you, and you colour it. We have a very precious word in Hindi. It is difficult to find a word like it in any other language; the word is *raag*. It means both infatuation and colour. All your infatuations are the result of the colour projected by your own eyes. You give a certain colour to things, and whatever you manage to colour is where your infatuation sets in.

Raag means that you have managed to colour something. It is not the woman who is beautiful, you have the colour of sexual desire in you, so she appears beautiful to you. A small child is not interested in a woman's looks because the colour of his sexual desire has not developed yet. The old man has lost his colour long before. He laughs at your foolishness, although he was doing the same foolishness himself. One day you will also laugh.

But the person who recognizes and understands his foolishness while doing it, will become awakened. There is not much point in laughing after the colour of your foolishness has left you. Then anyone would laugh! But when you are in the grip of your foolishness and the colour is in full force, if you can become aware in that moment and recognize that it is all a play from inside you that is being projected on the outside, that there is nothing on the outside, just an empty screen . . . *Inner being is the stage*; our inside is where the projector is, and it is from there that we keep projecting everything.

Essential self is realized by overcoming the mind.

This play that is happening will continue, and you will remain lost and wandering in it as long as you haven't overcome your mind. As the mind is conquered, reality is attained. The moment you realize that the whole drama of life is being projected from within, you will forget all about conquering the world. The world has never been conquered by anyone. There is nothing there anyway, it is only a screen.

If you overcome your mind, you have overcome the whole world. The moment you become aware that you, yourself, are the producer, the scriptwriter, the actor— you are everything, even the stage of the play that you are watching—then you no longer remain interested in changing the outside. You begin making efforts to find your inner mastery, and that is the mastery over the mind.

As you are, you are not the master of your mind. Your thoughts are not your servants. Rather, you are the servant of your thoughts. You go wherever your thoughts take you, and they never go where you want them to. Try to make even a very insignificant thought turn slightly, and it refuses. Tell an insignificant thought to be quiet, and it immediately rebels. You never pay any attention to this fact because it is so painful to realize that 'I am not even my own master.' Instead, you go on trying to be a master of the world! But how can you be the master of anything else when you are not even the master of your own self?

Become acquainted with your own mind, examine it closely. The first thing you will notice is that your mind has become the master, not you, not your being. The mind says, 'Do this!' and you have to do it. If you don't, then the mind will create problems. If you don't do it, then the mind will become sad, and its sadness will become your sadness. If you do it, you will get nowhere because the mind is blind: where can you get by obeying its commands? Mind is unconsciousness, unawareness. You will not get anywhere by listening to it.

You must have heard the proverb that when a blind man follows another blind man, they both fall into the ditch. But that is exactly what everyone is doing. Your mind is absolutely blind, it knows nothing, and yet you follow it. Just as your shadow follows your body, you follow your mind. You have simply forgotten that you are the master. It often happens when you have been working with slaves for a long time that, by and by, the slaves become the masters, because the more you depend on them, the more their mastery is proved. All spiritual search is for one thing only: to destroy the mastery of the mind.

What can you do to destroy this mastery? If you want to end the mastery of the mind the first thing is to stop being identified with it. When a thought arises in your mind, don't get identified with it. When you become attached to it, it gets energy. Just stand at a distance from it. Watch it as if you are standing by the side of the road, watching the traffic. Watch it as if there are clouds moving in the sky and you are watching them from the ground. Don't identify yourself with the thought. Don't say, 'This is *my* thought.' The moment you say 'my', you are identified, and the moment you are identified, all your energy will flow into the thought. This same energy makes you a slave of the thoughts; it is your own energy that does this.

Don't become identified with the thought. As you move away, as you break away and separate yourself from the thought, it will become lifeless, powerless, because it will not be getting any energy. Your problem is that you want to extinguish the flame in the lamp, but you also go on pouring fuel into it. On the one hand you blow at the flame to extinguish it, and at the same time you pour more fuel on it. The first thing is to stop giving more fuel. The old oil in the lamp will not last very long, so stop pouring more oil into it.

What is the fuel? Whenever a thought takes hold of you—for example, whenever anger takes hold of you—you immediately become one with it. You say, '*I* am angry.'

Now you have identified yourself so much with the anger that all your energy has become available to it. The anger has become the master and you have become its shadow.

No, when anger comes, stand apart from it and observe it. Let the anger come, let it spread all over your body; it will envelop you from all sides like smoke. Let it! Just keep remembering only one thing: 'I am not the anger!' And don't be in a great hurry to do something with the anger, because once you act on it, it will be difficult to pull yourself back out of it.

Just watch your anger. And make sure of one thing: even if you have to react to the person who triggered the anger in you, the person who abused or insulted you, make sure you do it only when the anger is gone and not before that. In the beginning it will be very difficult because you will have to learn to be very aware and alert, but gradually it will become easy. Just keep your mouth shut: 'I will answer only when the anger has subsided.' This *is* the right thing to do, because it is appropriate to answer only in a calm moment. How can it be right to answer in the moment of anger? It is just like someone reacting under the influence of alcohol.

When sexual desire takes hold of your mind, stand aside and watch. Create a distance. The greater the distance between you and your thoughts, the more your mastery will begin to be established. But you are so stuck together with your thoughts that you have completely forgotten that there can be any distance between the two of you.

Start this from today. The results will not come immediately because it is an identification of lifetimes; it cannot be broken in one day. The relationship is very old, it will take time to break it. But if you really make just a little effort, it *will* break because the relationship is false. If it were real it could never be broken. It is false, just imaginary. It is just your imagination that you are one with your thoughts. This very idea of being one with thoughts creates the problem.

When you are hungry, don't say, 'I am hungry,' say only this much: 'I see that the body is hungry.' And actually that is the truth—you are the watcher, and it is the body that feels hunger. Consciousness can never become hungry. Food goes only into the body; it is the body that needs the flesh and blood. It is the body that gets tired, never consciousness. Consciousness is like a lamp that burns with no fuel. No food, no fuel, is needed, nor have they ever been desired.

The body needs fuel—food, water. The body is a mechanism. Being is not a mechanism. Feed the body when it is hungry, but just remember one thing: the body is hungry, and you are watching it. If it is thirsty, give it water. It is necessary to give it—you have to give it to a machine. It is foolish to say, 'I am not the body and so I will not give it water.' If you are sitting in a car and you don't put petrol in it, then what will happen? If you don't want to put fuel in it then get out of the car because it is not going to move. But you can keep sitting in the car, trying to drive and insisting that you will not give it petrol. Only this much is enough: that you don't become one with the car. Be the master, but fulfil the needs of the car.

The needs of the body have to be satisfied; it is a mechanism that you have to use. And its use is tremendous, because the body is the ladder that leads you to misery and it is also the ladder that leads you to bliss. The body is a ladder. The speciality of a ladder is that one end touches the ground and the other end the sky. You can come down or go up on the same ladder. It is through the medium of the body that you have descended to hell, and it is through the medium of the body that you will reach heaven. It is through the body that you will be able to attain the ultimate liberation. The body is the medium: you have to take care of it, you have to provide for its needs—but there is no reason to become one with the medium! Let the machine remain an instrument. You write with your pen, but you are not the pen. You walk with your feet, but you are not your feet.

The body is a machine, so take care of it. It is a valuable machine—don't damage it. There are two types of people who damage their body: there are people who damage it through indulgence, and there are those who damage it through renunciation. Both are enemies of the body and both are foolish. Someone damages it by going to prostitutes his whole life, someone else by overeating. Then there are mad people at the other extreme who damage it by fasting. Either you fill the car with so much fuel that there is no space left for you to sit in it, or you don't put fuel in it at all. And you move between these two extremes. No, give the body just enough to meet its needs. You care for your servant also, but that doesn't make him your master.

Essential self is realized by overcoming mind. As you begin to become the master of your mind, you will start becoming more and more of a witness. You will find that the essence within you, your being, your real existence, has started to emerge.

When the mind is corrupted, it is the world, and when you overcome the mind, then it is the essential self. If the mind is the master, then it is the world, and if the mind becomes the servant, that is the transcendence of the world.

The mind is a ladder. It is not inevitable that you can only go down with it, you can also go up. But you can only go up as a master; as a servant you keep going down and down. And it is very dangerous to be a servant to the mind because it is not slavery to just one thing—the mind is a crowd: one moment it orders you to be angry, the next moment it orders you to repent. One thought tells you to enjoy the world, another says go seek nirvana. One thought says accumulate money even if you have to steal it, it doesn't matter, another thought says that's a sin. There are an endless number of thoughts, and the sum total of all those thoughts is the mind.

If your intellect were made up of just one thought, then too you could have some peace in your life. But it is not just one thought—it is a crowd, a marketplace. The mind is like a classroom in a school: as long as the teacher is present the children will sit quietly and study. All is peaceful. But as soon as the teacher goes out of the room all hell breaks loose! Fights break out, books are thrown around, slates are broken, tables are overturned, graffiti is written on the blackboard and abusive language is shouted. All these children don't have anyone over them in that moment, there is nobody to supervise them. When the teacher comes back into the room again there is absolute silence—all the books are returned to their place, all eyes look down and once again everyone is busy studying.

As soon as you are present as the master, the mind starts to behave in an orderly way. The moment you lose your mastery, the mind is a chaos. And it is difficult to follow this chaos because there is not just one voice, there are numerous voices. They lead you nowhere.

Mahavira has said that man is multi-psychic, that man has not just one mind, but many, and modern psychology agrees with this. It says that man has many minds. There is not only one mind inside you, there are numerous minds. It is just as if there is one servant with thousands of masters, and each master is giving different orders: that servant will go mad. 'Who should I obey?' You have also gone mad in much the same way.

Seek the one, so that the teacher can return to the classroom. Seek the one so that the servants, who are many, settle back in their places. When there is one master there will be direction in your life. You will realize your essential self, you will be able to know who you are.

Upon becoming self-realized spontaneous freedom arises.

Right now, as long as you go on allowing the mind to remain your master, you will remain a servant. As you realize your essential self, spontaneous freedom happens.

It will be good to understand what is meant by *spontaneous freedom.* Why has it not simply been called *freedom?* Why *spontaneous?* It is a somewhat subtle matter to understand.

There are two types of freedom. One is in opposition to. When freedom is in opposition to, it becomes reaction. This is not real freedom, you are only moving in the opposite direction. For example, your mind says, 'Be angry,' and you start moving in the opposite direction, doing just the opposite of what the mind is telling you to do. You say, 'No, I will not be angry, I will be forgiving.' Or the mind says, 'Kill this person!' and you say, 'No! I will not kill. On the contrary, I will offer the person my head to be chopped off.' Whatsoever the mind says, you will do just the opposite.

This is what your saints usually do: the mind says, 'Go look for a woman,' and the saint escapes to the forest. The mind says, 'Go after money,' and the saint refuses to even touch money: to touch money for him is like the sting of a scorpion or the bite of a snake. The mind says 'Rest, relax,' and the saint stands in the burning sun or sleeps on a bed of thorns.

This is not real freedom, because you are still listening to whatever it is that you are going against. That thing is still the master because you are still fighting with it. Try to understand this because it is a little complex: if you have become the master, then all fighting ends. A servant is a servant—why fight with him?

Imagine that you have a servant in your house and he has become the master: he asks you to sit down, and you sit down; he asks you to stand up and you stand up. Then one day you decide that from now on you will act against the servant's bidding—even then he will remain your master because now when he tells you to sit down you will stand up. It only seems as if you are not obeying him, but in fact you *are* obeying him because he is still controlling your action. If the servant becomes a little more clever, then when he wants you to sit he will ask you to stand up—and you will sit. You cannot escape.

Mulla Nasruddin had guests in his house and his little son was making a lot of noise. Mulla told him many times to keep quiet, but the more he told him the more rowdy the boy became. If Mulla told him to go out, the child would stay in. Finally Mulla got really upset.

When there are guests in the house, children make more trouble in front of the guests because now it is a question of proving in front of everyone who is the real boss, the father or the son. Normally, children don't make that much noise; they keep playing with their toys or get busy doing something else. But the moment a guest arrives the trouble begins because it becomes a question of ego, of the struggle for who is the boss. So seeing guests in the house, the child started creating a big scene.

At last the Mulla said, 'Look, do whatsoever you like. Whatsoever you want to do, do it! Now let's see how you can disobey me!'

The child must have found himself in great difficulty.

If you go against the mind, spontaneous freedom will not happen. A kind of freedom will happen which is not really freedom, but a reaction, a rebelliousness. But whatever we rebel against, we remain tied to. Whatever we fight with, we remain connected to. We are still not the master because the orders are still coming from the same source. Now we will do just the opposite, but the directions are still coming from the same source.

You may practise celibacy but it will make no difference because your celibacy is just a reaction; it is not spontaneous. Your mind moves in sexual desire and you start fighting with it. It is a fight—but do you need to fight with a servant? Someone who fights with his servant is still taking the servant to be his master. The fight should be with a master! What is the point of fighting with a servant?

So it may be that your saints are the exact opposite of you, but they are not in any way different from you. Your saints may be going in the opposite direction to where you are going, but as far as mastery of the mind is concerned, there is not even one iota of difference between you.

Spontaneous freedom is something totally different. The very meaning of 'spontaneous freedom' is that you are the master. Now whether to obey the mind or to disobey the mind is not the issue. Now to go in favour of the mind or to go against it is not the question. Now I give orders to the mind, I do not take orders from it! There are two ways of obeying the mind: to take orders from it, or to go against its orders—but in both cases you are still obeying the mind.

When the mind is the master, its mastery over you can be of two kinds, positive or negative. You can be a man of the world if you want or you can be a saint, but it makes no difference. This is why your saints are nothing but the mirror opposite of the worldly man—the worldly man in a headstand. There is no difference between the two. And your saints are in greater difficulty than the worldly man because it is easier to stand on your feet than it is to stand on your head, otherwise nature would have created you standing on your head. Your saints are doing the exact opposite of what you are doing: you are accumulating money, they are renouncing it; you are protecting your body, they are neglecting it; you are preparing a soft bed for your body, they are collecting thorns and pebbles to lie on; you are enjoying good food, they are fasting, rejecting food; you are wearing fine clothes, they go naked. This is not spontaneous freedom. This is a state of tension, there is no spontaneity in it.

That is why the sutra says: *Essential self is realized by overcoming the mind.* And: *Upon becoming self-realized spontaneous freedom arises.* Then you are really free. Then you don't look to the mind to tell you what you should do or shouldn't do. Then you don't look to the mind at all. Then your actions are simply spontaneous. Then you are really free from the mind. Then you are the decision-maker and the mind simply follows you. But this will happen only when you become the master, and you can become the master only when you have become the witness.

Don't fight the mind, otherwise spontaneous freedom will never arise. If you fight, then you have accepted the mind as your equal. You give an equal status to whatever you fight. Once it was a friend, now it has become an enemy, but you are standing on an equal footing. But a master is not an equal to a servant: the master is in the sky and the servant is always on the ground. When you are the master your freedom is spontaneous, and this freedom is a unique phenomenon.

I have heard that a Sufi mystic, Bayazid, went on a holy pilgrimage to Mecca with one hundred of his disciples. They had decided that they would fast for forty days. After five days of fasting they reached a certain village. Bayazid was a very well-known and respected mystic, and when they reached the outskirts of the village the people came and informed him, 'Bayazid, there is a devotee of yours here, who has exceeded all limits. He is a poor man, utterly poor. Except for his hut, he had nothing much. He sold his hut, his cattle and whatever little else he had and has now invited the whole village to a feast to welcome you.'

Now Bayazid and his disciples had decided to fast for forty days. Bayazid was undisturbed by this news but his disciples became very tense because they knew that there was no question of eating. But when they arrived there, Bayazid sat down to the feast. The disciples were really disturbed because when the master has sat down to eat, they too had to eat, although feeling very guilty.

They spoke among themselves, 'Has Bayazid forgotten? Has he lost his memory so easily? Has he been tempted by the food? He should have refused! We are observing a forty-day fast until we reach our place of pilgrimage, and only there are we supposed to end the fast. Now what is this? We took a vow and it has been broken in just five days.'

But they could not say anything in front of the crowd either, so they ate the food with much guilt, with a restless feeling. When they looked at Bayazid they saw him eating with immense joy, with no tension, with no guilt.

At night, when everybody had left, they went to the master and said: 'This is the limit! We were not supposed to eat, but you ate so we had to follow you.'

Bayazid said to them, 'Why are you so upset? He had prepared the meal with so much love that it was worth breaking the fast. Breaking his heart would have caused far greater harm. Breaking the fast has caused no harm. We will simply fast for five days more. We can add five more days to our fast. We were to complete forty days: now instead of forty, we will have fasted for forty-five days. If we had broken his heart we would never have been able to mend it.

If his heart had been hurt, there would have been no way to heal it. It is only a question of fasting. Forget those first five days; we will go on a fast for the next forty days.'

This is the difference: the freedom of those disciples was not spontaneous. They were troubled thinking that 'Oh! We have followed our minds! Our minds were already asking us to eat and we were fighting against it. Now we have followed our minds! It proves our slavery.' But Bayazid has mastery: the decision to end the fast or to keep it was in his hands. There is no rebellion against the mind in it, no opposition against the mind in it. He was not obeying the mind. It is simply that he is the master. If he wanted to keep the fast, he would have; if he decides to break it, he could—but the decision is his.

Both the master and the disciples were on a fast, but there is a very revolutionary and basic difference between the two fasts, in their attitudes about it: Bayazid's freedom is spontaneous. He can stay in a palace with no problem or he can stay in a hut. But his disciples would feel restless if they had to stay in a palace because that would be an indulgence.

Now this is a very interesting thing: sometimes you are attached to a palace and sometimes to a hut, but attachment as such never leaves you. Bayazid can move in either way, his freedom is spontaneous. There is nobody to stop him. The decision will be from his own being. The being will be the decision maker.

Only upon becoming self-realized, does spontaneous freedom arise. All the other freedoms before this are false.

Because of this freedom, which is his essential nature, the realized one can move even outside of himself; also while moving outside, he can remain within himself.

This sutra is precious: *Because of this freedom, which is his essential nature, the realized one can move even outside of himself...*

Kabir kept on weaving cloth. He was a weaver, and he remained a weaver. His disciples said many times to him, 'It does not look right any more that you weave cloth and go to the market to sell it. You are no longer a worldly man.' Kabir would laugh and say, 'It is all the play of the existence! The inner and outer are one.'

We cannot understand this because we are caught in the grip of the outer. We are so caught up that we think, 'How can the outer and the inner be one?'

Zen masters have said that sansara and nirvana, the world and liberation, are one. We are utterly shocked: 'How can this be? The world has a hold over us and we are suffering because of it. And liberation has to be just the opposite, where we would be free, peaceful, blissful, happy; where there would be no suffering.' Our 'liberation' is bound to be something opposite to our 'world'. But for the person who finds liberation, no opposites exist in the world any more. For him, all opposites disappear. For a person who finds liberation all the differences of outer and inner cease. All the differences are there because of the wall of ego.

What is inner and what is outer? Only the ego creates the separation. We can step into a river with an earthen pot and fill the pot with the water. We will then say that this water is inside the pot and the river water is outside. But what is the separation between the two? It is only the clay wall. If this wall were to be broken, then what would be outside and what would be inside? No, what is within is also without, what is without is also within.

This is why Kabir says, 'Sitting and standing is my worship. Walking and moving is my prayer.' Kabir no longer goes to the temple because for him there is no distinction between the shop and the temple. Now Kabir does not escape from the marketplace to the Himalayas because for him there is no difference between the marketplace and the Himalayas. Kabir does not even renounce his house, because now there is no difference for him between 'mine' and 'thine'. From what can he run away, to where?

All separation dissolves the moment the ego dissolves. Then there is no within and no without. Then there is neither matter nor spirit; then both are one. This is non-duality, where all becomes one and all boundaries dissolve. But this can happen only when spontaneous freedom has happened in your life. Then: *Because of this freedom, which is his essential nature, the realized one can move even outside of himself; also while moving outside, he can remain within himself.*

For him, there are no distinctions. He can live in a palace and yet he is a sannyasin, or he can be a sannyasin standing on the road and yet feel he is in a palace. Even if he has tens of millions of rupees, he is still a non-possessor. And if he has nothing at all he is still the greatest of possessors because the whole world is his. But it is very difficult for us to recognize this because we are familiar with only one part. The water that is inside the pot and the water that is outside the pot appear to us to be separate.

What is hidden in you is also outside of you. The space that is within you is the same as that which is without. Your body is no more than a vessel of clay which, with its thin wall, creates the illusion of separation.

Sansara, the world, and sannyas, the inner life, are not two things. They seem to be two because you know only the world; you don't know sannyas. This is why you also think of sannyas in terms of the world. Your concept of sannyas is also based in your concept of the world. Only when someone is the total opposite of you do you call him a sannyasin. You say, 'Look what a great sannyasin! He walks barefoot, he is naked, he stands in the sun, in the rain, and he sleeps on the grass or on straw. Such a great sannyasin!'

Your concept of sannyas also arises from your world. For you, a Janak cannot be a sannyasin. How can he be? He lives in a palace. For you a Krishna cannot be a sannyasin. How can he be? He wears a decorative peacock feather crown and plays on his flute. No, for you they cannot be sannyasin.

But, as your slavery to your mind ends and your essential self is released, you will know that liberation exists everywhere. Your shop is not a hindrance, because liberation is everywhere. An empire is not an obstacle because liberation is a state of your experiencing. The moment you experienced liberation, the world that is separate from you will disappear. Then there is no within or without, all is one. Then worship and work are one and the same. Then you accept life the way it is. There is no longer the need to make even the slightest distinctions in it. This is why it has happened that even butchers have become enlightened, that even worldly men have become enlightened. And it also happens that a sannyasin who escapes and renounces everything can keep on wandering and not become enlightened.

This sutra is ultimate in meaning: *Because of this freedom, which is his essential nature, the realized one can move even outside of himself; also while moving outside, he can remain within himself.*

Now he is free. Now he is beyond all definitions. Now if you try to define him, you will not be able to recognize him. Now he is indefinable, beyond all characteristics. Now it will be very difficult to say where you will find him because he could be anywhere.

Once it happened that just before the rainy season, one of Buddha's sannyasin went into a village and a prostitute became infatuated with him. The sannyasin was young and handsome, and besides that, a sannyasin radiates a unique beauty which an ordinary person cannot have. Someone who has let go of everything begins to have a kind of radiance. Flowers of the significant begin to bloom in someone who has dropped all that is insignificant; an aura of grace which ordinarily does not happen in people begins to manifest in his life.

It was very natural for the prostitute to fall in love when she saw that dancing, blissful monk. She was very beautiful and even great kings courted her, but not everyone had a chance to meet her. To be with her even for a moment was considered precious. But she herself went running to meet the monk on the road and said, 'Please accept my invitation to stay at my house for this rainy season.'

The monk said, 'I will ask my master—whatever he tells me, I will do.' The monk did not say yes or no, he only said, 'I will ask my master.'

The next morning the monk went to Buddha and said, 'I have received an invitation to stay with a prostitute. What should I do?'

Buddha replied, 'If the prostitute was not afraid of you why should you be afraid of her? Is my sannyasin so weak that a prostitute can frighten him? Go, accept the invitation! Stay with her during the rainy season.'

The other monks became very uneasy because many of them had seen her while passing on the road. She was very beautiful and many of them were filled with desire for her. Many of them wished that she had invited them instead.

One monk stood up and said, 'This is not right—a sannyasin staying in a prostitute's house! This is not right. There is every possibility that he will be corrupted.'

Buddha said, 'If you had received the invitation, I would not have given you my permission. There is every possibility that you can be corrupted because you still believe there is a difference between the inner and the outer. I am sending him knowingly: whether he stays with her or not makes no difference to him.'

Still the monks were not convinced, and they told Buddha, 'You are making a mistake. This will encourage a wrong code of conduct. All the rules of propriety will be broken.'

Buddha said, 'You wait. Let the rainy season pass and then we will see.'

Every day the monks started to bring news that he had been corrupted. He had been watching her dance, and the dance was happening at night while he was sitting there. Some said that he sat on velvet cushions, and some others said that he had changed his clothing. Some said that they even saw the two in an embrace. In this way they kept on bringing all sorts of news about him.

Buddha would say to all of this, 'Let the rainy season pass. What is the hurry? Why do you bring these rumours? What is your concern? It is not you who is being corrupted. The person who is being corrupted will return after the rains.'

After the rainy season the monk returned, and the prostitute came walking behind him. She said to Buddha, 'Please make me a sannyasin. Your monk has won and I have lost. I did everything I could and he did not object. Even when I embraced him he did not move away. When I made him sit on a velvet cushion he did not say, "I am a monk, how can I sit on a velvet cushion?" I gave him the best foods and still he never said that he could not eat this food because it would arouse desire. I offered him all kinds of invitations and he never said no. Whatever was happening, he just sat silently as if nothing was happening. I am immensely moved by his behaviour. I also long for the same bliss that he enjoys, where within and without have disappeared, the bliss which nobody else can interfere with.'

Buddha said to the other monks: 'You see? A person whose boundaries have dissolved, even if he lives with a prostitute, it is the prostitute who will be transformed. If you had stayed with her you would have become like her shadow.'

There is a goodness that is afraid of evil, but that goodness is not of much value. A false saint is afraid of a sinner, a true saint is not—he is beyond both. A true saint is one who is not changed by any circumstance. While in the outer world he is firmly rooted in himself; the world does not enter him even if he remains in it.

Buddha has said, 'The highest state of sannyas is when you can walk through a river but the waters don't touch your feet.' If you are afraid of the river, of getting your feet wet, it is not the highest state. It is a state of fear.

Remember these three sutras: you have to break the mastery of the mind. This will happen through witnessing. Witnessing will create a distance between you and the mind. You have to attain your mastery, but not by going against the mind, but by rising above it. Freedom will come, but if it has come through opposition then it is a false freedom. There will be tension and uneasiness in that freedom. It will not be peaceful, it will not be spontaneous.

Freedom should come by rising above, by witnessing, not by fighting. In religion there is no place for being a warrior. In religion you have only to rise above, not fight, because otherwise you will become stuck there, at the same level as whatever you are fighting. Don't make an enemy of your mind: you have to go beyond it, you have to transcend it. And the key to going beyond the mind is witnessing.

As you rise beyond the mind, a spontaneous freedom will happen, the ultimate liberation will happen. This liberation is not against anybody or anything. In this liberation you will come to a state where, whether you are in yourself or out, it will make no difference because the very distinction of within and without has disappeared. Sansara and moksha, the world and liberation, are one. All dualities have ended. All separation is lost. This is a state of non-duality, non-separation.

Enough for today.

7

Trust Is the Door

Meditation is the seed.
    Settled in oneself, one bathes spontaneously in the lake of pure consciousness.
    And one attains self-creation or the state of being twice-born.
    Ceaseless awareness is the cessation of the cycle of birth and death.

THE DISCIPLES OF Jesus asked him, 'How is the kingdom of God? What is its form and nature?'
    Jesus replied, 'The kingdom of God is like a seed.'

Jesus is speaking of the same seed we will discuss today.
    Meditation is that seed.
    A seed has no intrinsic meaning in itself; a seed is only a means. A seed is only the possibility of becoming a tree. A seed is not a state, it is a journey. When a seed reaches its fulfilment by becoming a tree, by having flowers and fruits—this is its fulfilment—then its potential is realized. In the same way, when the seed of meditation becomes a tree that bears flowers and fruits, that is the fulfilment known as godliness.

So it is very necessary to understand the state of the seed properly. You constantly ask about godliness, but it is a futile inquiry. Why ask about the tree when you haven't sown and nurtured the seed? And without sowing the seed, how do you expect to see the tree? Godliness is not some external phenomenon that you can see with your eyes, it is your own purified state, your own growth. You cannot see godliness through others. You will be able to see godliness only when the seed hidden within you sprouts and becomes a tree.

Buddha, Mahavira, Krishna and Shiva will not be able to reveal godliness to you, however hard they try, because your godliness is hidden within you. And right now it is just a seed, it is not yet a tree. You cannot see anything in a seed. But when the seed breaks open and the tree appears, when it grows—when you open and flower and the flame within you is kindled—only then will you know what godliness is.

This is why it is difficult to win a debate with an atheist. Actually, no one has ever been able to win in a debate with an atheist. The reason is not because the atheist is right; the reason is that he is asking a wrong question, so whatever answers are given will prove to be futile. He asks, 'Where is this God? Show it to me.' Now godliness is hidden within the person, godliness is hidden within the questioner. And no one else's godliness can be revealed to you, it is an inner happening. Only when your own seed sprouts will you know it.

Right now you are like a seed. But you have not yet understood this, so you go on seeking on the outside. And as long as you go on seeking outside of yourself, your seed will just remain dormant in you, it will not sprout. The seed needs water, soil, sunshine and love—the same as a small child. When you turn your eyes in, when your awareness flows inward and your life energy turns inward, only then will this seed receive life. Only then will this seed come alive and sprout.

Meditation is the seed.

People come to me and ask, 'We are restless. How can we become peaceful?'

Early one morning Mulla Nasruddin came to me. Just looking at his condition I was about to say something, but before I could say anything, he blurted out: 'Now, you must help me!'

'What is the problem?' I asked.

'It is a very complex problem,' said the Mulla. 'About ten to twenty times a day, sometimes even more, I keep having the strong urge to shower! This obsession is driving me mad. I can think of nothing else. Please help me!'

I asked, 'So when did you last have a shower?'

'As far as I can remember, I have never taken a shower.'

If you never take a shower and an urge to do so catches hold of you, then the problem is not about the shower, the problem is with you. You are restless, but you are not aware that you have never meditated—you have simply never bothered with it—and yet you want to get rid of your restlessness! But it will never happen unless you bathe in meditation. That is what you have: a restless urge for it.

Meditation is an inner bath. Just as the body becomes fresh after a bath—all the dust and dirt is washed away and it feels clean and fresh—similarly, meditation is a bath of your inner being. And when everything becomes fresh within, where is restlessness, where is misery, where is anxiety? Then you are delightful, you are cheerful and blooming. There are dancing bells on your ankles and your life becomes a dance! Before this you were sad, tired and distressed.

You are befooling yourself if you think the causes of your restlessness are on the outside. There is only one cause for your restlessness and that is that you have not allowed your seed of meditation to grow into a tree. You may try a thousand and one ways: 'Maybe if I get more money, the restless feeling will go away,' 'Maybe if I have a son,' 'Maybe if I become famous, prestigious, or have better health, or a better body, or long life'—but even if all this happens, your restlessness will not leave you. In fact, the more you acquire these things, the more intensely you will notice your restlessness.

A poor man is not as restless as a rich man. Why does restlessness grow with wealth? It doesn't—the poor man is also restless, but so much of his energy goes into getting food that no energy at all is left for him to notice his inner restlessness. All the outer needs of a rich man are fulfilled, so all his energy is free and he notices his inner needs. A poor man is just as restless, but he has no space to feel it. A rich man's restlessness begins to hurt like a thorn and he becomes obsessed with it.

When you have satisfied all your so-called needs, you will suddenly realize that the real need was only one: the need for meditation. All the other needs were only of your body, not yours.

This sutra says: *Meditation is the seed.* On your inner journey, on your quest for life, on your pilgrimage to the temple of truth, meditation is the seed. And what is meditation, that it is so valuable that you will become godly if it flowers, and if it remains dormant your life will become a hell?

What is meditation?

Meditation is a state of thoughtless consciousness, where consciousness is totally there, but there are no thoughts; meditation is where you are, but there is no mind. The cessation of the mind is meditation. Right now *you* are not there at all, only the mind is. Just the opposite should be the case—that you and only you are there and not the mind. Right now, the mind consumes all your energy. Right now the mind is absorbing all your life energy.

Have you ever seen the *amarbel*, the creeper that never dies? It attaches itself to trees and lives off of them, feeding on their life juices. The tree then starts to dry up and die, and the creeper keeps growing and spreading. This creeper is really something! It is exactly like the mind. It has no roots; it needs none because it thrives by exploiting the plant it lives on. It sucks the tree dry as it nourishes itself. Hindus have given it an apt name: 'amarbel', the undying creeper. It does not die. As long as there is nourishment available to exploit, it can live forever.

Your mind is the same—an undying creeper. It does not die, it can live on forever; and it will follow you for countless lives. And the interesting thing is that it has no roots, no seeds. Its existence is rootless. It should die this very moment, but it doesn't. It lives on exploitation.

And your mind has enveloped you from all sides. You are completely buried under this undying creeper. All your life energy is sucked up by the mind, nothing remains. You live almost dried up, impoverished. Your mind lets you live only as much as is necessary for its own life. The creeper also does not completely kill its host tree, because if it did then it too would die. It leaves the tree with only enough life juice that it needs to keep it alive. The owner of a slave also does not kill his slave totally; he gives the slave only as much food as is essential to keep him alive.

Your mind gives you just enough so that you can survive, and it sucks 99 per cent for itself. This is the non-meditative state: you are just 1 per cent and your mind is

99 per cent. When you become 99 per cent and your mind only 1 per cent, that will be the state of meditation. And if you become 100 per cent and the mind is zero, it is the state of samadhi, of superconsciousness or enlightenment. You are liberated. The seed has become a full-grown tree and now there is nothing left to be attained. All that could be attained has been attained, all your potential has become the reality, all that was hidden has become manifest.

Then existence is filled with your fragrance. Then the music of your dance can be heard in all corners of the earth, as far away as the moon and the stars. Then it is not you alone who is thrilled—with you, the entire life-stream of the universe is thrilled. The existence goes into celebration. Whenever a buddha is born, the whole existence celebrates because the whole of existence is eager to help you transform your seed into a tree.

Meditation is a state where the mind is almost not there at all. Enlightenment is a state where the mind is completely empty and only you remain.

This sutra of Shiva says: *Meditation is the seed.* So you will have to start with meditation. Right now, asleep or awake, conscious or unconscious, the mind has you in its grip. Thoughts invade you in the day and dreams in the night. Around the clock your mind is in a state of deliberation, thinking. And the most amazing thing is that nothing comes out of it. No matter how much the chattering continues, nothing is achieved through the mind. What have you achieved? Where have you reached through your thinking for all this time? Think about this. Pay attention to this fact: that you have made such a long journey, and where have you reached? What have you achieved by thinking?

The great philosopher Immanuel Kant was returning home one evening when a small boy stopped him on the road and said, 'Good evening, sir. I have just been to your house. Tomorrow I am going on a picnic with my family and I came to borrow your camera. You were out for a walk, so I asked your servant and he flatly refused. Is it right that a servant should say no, just like that?' The child was boiling with anger.

Kant said, 'It certainly is not right. Who is that servant to refuse you when I am here? Come along with me.'

The child was very happy. They reached Kant's home and Kant called the servant and reprimanded him before the child, who was enjoying the scene very much. He said to the servant, 'Who are you to say no while I am here?' He even turned to the child and asked, 'Now tell me, who is he to say no when I am here?'

The child said, 'You are absolutely right. And this man said no in a very rude manner.'

Finally, Kant turned to the child and said, 'Now I will tell you something, the fact is that I don't own a camera.'

All the joy and the thrill of the child, all the anticipation that he was going to get the camera, all that noise and fury, only to discover in the end that Kant didn't even own a camera.

This is the state of your mind: all your life you will run, you will shout, you will hope, you will work hard and, in the end, your mind will tell you that it doesn't have what you have been seeking. The mind has always said this, and it *really* doesn't have it. This is why the mind always gives you false hopes. It consoles you. It always says, 'Not today. How about tomorrow? Tomorrow, by all means, yes.'

Nothing can be more reassuring than the mind. And you are a fool, because if the mind had anything to give, it would have given it today. It talks about tomorrow and you believe it. How many times have you believed the mind? Every day tomorrow comes, and again the mind postpones it for the next day. By now this has become your unconscious habit—you have become accustomed to hearing about tomorrow. This habit has become so deep-rooted that you don't even think twice about it. Even in your unconsciousness, in your dreams during the night, your mind keeps postponing things to the future.

Mulla Nasruddin was very sick. His wife told me, so I went to see him at his home. He was lying unconscious with a very high fever; it must have been 105 or 106 degrees. He was absolutely unconscious and his body was burning as hot as fire.

I asked his wife how long he had been in this condition. His wife said, 'Just now, maybe for an hour.'

I said, 'Put the thermometer in his mouth and check.'

His wife put the thermometer in his mouth, and even in that unconscious condition, do you know what he said? He said, 'Give me a match, please!'

Mulla was a chain-smoker and he had always lit the new cigarette with the previous one. Even running a fever of 105, when he couldn't remember anything, when he wasn't conscious of anything, the moment his wife put the thermometer in his mouth, the first thing he remembered was a cigarette. He said, 'Give me a match, please!'

Even while dying, your condition will be exactly like this: 'Give me a match, please.' It is the old habit of your mind to keep spinning its plans, even when you are unconscious. Even at the moment of death you will be filled with the mind. Whether you worship, pray, go to the temple or go on a pilgrimage to holy places, your mind is always with you. And whenever the mind is there, you will not be able to make any contact with your self-nature.

There was a Mohammedan fakir, Haji Mohammed. He was a saintly person. One night he dreamed that he had died and was standing at a crossroads where one way went to heaven and the other to hell; one road went to the world and the other to moksha, the abode of liberation. There was an angel standing at the crossroads guiding and directing each person on their way according to their actions.

Haji Mohammed had nothing to fear because all his life he had been a pious man. He had offered his prayers five times each day, and he had been on the Mohammedan holy pilgrimage, the hajj, sixty times. In fact, that is why he was known as Haji Mohammed. When his turn came, he stood with his chest out before the angel.

'What is your name?' the angel asked.

'Haji Mohammed!' was the reply.

The angel pointed towards hell, 'This is the road for you.'

Haji Mohammed said, 'Maybe you have misunderstood. Surely there is some mistake. I have been on hajj sixty times during my life on earth.'

'That was all a waste,' said the angel, 'because whenever anyone asked you your name, you would say with great pride, "Haji Mohammed". You have already taken enough advantage of your hajj on earth by adding "Haji" to your name. You have become very arrogant because of that. Have you done anything else?'

Haji Mohammed became a little shaky. When sixty pilgrimages counted for nothing, all hope was lost. But he persisted, 'I have said my prayers fully and religiously five times a day.'

'That also has been a waste,' said the angel, 'because you prayed louder and longer when people were around and made it short when no one was around. Your attention was on the people, not on God. Once some people came to your house and you went on praying for a very long time. That prayer was false. Your focus was on the people, not on God. The people were watching so you went on praying so they could see that you are a religious person: Haji Mohammed. Do you have anything else to show?'

Haji became so terrified that he woke up! This dream changed his life. He stopped using the word 'Haji' in his name from that day on, and he also began to pray in secret so that no one else would know. Word went around the village that this Haji was no longer religious: 'He has even stopped saying his prayers, he has become senile in his old age!' But Haji never refuted what people were saying; he continued to pray in secrecy. His prayers started becoming meaningful and sincere. It is said that he went to heaven after his death.

Your mind, even if it prays, will not allow prayerfulness to happen. Your mind will start feeding the ego even with prayer.

Don't talk about your meditation, keep it a secret. Protect it just as you would protect a precious diamond that you have found: you don't flaunt it around, you always bury your treasures. In the same way, bury your meditation deep underground. Don't talk about it and don't use it to feed your ego. Otherwise, the creeper of the mind will reach there too and suck away at it. Wherever the mind reaches, there can be no meditation there. Where the mind does not reach, there meditation exists.

The mind is an extrovert: its attention is on the other, not on itself. Meditation is introversion.

Meditation means that your focus is on your own self, not on the other. Mind means the focus is on the other. Watch it: even if you give two cents to a poor man, you look around to check if people have seen it or not. Even if you build a temple, you take care to inscribe your name in bold letters on a marble slab. Even if you make a donation, you see to it that it is mentioned in the newspapers. It all becomes meaningless. You cannot reach anywhere by becoming a Haji Mohammed. Don't keep an account of your fasts and austerities. The realm of the inner is not a realm of business; your accounts are of no use there. If you go there with your accounts book, you will lose. Calculations are useful only in the outer world.

Just observe: every year the Jaina monks publish how many days they have fasted, how many days they did not eat during the rainy season, how many vows and disciplines they have undertaken. They are keeping an account of all of this! They are really shopkeepers gone to sit in temples. Their minds have not let go of calculations. Their fasts and their so-called meditations are all a waste of time. They are becoming Haji Mohammeds.

No, don't be concerned with the outside world, with whether people think of you as a religious person or not. What others say is not at all worth being concerned about, because it is your mind that is related to other people, not you. The day the mind is no longer there, you will become *asang*, not related with anyone.

It is the mind that binds you to the other. As long as the mind ties you to the world, you will remain separated from existence. When you are finished with the world, the mind will disappear on that very day and you will become one with existence. Then all your ties to the world of relationships will be broken and your connection with godliness will happen. Your eyes will close to this world and they will open to godliness. *Meditation is the seed*. And meditation means consciousness without any thought.

The second sutra:

Settled in oneself, one bathes spontaneously in the lake of pure consciousness.

This sutra is revolutionary. It is easy and also very difficult: *Settled in oneself, one bathes spontaneously in the lake of pure consciousness.* The tradition of Zen masters in Japan is that if you ask them what you should do to meditate, they say: 'Do nothing. Just sit.' Now remember, when they say do nothing it means to do *absolutely* nothing, simply sit. Do only this much: sit and do nothing at all, because the moment you do something, the mind will come into play. It seems very easy, but in fact it is extremely difficult. The problem is that to sit silently in itself is difficult. The moment you close your eyes the mind goes into action, its race begins. Your body appears to be sitting still, but your mind is racing wildly.

If you just sit and do nothing—that is meditation. You are just sitting, centred, just sitting doing nothing, not even chanting 'Rama, Rama', not even praying 'Krishna, Krishna', doing nothing at all; not a ripple of thought occurs because that too is an activity. You do absolutely nothing. You don't even try to stop the thoughts because that too is an action, that too is just another thought. You are neither remembering godliness nor are you remembering the world, because those are also thoughts. You are not repeating inside, 'I am the soul,' 'I am the Brahman,'—this is all nonsense. Nothing will happen with these repetitions, because they are all thoughts. You are not doing anything at all. You are just sitting as if you are a rock where nothing is happening inside and nothing is happening outside: that is the state of 'just sitting' or 'just sitting centred'. In Japan this is called zazen, 'just sitting'. Zen masters use this method. Sometimes it takes twenty or thirty years before a person can reach the state where he is just sitting.

This sutra seems to be easy, but in fact it is very difficult. The easiest things are often the most difficult things in the world. If someone asks you to climb the Himalayas, you could do it; it would not be much of a problem. You would perspire and get tired, but you would be able to climb. But if someone tells you to do nothing, suddenly you will be face-to-face with a great problem, even though the only thing being asked of you is to just sit and do nothing.

What will happen if you just sit silently? First of all, as soon as you sit you will notice that all kinds of movements are happening in different parts of your body. You might feel needles pricking your feet, or you may start feeling itchy in some other part of the body, or you might suddenly feel a pain in the back or in the neck. A moment before, nothing like this was happening, you were absolutely okay. Suddenly, your body is in revolt from every part. It is telling you to *do* something—if nothing else then at least scratch yourself, but do something. If nothing else then at least change your position: you have your legs this way, put them the other way, or lie down—but do something!

Life in this world is based on action. The moment you are empty of action, this world is lost to you. As soon as you want to sit still and silent, the body will urge you to do something.

People come to me and say, 'We are not usually aware of aches and pains, but whenever we sit for meditation, all kinds of troubles start.' You suddenly feel like coughing whereas before you were all right, there was no urge to cough at all. The moment you sit silently, your body will start to react. Be aware of this and don't listen to what your body says. You are the master, and if you don't listen, your body will settle after a few days. How long can it go on protesting? It is you who goes on giving it attention and encouragement. Just tell your body that whatever happens, you are not going to do anything at all for this one hour. At the most, the itching will persist, but what harm can that do?

Have you ever noticed that if you can be brave and not scratch for a minute or two, the itching stops on its own? In any case, has scratching ever stopped any itch? No, it increases it.

The moment you make a firm resolution that your body is the servant and that it has to obey you, that you are not going to obey it, you will suddenly find that your throat has settled and the urge to cough has disappeared. You will have to assert your mastery for a few days, because you have allowed this servant to be the master for a very long time. When it feels that its power is being taken away, it will create a hindrance; it will tell you that it won't allow this to happen: 'I am occupying the throne.'

If you have decided to sit silently for an hour, what harm can happen? If the feet itch, let them—you are not going to die, it's only an itch—and very soon you will find that as you remain firm in your resolve, your feet will stop insisting. That insistence was only a trick to make you give in. If you had paid attention and dealt with its request, the itching would have shifted to some other part of your body. If you ignore the itching, it will disappear. If the house is empty, the beggar will just give up after knocking a few times and go away. But if you make the mistake of saying even this much, 'There is no one here. Go somewhere else,' then he will not budge from your door. Once you respond, once you react in any way, he is sure to remain there.

A beggar was begging for alms at the house of a miserly Marwari. What a wrong place to go to! He called out and begged for a slice or two of bread.

'There is no bread here. Move on!' the Marwari said.

'Then give me a few pennies,' cried the beggar.

'There is no money here. We don't give anything here,' said the Marwari.

'Then give me anything—even a piece of cloth will do.'

'Didn't I just say that there is nothing here?' shouted the Marwari.

'Then what are you sitting here for?' answered the beggar. 'There is no bread, no money and no cloth. Why don't you come with me and we can both go begging together!'

The moment you react, you are caught. Your reaction means that you are there and that you are willing. At least you are reacting, that is enough. No, if the body feels itchy, just go on watching and don't respond. After a while you will be surprised to find that the itching sensation has gone. If pain comes, just go on watching it and the pain will also go away. It will take about six months to bring the body to the point of just sitting centred.

Choose any posture in which you feel comfortable, in which you can sit for a longer time. Don't choose a posture that might unnecessarily give you trouble: choose a relaxed posture, so that you can sit comfortably. Your body should not be deliberately tortured, that you sit on stones and pebbles or that you make a bed of thorns. As it is, the body will give you enough trouble, there is no need to invite more trouble.

Sit in an easy posture. If you decide to sit for an hour, then for that one hour, don't listen to the body at all. You will be amazed that if you keep your resolve and don't give in to the body, within three weeks you will find that the body has stopped creating distractions. Turn your attention towards the mind only when your body has first stopped disturbing you. Don't worry at all about the mind. Right now it will not be good to get into a tangle with the mind. First, let the body become quiet.

When you feel that now the body no longer gives you any trouble, that now it is ready to sit still, you will know that half the journey is over. In fact, more than half the journey is over, because the mind is also a part of the body. If now the whole body is ready to sit, then the mind cannot hold out for very long. Although the mind is the most rebellious, it is still a part of the body. And when the whole body has settled into just sitting, centred, the mind cannot wander around for long; it too will settle down.

To bring the body to a point of 'just sitting, centred' means that all the disturbances of the body have calmed down. Now you sit as if you are bodiless, as if there is no body. You don't notice the body at all, you just sit.

Now pay attention to the mind. The method is exactly the same: whatever the mind says, don't listen to it, don't react to it. If thoughts come to the mind, watch them with an indifferent attitude, as if you have nothing to do with them, as if all these thoughts are going on in someone else's mind and they are very far away from you; as if it is just some noise on the road, or as if they are clouds passing by in the sky and you have nothing to do with them. Keep on watching indifferently.

First, let the body become silent. Then slowly, slowly . . . the body will take three weeks to settle, the mind will take approximately three months. It can be a little more or a little less, it all depends on your intensity—but within a period of six months this state of 'just sitting, centred' will have happened. Then neither the body nor the mind do anything.

Don't fight with the mind, don't try to suppress it. Don't ask it not to think, because, remember, this too is a thought. Even this small thought can keep the mind going. The mind can brew up many troubles, so don't fight because fighting means that you are willing to at least react, that you could not remain indifferent.

Indifference is the key. Just go on watching, don't say anything. It will be difficult because the habit is old: it has always been your habit to talk to the mind, to react, to answer back. Gradually, by and by, simply by continuously watching, you will come to a moment where you are just sitting and there is nothing happening in the mind; there is no movement in the body or in the mind. When all the activities of the mind and body have come to a standstill, it is called the state of 'just sitting, centred, settled'.

The word 'asana', settled body posture, does not mean practising some intricate yoga posture. If you are practising yoga, it will be helpful because it will increase your capacity to sit, but it is not really needed, it is not a necessity. If you simply start sitting and can learn only how to sit, that is the ultimate asana.

Also, it is not necessary that you should sit only on the floor, you can sit on a chair too. The only thing to remember is that in whatever posture you choose to sit, remain in it throughout the whole sitting. Sit comfortably so that your body can't complain that you are unnecessarily torturing it. Sit comfortably, make all arrangements for the body's comfort. If it is cold, use a blanket; if it is hot, switch on the fan—arrange for the body's comfort. Don't torture the body unnecessarily, because that is just cruelty. Whether you torture someone else's body or your own, both are acts of violence—and nobody has ever experienced godliness through violence. This body also belongs to existence, there is no need to torture it. Make yourself comfortable in every possible way. But once you sit down, don't listen to the body's demands and complaints any more, just go on sitting and be indifferent to the mind as well.

In the beginning the mind will create a lot of trouble, perhaps more than ever before. People come to me and say: 'Before we started meditating the mind was never this restless. Now it has become much more restless. Now it creates so much noise and disturbance.'

This noise and disturbance were also there before, only you were not aware of them because you had never paid any attention to it. You were so involved on the outside, but the chaos within you was the same. Sitting silently has nothing to do with an increase in chaos. The chaos can only become less—how can it possibly increase? But you were so entangled in the outside and your whole attention was extrovert—in the marketplace, in business, in money—your attention was so engaged there that you had no chance to look inside and see the chaos that was happening there. Now that you have closed your eyes to the outside, your whole attention, your whole focus, all your light, is focused inward. When your light turns in for the first time, you become aware what a chaos there is inside.

But remember to be indifferent. You have to remember only one thing: let go of all expectations of the mind. If you keep any expectation, you will not be able to remain indifferent. Drop all expectations. Cherish no hopes and sit in total indifference. Become utterly neutral. However difficult you may find it in the beginning, it will become easier if you go on sitting.

If it doesn't happen today, it will happen tomorrow or the day after. Don't worry about when it will happen, because the more you hurry, the more it will be delayed. Haste is the nature of the mind. If you hurry, the mind will defeat you. If you are patient and don't hurry, if you are prepared to wait for the happening whenever it comes, if you are not worried about it and continue to sit, you will find that within about six months the mind will also become peaceful.

The state of 'just sitting, centred' means that there is no activity in the body, no thought in the mind. This sutra of Shiva is tremendously revolutionary. It says that the moment you find the state of 'just sitting, centred', you are immersed in the lake of pure consciousness. That lake is within you.

Energy cannot flow out when all movement of the body stops. And when all the movements of the mind come to a halt, all the outlets for energy are sealed. For the first time, the bucket of your mind has no holes: all the holes are closed, nothing can flow out. Then all your life energy goes within— and within you is the great lake. Your energy flowing within merges with that great lake and you, the 'drop' that is you, begins to merge with the inner ocean. A natural merging with the pure lake of consciousness happens, and that is the state of godliness.

You have lost yourself by going out; going in, you will reach the destination. You are searching on the outside for what is hidden within you. You are searching for that which you, yourself, are, and this is why you have not been able to find it. What you are searching for has always been inside you—and that is the difficulty, that is the complexity, because you don't look for it inside you. And it is not where you look for it, so you keep wandering endlessly.

Late one evening Mulla Nasruddin was searching for something on the road outside his house. Other people gathered around him. 'What are you looking for?' they asked.

The Mulla said, 'I have lost my needle.'

They started to help him search; after a while one of them asked, 'Mulla, where exactly did you drop the needle?— because the road is so wide and the needle is so small.'

Nasruddin said, 'Don't ask that question. That is a sore point.'

His friends were puzzled. 'What do you mean?' they asked.

Nasruddin said, 'I lost the needle in the house, but there is no light in there. It's so dark there, so terribly dark, and I am afraid to go in even in the daytime. I spend my nights outside. In the daytime I go in once in a while, but in the night, never! So I am searching outside.'

'You are mad, Mulla!' they exclaimed. 'How can you look outside for what you have lost inside?'

Nasruddin laughed loudly and said, 'Everybody is doing the same—what they have lost within, they seek without. And you think *I* am mad?'

What is it that you are seeking? Certainly, you are seeking something, but what is it? If you were to find the essence of all your quests, you would discover that you are seeking bliss. Somebody may be searching for money, but through that too he is seeking bliss. Somebody may be searching for love, but through love, he is seeking bliss. Somebody else may be searching for fame, but through that he is only seeking bliss. Your searching may have different names, but there is only one thread hidden in all of it and that is your search for bliss.

You are seeking bliss. A man going to the tavern and a man going to the temple are searching for the same thing: both are seeking bliss. Whether a man is doing virtuous acts or sinful acts, the search is the same—they are seeking bliss. The good people and the bad people are both searching for only one thing and that is bliss.

But have you ever asked yourself where you have lost bliss? Search for it where you have lost it! You are searching in places where you have not lost it. You have certainly not lost it somewhere on the outside. It is a taste somewhere inside you, and you know its flavour well.

Psychologists have made a very significant statement: they say that a child is in the most blissful state when he is in his mother's womb. It should be so—he has no worries, no responsibility, no anxiety about food or about the weather. The temperature in the mother's womb is constant. It makes no difference to the child whether it is raining or hot or cold outside—the temperature inside the mother's womb remains the same, it does not change at all. There is no problem for the child if there are changes in the climate outside. The mother may be hot and sweating, but for the child there is no heat, no cold. The mother may be facing hunger, but the child does not face it. What is happening to the mother does not make any difference to the child; the child remains fully protected and just keeps floating in the womb.

Have you ever seen the picture of the god Vishnu floating in Kshirsagar, a sea of milk? This is the state of the child, of every child in the mother's womb. Just as Vishnu is resting in bliss in an ocean of milk, each child is resting in the same way. That picture of Vishnu is, in fact, a representation of a child resting in the womb of his mother. And just as a flower is blooming from Vishnu's navel, in the same way, a child is connected with the mother through the navel. The entire source of life is from there. And the water in the mother's womb is the same kind of water that is in the ocean—even the ratio of salt is the same. This is why when she is pregnant, a woman often has the urge to eat more salty things, because the salt in her body is being absorbed by the womb. She might even start eating clay if it has the taste of salt in it because all the salt in her body is being absorbed by the womb.

Scientists say that there is exactly the same ratio of salt and water in the mother's womb as there is in the ocean. The child floats in this water inside the mother's womb: the temperature is constant and he goes on blissfully floating there. There is no worry, no responsibility. There is no need to even cry because even before he is hungry, he is fed. The child doesn't even breathe on his own because the mother breathes for him. The child is connected with the mother, he is not yet separate. There is no ego yet, not even a consciousness of being. The child is totally merged with existence, and the bliss he feels in the womb is the bliss he goes on searching for his whole life.

Psychologists say that your whole life's search is, in fact, a search to return to the womb. We try in a thousand and one ways to recreate it. If you look closely, you will find that all your efforts are for the same thing—to recapture that bliss.

You like to have a comfortable bed to sleep in, but it is comfortable only when the temperature is almost the same as it was in the womb of the mother. When you sleep in the bed, you sleep almost in the same posture as a child curled up in the mother's womb. People who sleep well often sleep in this curled-up posture of a baby: they have become babies all over again.

All your life's efforts are simply aimed at one thing—to be relieved of all responsibilities, all worries. This is why you seek money, because if you have money, there will be no worries about the future. You look for friends everywhere, you look for love, so that all these things together create a womb and you feel safe surrounded by them. You are afraid to be alone because all around you there are unknown people, unfamiliar people, enemies. You feel good when you are among friends. You make a house for yourself and you create a world of your own inside the house. If you look closely at it, you will see that you have created a womb again, and within its walls you feel safe.

The child, every child, experiences a taste of bliss in the mother's womb. Then for his whole life he searches for that same bliss. This is why whenever you get even a small glimpse of that bliss, you feel happy. All your moments of happiness are simply glimpses of that bliss.

Psychologists say that the search for the state of liberation is in fact a search for the womb. On the day that this whole existence becomes like a womb and you become one with it again, when your ego dies and there is no worry, no anxiety, then you will find this bliss again. This bliss is right there inside you, and you have lost it. And because you look for it on the outside, you are not able to find it.

In the state of just sitting, centred, in the state of meditation, your own body becomes a womb for you. In the state of just sitting, centred, when all activities quieten down, when all thoughts are gone, your body and your mind become the circumference and, at the centre, you enter the womb again. This is why we call a person of meditation dwij, one who is twice-born—he has found his own womb. There is one birth that happens through your parents and there is a second birth that you give to yourself. It is this second birth that will make you a dwij.

Settled in oneself, one bathes spontaneously in the lake of pure consciousness. Then there is the ocean of consciousness. When there is so much bliss in the ocean of the body, in the womb, then imagine how much greater the bliss will be in the ocean of consciousness. You cannot even imagine it. It is infinite, infinitely times more; it is boundless. The small taste of bliss that you had in your mother's womb was only the bliss of merging with the body. When you merge with your being, the bliss that you will experience is the only bliss there is. That is the supreme bliss. Hindus have called it Brahman. There is no taste that can equal it. It is *sat-chit-anand*—truth, consciousness, bliss.

And one attains self-creation, the state of being twice-born.

The moment you merge with the inner ocean you become a dwij, a twice-born, and for the first time the being is born. Right now your being is hidden in a seed—it is present and yet it is not present. It is present only as a seed, not as a tree. Right now you are only a potential, a hope of becoming: you have not yet become. This is your anguish. This is what keeps you trembling in anguish.

If you understand it rightly, all this pain is the pain of birth—and until you are reborn, this pain will continue. And for the person who has entered this second birth, the first type of birth will cease because now it is no longer needed. Otherwise, you will continue to be born in a physical body again and again; you will come back in the body again and again. But if you have become twice-born, there will be no need for you to return to another body.

We call those who are Brahmin by caste a dwij, but the correct thing would be to call a dwij a Brahmin. All Brahmins are not dwij, although all those who are dwij are Brahmins. You do not become a Brahmin just by being born into a Brahmin family. Until you are reborn into Brahman, the ultimate reality, you have not become a Brahmin. Until you merge with Brahman, you have not become a Brahmin.

Hindus have a really unique concept: they say that everyone is born as a Shudra, the lowest caste, and only a few become Brahmins, the highest caste. So everyone is born a Shudra, whether they are born in a Brahmin family or a Shudra family. At birth, everyone is a Shudra. This is why a child born in a Brahmin family is later initiated with a sacred thread. It is simply a formality to make him aware that now he is no longer a Shudra, now he is a Brahmin: 'You too have been born a Shudra, but now that the sacred thread has been put around your neck, you have become a Brahmin.'

To be a Brahmin is not so cheap that it can happen just by putting a thread around someone's neck! To become a

Brahmin is the most difficult process in the world: it happens only by merging into yourself. A person who gives birth to himself is a dwij, a twice-born. He has been reborn. Now he is his own mother, his own father. Now his birth has not happened through another. Now his connection with the world is broken and he has become connected with Brahman, the ultimate reality.

This sutra says: *Meditation is the seed.* Someone who attains the state of sitting settled in his being bathes spontaneously in the lake of pure consciousness, becomes twice-born.

Don't fall prey to cheap tricks—don't sit holding your sacred thread. If only it were so cheap and easy to become a Brahmin! But we always invent easy methods to console our minds. How long will you go on consoling your mind? Truth cannot be found by consolation! Drop all your false hopes, break all your sacred threads: they will not be of any help. A real rebirth is needed. And the real rebirth will happen only when you become your own womb. The body settled in itself, and the mind in the meditative state, together they create that womb.

Nicodemus asked Jesus, 'When will I attain the kingdom of God?'

Jesus said, 'When you die and are born again.'

You must die as you are and be reborn as your potential— only then can you enter the kingdom of God.

It is absolutely clear: die as a seed and be born again as a tree. As you are now it is only a dream, a hope, a potential that some day godliness can blossom in you. Plant this possibility in the soil like a seed. What is the fear? The fear is that the seed is afraid it will no longer be. I can understand the seed's difficulty: it does not know whether it will become a tree or not. And the seed will never be able to see the tree, because only when it is no more will the tree come into being. The seed will never come face-to-face with the tree—it has never happened. How can the seed be absolutely certain that an immense tree will come into being when it dies? All that the seed can see is that whatever it already is, even that will cease to be. Where is the certainty that it will become an immense tree?

That is your anxiety. When you come closer to a Buddha, a Mahavira, a Shiva, your difficulty is only this. You also ask this same question: 'What if I lose what I have and what you promise does not happen?'

The fear is natural. This is why you are afraid when you come close to a master. And if you don't experience this fear near a master, then he is worthless. Then run away from him, because only with a real master will you feel the fear. He will make you afraid; because to you he will look like death itself. He *will* destroy you. The moment you start to dissolve, your mind will say, 'Escape from here!' The place your mind tells you to run away from, don't run from there. Where the mind tells you, 'Be here; what a beautiful satsang is happening here'—immediately escape from there. Wherever the mind is afraid of, know that something is about to happen, because the seed is afraid only where it faces its death, not before that.

This is why you are not afraid of your priests, you are not afraid of your temples. You are not afraid of your holy places; you can go there with no fear. There is no longer anyone there in Bodhgaya or in Girnar or in Jerusalem to demolish you, you can go there without fear. All your holy places of pilgrimage are dead. They always die, because life is not in the holy places themselves, life is in the awakened ones around whom they developed. The awakened one is gone and you create a place of pilgrimage after he is gone.

Then it is a dead pilgrimage place, it is a corpse; it cannot demolish you. No dead master can demolish your ego. This is why the mind likes to worship the dead masters.

You enjoy worshipping Mahavira because you know very well that a stone statue cannot do anything to you. After all, you have purchased it, it is in your hands, and you can throw it away whenever you want. Hindus are clever: they make their idols out of clay, because after worshipping them for two or three weeks, they can just throw them in the river. One thing is certain—you are their creators and you are their destroyers. What harm can your statue do to you? Even the worship you created the statue for is out of your own choice. They are part of your game. Their value to you is no more than that of a doll. Indeed, they have no value.

When a Mahavira, a Rama, a Krishna, are no longer alive, then they are worshipped. When such a one is alive, you are afraid of him. You are afraid of a living master, who is the very embodiment of sacredness, but you are very eager and very happy to go to a place of pilgrimage that has been created in his name. Just see the point. Tens of millions of people flock to the Kumbh Mela, the gathering of pilgrims and holy men that happens once every twelve years. Have people ever gathered in such great numbers around a Mahavira or a Buddha or a Krishna? Never! The Kumbh Mela does not come to your door, you have to go on a journey to it. But when a Mahavira or a Buddha even come knocking at your door, they find the door closed. You are afraid of them because these people are dangerous, they say: 'Die as a seed and become a tree.'

This is why trust is so important. If you listen to logic, it will tell you, first, to be certain about what outcome is being promised. And logic is right in saying that, first, there should be some guarantee about what you can become and only then should you let go of what you are now, lest the real that is in your hands gets traded for some false hope, lest the little that you have in your hands be lost for a promise of what is yet to come. Logic always says that one bird in the hand is better than two in the bush. It is true that you have only one, but at least you have it, and you should let go of it only when you first get two in your hands. If you follow logic . . . and logic seems to be absolutely right.

Mulla Nasruddin wanted to learn swimming, so he found a teacher in his village and asked, 'Will you teach me how to swim?'

The teacher said, 'Come with me, I am just now going to the river.'

As luck would have it, the Mulla slipped on the bank of the river and fell into the water. He went down a couple of times, but somehow he managed to struggle his way out of the water and started to run away.

The teacher ran after him and shouted, 'Where are you going? Don't you want to learn to swim?'

'First teach me how to swim,' said the Mulla, 'and only then will I get back into the water. Until I have learned how to swim I am not going to put my foot into that water.'

'That's impossible,' said the teacher. 'How will you learn if you don't enter the water?'

The Mulla said, 'Not again! I have made that mistake once, but never again in this life!'

When you bring logic in, your logic also is saying the same thing—and the logic is absolutely right. As Nasruddin says, 'I will only step into the river when I have learned to swim, otherwise it is dangerous. It was sheer good luck that I was saved from drowning! First, I will learn how to swim properly, only then will I enter the water again.'

One day I saw Nasruddin standing by the side of the road. His wife was sitting in the car and he was teaching her how to drive. I watched for some time and saw that he was running alongside the car and shouting out instructions: 'Go left!' 'Press the clutch when you change gears!' and so on.

Later on I asked, 'Nasruddin, I have seen many people teach driving, but yours is a unique method! I have never seen anyone teaching from outside the car.'

The Mulla said, 'The car has insurance, but I don't, so I am not getting into that car!'

Logic always demands insurance, it wants guarantees. The seed also demands some guarantee that it will become a tree—but how is it possible to give assurances to a seed?

This is why trust has such value. There is no way to assure you. Trust is a leap into the darkness. Hence, people who trust reach the goal, but the logicians never do. The intellect leads you astray and the heart takes you to the goal.

When you are in love, you never listen to intellect. When you are in prayer, then too—only if you don't listen to intellect will you be able to experience anything. If you listen to intellect, what it says seems to be right, 100 per cent right, because intellect always functions logically. But in the final analysis all goes to waste, all becomes futile. The seed will remain a seed and will begin to rot.

Ask yourself one thing: Whatever you have, is it really something of worth? What is it that a seed has? Don't ask if the seed will become a tree or not. Instead, ask what the seed has that it is so afraid of losing. What do you have that you are so afraid of losing? Ask this. This is what trust always asks: 'What do I have that I am so afraid of losing?' Do you have anything that will leave you empty if you lose it? No, you have nothing like that. You may have your worries, your sadness, your anguish and misery. Why are you afraid to lose them?

Do you have any bliss in you? Have you known the dance that, if lost, will leave you feeling empty, poorer? No, you have nothing. You are like the naked man who won't bathe because he has nowhere to dry his clothes. He has no clothes, so there is no question of washing and drying them. But the mind is caught in these anxieties.

You have nothing to lose, absolutely nothing, and everything to gain. This is trust. Trust always asks, 'What do I have?' and logic always asks, 'What will happen in the future?' Logic is future-oriented, and trust looks into the present: 'What do I have right now?'

People come to me, and when I tell them to take the jump into sannyas they say, 'Not now, in a year'—as if I am taking away something from them, as if they need a whole year to gather courage. They say, 'Please wait! Right now it is difficult.' It is as if I am asking them to renounce something! They don't have anything, absolutely nothing, no true wealth except misery and poverty. I want to give them the glory of sannyas. I am not taking anything away from them; rather, I am giving them something because I don't consider sannyas to be a renunciation. It is the door to ultimate enjoyment. By becoming a sannyasin, you become an emperor for the first time in your life—but you consider your beggarly state as a great treasure.

Whenever I tell someone to take the jump into sannyas, he looks at me as if I am snatching something away from him. I am amazed! If he has something to lose then I can understand it. You have absolutely nothing, not even rubbish! Whatever you have is a Pandora's box filled with scorpions and snakes, not even rubbish. Except for your anxiety, your suffering, your worry and anguish, you don't have anything else. Even this you don't let go of, this too you go on holding on to. What is the reason for it? No, you don't look in that direction at all. What you look at is: what will you gain?

People ask me, 'What will we gain by meditating?' And that is their mistake. I want them to ask themselves what they have gained by *not* meditating. You cannot be sure of what you will gain because the future is unknown. In any case, the seed and the tree will never meet. A seed is a seed—how can we make the seed meet its future? Only with the death of the seed does the tree come into being. By the time the tree grows, the seed is no more. We will not be able to show the seed that 'Look! This is what you have attained.'

This is the great problem: how can you show the seed what it will find? As long as you are a seed, you are a seed; when you become a tree, you are a tree—the seed and the tree will never meet. Right now you want a guarantee for the future. To whom should it be given? The seed will no longer be there—you will not remain.

No, the trusting person will ask: 'What do I have?' Then he will look and find, 'I have nothing, I am naked, and I am just afraid about where I will dry my wet clothes.' Once this realization comes that you have nothing, then you are ready to go on the pilgrimage towards the unknown because then you will not be afraid that you have anything to lose. If something is gained, it is okay; if nothing is gained, that too is okay. But in fact there is nothing to lose. Whatever you are, you cannot be any worse off. Or do you think you can be? There are people who always live in the fear of being in a worse situation than the one they are in.

Mulla Nasruddin had a habit of saying, 'It could have been worse.' Whenever anyone said anything, the Mulla always would say, 'It could have been worse.' His friends were tired of hearing this. There was no conversation where he would not say, 'It could have been worse.'

One day an incident happened in the neighbourhood, and his friends were certain that in this the Mulla would not be able to use his pet phrase.

It so happened that the Mulla's neighbour had been out of town, and when he returned two days earlier than expected, he opened the door and found his wife in the arms of a stranger. The husband picked up his gun and shot them both. When Mulla went out of his house the next morning, the neighbours surrounded him and said, 'Now, Mulla, what do you have to say about this?'

'It could have been worse,' the Mulla said calmly.

'What could have been worse than that!' they all shouted together.

The Mulla said, 'If he had returned a day earlier it would be me who is now dead!'

But I say unto you, it cannot be worse than this. Give up this phrase. The state that you are in is the worst state that you can possibly be in. What could be worse?

Trust always thinks, 'What do I have?' What does the seed have? A seed is just a shell, it has nothing. It can become something—but only when its shell breaks.

You are a shell . . . let the shell break. Then everything becomes possible. Godliness within you becomes possible.

This is why Shiva says: *Meditation is the seed*. And when the seed has disappeared, you attain the state of being twice-born.

> *Ceaseless awareness is the cessation of the cycle of birth and death.*

On the day the twice-born state flowers within you, you will be born again. Then the knowing within you will never cease; it will become a constant flow. You will become a current of knowing. Everything within you will become this knowing, will become conscious. When the seed of meditation breaks open, there will be nothing but consciousness, only consciousness left in you. You will be transformed into a state of awareness and of witnessing where knowing is indestructible—it cannot be destroyed. Right now your consciousness is almost non-existent. You live as if you are asleep. Right now, whatever you do, you do unconsciously.

A man was sitting in front of Buddha. He was wriggling his big toe, and Buddha said, 'Brother, why does your big toe move so?'

The moment Buddha said this, the wriggling immediately stopped. The man was surprised and said, 'I myself don't know. By asking about it you have put me in trouble. I was not moving it consciously, it was just moving.'

'Your whole life is like this,' said the Buddha.

What have you ever done consciously? Have you ever been angry consciously? Have you ever loved consciously? Have you ever been greedy or in attachment consciously? What have you done consciously? Just as the big toe goes on moving unconsciously, your entire life is like this. You have set up a house, raised a family, given birth to children, but what have you done consciously? All this is just happening and you are simply caught up in it, mechanically.

What have you done consciously in your life? Can you find even one act that you have done with awareness, which may have come out of your consciousness? No, you will not be able to find a single act that you have done consciously. You fell in love—it happened; you did not do it. You had a fight with someone—it just happened mechanically; you did not do it. You see other people and you immediately reach some conclusion, involuntarily: someone you like, someone you dislike. But if looked at consciously, who is good and who is bad?

Whatever you have become in life appears to be just accidental. You have not done anything with awareness: things are happening around you and you are unconsciously flowing with them. You are like a straw floating in a river that goes wherever the current takes it, although the straw too must be thinking, 'I am the one making the journey.' In the same way, you think that you are doing something—but how can there be a doer when there is no awareness?

This sutra says that knowing becomes non-ceasing only when the seed of meditation breaks open and a constant current of consciousness remains present in you. Then asleep or awake, you are never asleep. Then sitting or walking, you are never asleep. You are always conscious inside. Then when you love, you do it with total awareness. When you eat or drink, walk or talk, it is in total awareness. Your whole life becomes an expansion of consciousness. This is what we call buddhahood. Buddhahood means a person is living in total awareness.

Non-cessation of knowing . . . Now the knowing is uninterrupted. Now the awareness never fades. Now the flame inside never burns low: it continues to burn constantly, uniformly, without a flicker. When this happens—when the seed of meditation has opened and become a ceaseless knowing, when the flow of awareness is a continuous stream within you—then the cycle of birth and death is finished. Then there are no more births for you. Then you will not return in another body.

You reincarnate in a body only in a state of unconsciousness. You are asleep, so you descend again to a body. Descending to a body is because of your unconsciousness. When your awareness becomes continuous, your incarnations will end.

No longer will you descend into the confines of the body. It is a prison—no one who has awareness will choose to descend into a body. It is a bondage—chains that you, yourself, have forged around you. It is an imprisonment, a slavery. You are lost in darkness. When you become full of light, conscious, you will stop returning to a body.

Then where will you be? You will be one with the formless vastness. We call this Brahman, the ultimate reality. Some call it the universal being, some nirvana, or moksha. Give it any name, it makes no difference. In different religions, the difference is only of words. And all these words are true because each describes one quality of the ultimate state.

The word 'nirvana' means extinguishing the lamp. Buddha loved this word. He used to say, 'It is as if a lamp is extinguished and you ask where the flame has gone.' What would you say about where it has gone? You will not be able to point to a specific place. It must be somewhere, because nothing in this existence is ever eliminated. What is, is; whatever is not, is not. That which exists not, there is no way for it to exist; that which exists, there is no way for it not to exist. That flame is bound to be somewhere or the other. You extinguished the lamp, but the flame cannot be finished—finished up, where will it go? No, it has become one with the vast. Up to now it had a form, now it has become formless. Now it is free from the lamp, but that does not mean it is non-existent.

The lamp is made of clay, but the flame is totally separate. What does the flame have to do with the clay? There is no relationship between the two. The flame is not the lamp; the lamp has not become the flame. The lamp is just the body that contains the flame. You blow the flame out, and the connection between the fuel and the flame is broken. The flame disappears into the vastness and becomes part of the ultimate light. This is why Buddha called the ultimate state nirvana: here, the lamp is extinguished and the flame becomes one with the ultimate light.

Mahavira calls it *kaivalya*, absolute aloneness. He says, 'The moment your attachments break, the darkness disappears. False knowledge and ignorance disappear. Then there is just you and you alone—there is no one else. Only consciousness remains, which has no beginning and no end.'

Mahavira does not talk about a supreme being. He says that the being itself becomes the supreme being. They are one and the same thing. Either you can say that the drop is lost in the ocean, or you can say that the ocean is lost in the drop—what difference does it make? A drop falling in the ocean . . . Hindus say that the drop disappears in the ocean, Jainas say that the ocean disappears in the drop. It is the same thing, only the expressions are different. Mahavira gave it a word which he liked, kaivalya: just you and only you remain, no one else. Just pure consciousness, pure awareness remains.

Hindus call it moksha, ultimate liberation, because the body is a prison and you have become free. Jesus has called it the Kingdom of God because you are no longer poor and miserable, you have become an emperor. The difference is only of words, but the basic truth is one: if the seed can break, you will become the tree.

Be courageous! Great courage is needed. There is no greater courage than this in the world. There is no greater challenge than religiousness. Don't think it is the weak who become religious. The weak can never be religious; only the very strong can walk the path of religiousness. And wherever you see weak people being religious, know that there is no religion there. The people you see kneeling down in the temples and in the mosques are not religious. They kneel down because of their inner weakness. They are still worldly.

Religiousness is the greatest courage. What is this courage? It is this leap of the seed, its readiness to die only in the hope, with no guarantee that it will become a tree. It is the dissolution of the known for the unknown, letting go of the known and the familiar, for that which is unknown and unfamiliar. It is choosing to leave the well-known and well-trodden path of long association to wander off into the vast wilderness. It is choosing an unknown footpath for which there are no maps. It is letting go of the world and setting out in search of the ultimate reality. It is to leave the world of maps behind and enter into a world where there are no maps.

There are no maps to take along, no guides. No printed books will be of any help there. All your books will be left behind in this world, because they are all a part of this world. Not even the master can go with you—he can only push you while he himself stands on the shore. After all, when someone teaches you swimming what does he actually teach? He just gives you a push! You know that the teacher is standing close by, so you can jump without fear.

But the ability to swim is within you. The very first time, you will just throw your arms and feet around haphazardly—but that too is swimming, unskilled! In a few days you will get the knack of how you should move your arms and legs in the water. It was already there within you. If you had the courage, you could have jumped on your own, but alone, on your own, you are afraid. With someone standing on the shore, you feel safe: in case you start drowning, in case some danger happens, there is someone there to help you.

The master stands on the shore to assure you. He will not do anything because there is nothing to do. Everything is hidden within you, and it all has to manifest from within you. But the master's presence assures you that there is no danger. You feel confident that someone is present, and if you shout and call for help he will hear you and he will help. And the master says, 'Don't be afraid, just jump in!' But the moment you jump in, you will start thrashing with your arms and legs. At first you will thrash out of fear and confusion, but this is what will turn into the art of swimming.

What is the difference between swimming and thrashing your limbs around haphazardly? It is only the difference of a little experience. For a few days you will thrash around and then you will have grasped it through your own experience. You will stop thrashing around haphazardly and you will begin to swim in a coordinated way. And as you learn how to move more effectively, your self-confidence increases; in a few days the master will say to you, 'Now there is no longer any need for me to be standing here on the shore. Now, if you want, you can even teach swimming to others.'

This is what the master is doing through meditation: he is giving you a push. And if you can trust, the seed inside you will break open and the tree will be born. If you hold on to logic, you will go on wandering aimlessly. Trust is the door.

Enough for today.

8

The Mysterious Fourth State

*The fourth state of consciousness is to be nurtured into
the other three states like oil into the body.*
  Through this delight, one enters one's own being.
  *With the tidings of prana, life energy, that it is all-
pervading, one knows all things and all beings to be equal.*
  One becomes equal to Shiva.

THROUGH THE THREE states of consciousness—the waking,
the dream and the deep-sleep states—turiya, the fourth, runs
like a thread through the beads of a necklace. Even while
you sleep, there is something within you that is awake. Even
while you dream, there is some witness in you who remains
outside the dream. Even when you are awake and doing
your daily routine, there is a witness present inside you. This
is bound to be so because you cannot lose that which is your
intrinsic nature, no matter how deeply you are asleep. Your
essential nature is bound to be present. It may be suppressed,
hidden or forgotten, but it cannot be destroyed.

So whether you are asleep or dreaming or in your so-
called waking state, deep within you, turiya, the fourth, is
ever-present. Deep within you is always a buddha, eternal
consciousness. However much you may go astray, all your

straying is peripheral: it belongs to the waves on the surface. Deep within, you have never gone astray, because deep within there is no way to go astray.

Hence, the fourth state is not to be attained, but only to be discovered. Turiya is not to be achieved but only to be uncovered. It is hidden within you like a buried treasure: simply remove a few layers of soil and you become an emperor. You don't have to go and seek it anywhere else, your treasure is within you. You are always having glimpses of it, but you pay no attention to those glimpses.

When you get up in the morning, you say, 'I had a deep sleep last night. It was very blissful, very pleasant.' When you say this, have you ever paid attention to who it is who knows that your sleep was very peaceful and pleasant? If you were totally asleep, then who would remember this in the morning? If you were totally asleep then who would have a memory of it? Who is it who says the sleep was deep and refreshing? Surely, even in the depth of sleep, someone was watching; some glimmering light was shining even through the depth of sleep. The darkness was not absolute; it has been observed.

You dream at night and in the morning there is the memory: some glimpse stays with you. When you wake up you say that you had a bad dream—so this watcher was separate, and you were not completely lost in the dream. You had not become one with the dream, you were a spectator. The dream may have been playing on the stage of your mind's screen, but you were out of the play. Otherwise, there could not be a memory of it.

In the day, when anger grips you, then it is not that you are totally asleep: you glimpse it from deep inside. When anger catches a hold of you, you can see it arising. Even before it catches a hold of you, when the smoke of it is just beginning to rise, you know that anger is about to come. Just as the sky becomes overcast before it rains, you start feeling the same way—that now anger is about to come. When attachments fill your mind, then too; when you are peaceful, then too; when you are not at peace, then too there is someone within who is noticing all this. But you have never paid any attention to this watcher.

Your attention is flowing towards the scene, and you are engrossed in what is visible to you. You never turn in and see the one who is seeing. If you only do that much, your unconsciousness will be broken, the fourth state will be attained. Someone who has reached the fourth has attained all. And a person who has not reached the fourth, the awakened state of meditation, although they may have earned everything else, accumulated everything else in life, at the time of death they will find that whatsoever they have earned, whatsoever they have accumulated, has not been of any value at all.

I have heard that one day Mulla Nasruddin ran to the bank of the river to catch a boat. He was going on a journey and he was in a great hurry not to miss the boat. He was just a few steps away from the river when he saw that the boat had just left the shore. He happily took a big jump and landed on the boat deck, but in the process he slipped and fell flat on his face. His elbows were bruised and bloody and his clothes were torn. Even then, he happily got up, looked around, beaming, and said to his amazed fellow travellers, 'I made it at last! Although I thought I was late, I have caught the boat.'

The other travellers said, 'We don't understand, Mulla. Why such a hurry? This boat isn't going, it's coming.'

In your hour of death you also will realize that despite all the running around you have done all your life, your racing to get somewhere, the boat is not going anywhere—it is coming back to the shore. By then it will be too late, and you will not be able to do anything about it.

But *now* there is still time. Right now something can still be done.

For the person who awakens before death claims him, there is no death. And there is no life for the person who goes on sleeping until his time of death. For him, life is one long dream that death will shatter. For the person who awakens while living, death does not exist: he has seen his inner nature and has known that he is immortal. But you go on living as if you are drunk. You move in drunkenness: it is not very clear where you are going or why you are going.

Two beggars were having a conversation by the side of the road. I happened to be passing by and I overheard them.

One said, 'I wonder what the purpose of life is. Why does life exist?'

The other said, 'Anyway, what else can you do except live?'

You will also agree with the second beggar: what else can you do in life but live? And even living is not in your hands: it is dependent on an infinite number of circumstances, and they are all in the realm of the unconscious. Why do you feel sexual desire? Why do you raise a family? Why are you greedy? Why do you have to accumulate money? Why do you get angry? Why have you created enemies? Why do you commit crimes? Why are you dishonest? Nothing whatsoever is clear. It is as if you are just a puppet and your strings are being pulled by someone else. It is as if someone else makes you dance and you are just in the illusion that you are dancing.

If you look closely at your life, you will find that you are nothing more than a puppet. And can anything real, any experience of truth happen in the life of a puppet who is not even his own master?

One evening it happened that Mulla Nasruddin hurried to the train station with two of his friends to catch a train. All three of them were dead drunk. The Mulla tripped and fell so he missed the train, but the other two managed to get on the train. The stationmaster helped the Mulla to his feet and sympathized with him for missing the train.

Mulla said, 'Don't feel sorry for me. Those two who got aboard had come to see me off. I can always catch another train, but what will happen to them?'

This is very amusing. Don't take it for granted that the person who has managed to get aboard has succeeded, that he will get somewhere. And don't take it for granted that the person who has not succeeded, who could not get aboard, has missed something. In life, whether it is the one who has managed to get aboard or the one who couldn't, the successful or the unsuccessful one, the victorious or the defeated one—they are all equally unconscious. All accounts are balanced at the end of life: successful, unsuccessful, rich or poor, all become equal. Death wipes everything clean and makes everyone a blank slate.

There is only one whom death cannot make equal, and that is the person who has recognized the fourth state of consciousness that runs through the other three states as well. There is no death for such a person. Only he is successful, everyone else is a failure. Be it an Alexander or a Napoleon, they are all failures. Only once in a while, in an awakened one, is there success.

There is only one success: to have known the deathless. Consider whatever can be destroyed by death to be failure, make it the definition of failure. Do you have anything that death will not be able to take away from you? Keep reflecting over it: 'Do I have a single thing that death cannot take away from me?' And if you find that there is nothing, then don't waste time. If you find that all that you have will be taken away by death, don't waste any more time. It is time to wake up.

These three—what you call the waking state of your day, the dream state of your night, and your deep-sleep state where even dreams disappear—all three will be extinguished in death. These three states have nothing to do with you. It is like when clouds surround the sun, in the same way, these three states have surrounded your sun. If you have spent your whole life in only these three states, at the moment of death you will find that you are dying in misery and helplessness. But if you are able to catch a glimpse of even a single ray of sun, even one ray, then the sun itself is not far away. Then you will soon be facing the sun and the clouds will be left behind.

The first sutra:

The fourth state of consciousness is to be nurtured into the other three states like oil into the body.

In all three states, whether you are awake, dreaming or in deep sleep, you should keep the remembrance of the fourth state alive. Your attention should be on the fourth. Whatever may be happening on the periphery, your attention should be on the centre. Sitting or standing, keep your awareness. Eating, going to your shop, going home, keep your awareness.

Always remember one thing: I am the watcher, I am not the doer. Don't take life to be anything more than acting. Don't become too identified with the acting. Whether you are a wife or a husband, a shopkeeper or a customer, don't get too lost in the role. Your being a wife or a husband, a shopkeeper or a customer, is part of the acting. Inside, you remain out of it. Go to the shop, it is necessary. And the play is enjoyable—there is no need to renounce anything—but it is enjoyable as a play; it is fatal if you take it to be life. It is fine; fulfil the role that life has given you. Don't be an escapist; there is no need to run away in the middle of the play.

Escapists are always weak people. And the people whom you call your sadhus and sannyasin are often escapists. They are weaklings—people who could not face life as it is and could not take care of the watcher within—that is why they have escaped. You do not become a sannyasin simply by running away: running away only shows that the world was too strong and the person was weak. He could not become aware while at the shop or at work, and that is why he has run away.

But if you cannot become aware in your shop, then how will you become aware in the mountains? The process of being aware is one and the same, it has nothing to do with where you are. It also has nothing to do with what you are doing, that is irrelevant. The process of awareness is one. Whether you become aware sitting in your shop or you become aware sitting in a temple, whether you become aware sitting on a velvet cushion or sitting under a tree, the process of awareness is one.

And the process of awareness is this: whatever activity is happening, I am separate from it. Whether that activity is in a shop, at work, in prayer or worship, it makes no difference: the action is separate from me—it is a part of the world and I am the watcher. Don't become so engrossed in the activity that only the activity remains and the witness is lost. Right now, this is what is happening to you.

This sutra says: *The fourth state of consciousness is to be nurtured into the other three states like oil into the body.*

By and by, with continuous care and nurturing, the tree of the fourth state will sprout. First start with the waking state, because that is the closest to the fourth. It has a slight ray of awareness in it, a little consciousness. Make use of that ray. As far as the state of deep sleep is concerned, how can you become aware in it all of a sudden? How can you become aware in the dreaming state directly? So begin with the waking state.

Your waking state has 1 per cent consciousness in it and 99 per cent unconsciousness. Make use of this 1 per cent and nurture it. Whenever there is an opportunity during the day, shake yourself awake. Again and again you will lose it, again and again you will forget it, but each time give yourself a shake and wake yourself up. It is like when a person goes shopping in the market: he ties a knot in his handkerchief to remember an essential item, so that he doesn't forget it. In the same way, in order not to forget about the watcher, tie a knot of self-remembering in your awareness. Each time, in every situation, no matter what you may be doing, remind yourself that 'I am not the doer, I am just a watcher.'

The moment you remember this, you will notice that all your tension has disappeared. All tension is of the doer, of the ego. The moment you remember that you are the watcher, all your tension will disappear. If it disappears even for a moment, you will have a glimpse, and waves of the inner ocean will start pulsating.

Again and again, this state will be lost because for lifetimes you have cultivated unconsciousness, so it will take time to overcome this. But if you nurture it often and if even a dozen or two dozen times in the day, you manage to remain aware for a short while—walking on the road you suddenly stop and become a witness; eating your meal you suddenly alert yourself and become a witness; sitting in the shop, talking to a customer, you are about to lose yourself in unawareness and you suddenly stop yourself—then slowly, slowly, you will find that it becomes easier each day. You will start getting glimpses of the fourth state while you are awake in the day.

When the fourth has become easy during the day, then you will also be able to take it into your dreams. Then at night, when you are about to fall asleep, stay with only this remembrance inside: I am the watcher. As sleep begins to take you over, let only one feeling resonate in you: I am the witness, I am the witness, I am the witness . . . Fall asleep repeating this up to the point where you don't even know when you fell asleep and the current of feeling was broken. But if you go on nurturing it, an undercurrent of this feeling will continue even in your sleep because the current of feeling is in you, and it is only the body that sleeps.

If this process continues, then one day suddenly you will experience that you are the watcher even when you are dreaming. As you experience this, a unique thing will happen: the dream will instantly be broken. The moment you remember in a dream that you are the watcher, the dream will stop. The dreaming happens only because of your unconsciousness.

And when this starts happening in your dreams, the third occurrence also will become possible. If you go on watching the dream, remembering inside that you are the witness, the dream will disappear. But as you keep the remembrance inside—I am the witness, I am the witness—you will fall into sleep again, and now this current of remembrance will also enter into your deep sleep. The day this current—I am the witness—also enters into your deep sleep, the key to the supreme treasure has fallen into your hands. Now nobody will be able to make you unconscious. A person who has become conscious in deep sleep even for a moment will find that his unconsciousness has gone forever.

On the day you are aware and awake in your sleep, you have become a yogi. Nobody becomes a yogi by doing asanas, yogic body postures. These are just exercises. They are good and useful to keep the body healthy and there is nothing wrong if you practise them. But if you take these exercises of the body to be yoga, you are deluded. Yoga is when you are awake even in sleep—only then you are a yogi; without this, no one is a yogi.

This sutra says: *The fourth state of consciousness is to be nurtured into the other three states like oil into the body.* One day or another, that rare happening will take place. When you can remain awake even in deep sleep you will have settled in the fourth state. When you are settled in the fourth, it is as if a lamp is lit and there is no breeze at all, just an unwavering flame. Then your wisdom, your knowing, your being will be unwavering, full of light. Then many things will be transformed in your standing and sitting, in your waking and sleeping—a total transformation.

The first thing is: the dreams of one who has become aware in their deep sleep will end forever. Awakened people don't dream. So this is the first thing that will happen when you can remain awake in your deep sleep. By remaining awake in your dreaming, only the dream in which you are aware will end, other dreams will continue. By remaining awake during sushupti—a deep sleep where there is no dreaming—by remaining awake in such a state, all dreams will disappear. Then you will not see dreams at all. This will happen: all dreams will vanish, because it is only a mind full of desires that dreams.

What is a dream? Whatever you have not been able to fulfil in your waking state during the day, you fulfil in your dream in the night. Everyone can't be an emperor because there is great struggle, tremendous competition, so in sleep, beggars, the people on the streets, dream of becoming emperors. The overall total becomes balanced. And someone who has been an emperor during the day will have to sleep for some hours in the night, and he is bound to dream. And in his dream he will lose his whole empire! The beggar sleeps for a few hours in the night and dreams that he is an emperor—thus in the final balance, all is equal.

It happened once that the Mughal emperor Aurangzeb was very angry with a Sufi mystic. One day the emperor had the mystic arrested and brought to the palace. People had told Aurangzeb that it was impossible to even annoy this man. He said, 'We shall see.' It was a cold night, a cold Delhi night, and he had the mystic stripped naked and made to stand in the waters of the Yamuna river near the palace while the revelries in the palace continued non-stop. Aurangzeb said, 'I will ask him in the morning.'

The naked mystic spent the whole night standing in the icy cold river. In the morning, Aurangzeb sent for him and asked, 'How was it with you last night?'

The mystic replied, 'Part of it was the same as yours, and part of it was better than yours.'

'I don't understand,' said Aurangzeb.

'I kept dreaming,' said the mystic. 'And in my dreams I was an emperor. I was in a palace where non-stop revelries were happening. There was not even the slightest difference between those dreams and the revelries that were going on in your palace. I enjoyed everything as much as you did. So my night was in part like yours, and partly it was better than yours because once in a while I would become aware, conscious, and the dream would end. But you—you are still not aware at all.'

At night you complete what has been left half-finished during the day. The incomplete actions of the day are completed during the night. You could not fulfil all your desires during the day because there were many difficulties in the way. Besides, it is not easy to fulfil desires for they are really unfulfillable: they are such that there is simply no way to fulfil them. By their very nature, they remain unfulfillable. Even if you accumulate all the wealth in the world, your desires will not be satisfied.

It is said that Diogenes told Alexander, 'The day you conquer the whole world you will find yourself in great trouble. Forget about this whole business. Until you have conquered, you will be in trouble, but after you have conquered the world, you will find yourself in even more trouble.'

It is said that Alexander became sad and said, 'Please don't talk like that, because just the thought of having conquered the whole world makes me sad. Then there will be no other world to conquer! My mind will not be satisfied even after I have conquered the whole world. My mind will say what next? What to conquer now? And I will be sad.'

In this life emperors dream and beggars also dream, because what was left incomplete has to be completed in the dream. Dreams have one quality: they are very kind people. Dreams do you a great favour. If you have fasted during the day—say, you fell into the wrong company of some saints, fasting and almost dying of hunger—then in the night you will see yourself as a guest at a royal feast. Dreams are certainly more compassionate than your so-called saints! The dream will invite you to a royal feast and you will eat the most delicious food that you have ever eaten—delicacies beyond description. And there won't even be any difference in the taste of the food in your dream and real food—perhaps the food in your dream will be even tastier! If you have been chasing after women and been unsuccessful, then in your dreams you will be able to possess them—the most beautiful women in the world will belong to you or the most handsome men in the world will be yours.

A dream opens the door for you to fulfil all your desires. And if someone lives for sixty years, he spends twenty years sleeping, twenty years awake and another twenty doing other things. Now, if in your dream you remain an emperor for twenty years and someone else is an emperor for twenty years in his waking state, then what is the difference? The sum total is the same. Perhaps the man who is an emperor during his waking state can't remain an emperor all the time because of a thousand and one worries on his mind, whereas you can be an emperor in your dreams without a care.

Dreams will disappear only when you are awake in your sleep. At this stage, dreams become meaningless because someone who is awake in his sleep has no desire left. All desires are part of unconsciousness, of unawareness.

Once Mulla Nasruddin got off a train looking very sick and couldn't even walk straight. 'You look terrible! What's the matter?' a friend asked.

Nasruddin replied, 'Whenever I travel in a train and don't sit facing the direction in which the train is going, I feel sick and dizzy.'

The friend said, 'Mulla, you should have asked the man sitting opposite you to change seats with you!'

'I also thought of it,' said the Mulla, 'only there was no one sitting in the opposite seat, the seat was empty. But I did think about asking.'

Whatever you are doing in your life is almost as unconscious. You are in a deep intoxication. Somehow you will have to break this intoxication. Where will you begin? Begin with the waking state.

Wake up in the morning with only one thought: 'Today I shall practise witnessing all through the day.' And first thing in the morning when your eyes open, then your mind is very light and fresh: there are no dreams, no thoughts. After a full night's rest there is a dawn within you, just as there is a dawn on the outside. There are no tensions, no clouds in the sky of your mind; you are light. But soon your worldly activities will start, the race will begin and then it will be difficult. So as soon as you realize that your sleep is over, don't be in a hurry to open your eyes. In that moment, the consciousness is very sensitive. As soon as you wake up, remember, 'I am the witness.'

Each morning when you wake up, lie still for five minutes and keep your eyes closed. Don't open your eyes. The moment you open your eyes, the outer world becomes visible and you might be lost in it. Just keep your eyes closed and let there be only one thought: 'I am the witness, not the doer.' Then get up immersed in this feeling: 'May I be able to keep the witness throughout the day; may I be able to remember it again and again all day long.'

Try to support this for a while, because at the beginning of the day it is so much easier. As you get up, put your feet down on the floor in awareness; as you go for a shower, shower with awareness; as you eat your breakfast, eat with awareness.

'In awareness' means to remember that all this is happening outside of you, this is the need of the body, not of you. You have no need at all. Indeed, there are no needs because you, yourself, are the whole—what could be your need? You are the whole, the Brahman. All is yours, you don't have any needs. Being has no requirements, it needs no fuel. Its flame burns with no wick and no oil. You have no needs; all needs are the needs of the body: the bath, food, work, movement . . .

Try to nurture this. Stretch this thread of witnessing for as long as you can. Soon you will lose it in the hustle and bustle of the world—that is your old habit—but nourish it each day. Slowly, slowly, this plant will grow. You will not be able to see it growing because it will grow so slowly. But suddenly, one day, you will find that a ray of light is present all through the day, like a thin thread within you. This ray of light will bring an alchemical change in your life. You will be angry less often, because how can a witness be angry? Your attachments will be less and less, because how can a witness have attachments? Things will happen— there will be successes and failures, there will be sorrows and joys—but you will be less affected by them, because how can the witness be affected? Joy will come and you will watch it, sorrow will come and you will watch that too, and a continuous stream of 'I am a witness, not the doer or enjoyer of all this' will be present within you.

No one can say how long it will take. It will all depend on your intensity, your sincerity, on the depth of your thirst and longing. It will depend on how you move, on whether you run or crawl like an ant, because when it comes to the world of religion, people generally walk at such a slow pace, as if they are part of a marriage party strolling to a bride's home. In that way you will not reach anywhere. That slow pace is fine for a marriage procession because it is not going anywhere: it just goes around the village and comes back to the same place!

Aesop is a storyteller whose fables are still the best the world has ever known. He was a man of great wisdom.

One day Aesop was sitting by the side of the road when someone who was passing by asked him, 'Could you tell me, sir, how far is the village and how long it will take me to get there?' Aesop didn't say anything—he simply got up and started walking with the man. The man was a little frightened. He told Aesop not to trouble himself because all he wanted to know was the distance and the time it would take him and then he would be on his way.

Aesop still didn't say anything and continued walking with the man. After fifteen minutes or so, Aesop stopped and said, 'It will take you two hours.'

The man said, 'What a crazy person you are! You could have told me that from the beginning! There was no need to walk a mile with me.'

Aesop answered, 'How could I tell you the time it would take you before knowing how fast you walk? The time it will take isn't decided by the distance, but by the speed of the walker. Now I can tell you definitely that it will take you two hours.'

It all depends on your pace: if you run you, will arrive very soon; if you walk like a member of some marriage party, then it will be difficult to say when you will arrive. You may even move so fast that it becomes a quantum leap. You can also move in a half-hearted, lukewarm way: then it will take you many lifetimes and still you may not arrive. If you risk all with your total intensity—wholeheartedly, with your total being, without holding anything back—you can arrive right now, this very moment, because this journey is not an outer journey, it is an inner journey to where you already are; it is just a matter of turning your eyes in that direction. There is no distance at all. But if you delay turning in, postponing for tomorrow or the day after or the day after that, then infinite lifetimes have already passed and infinite more can pass.

Remember, nature is not at all interested in your spiritual attainments. Nature will lead only as far as man has already reached. If you want to go beyond this, then only your own effort will take you there. Nature makes you into an animal and no more; nature does that much. Humanity has to be earned. This is why man is in such difficulty, why he lives in such great difficulty.

All animals except man are in peace because nature has finished its work on them and they have no further to go. You cannot say to a dog that he is less of a dog than the other dogs. All dogs are equally dogs: they may be thin, fat, strong or weak, it makes no difference to their being dogs. This is not so with man. There are differences in the degree of humanity. A thin man can also be a great man, while a strong, well-built person can be very ordinary.

With man, a new quality begins. What is the deciding factor? The more conscious a person is, the more the humanity in him. And the day you become totally aware, you will become godly. There is great risk involved, because you can rise to the heights and you can also fall to the depths—only someone who can fall can rise. A person who cannot rise cannot fall either. This is why you cannot find a Buddha or a Krishna or a Mahavira among animals, but you will not find a Hitler or a Genghis Khan or a Stalin among them either. If buddhahood cannot happen, then there is no possibility for a Genghis Khan to happen either. The valleys exist only where there are mountains and high peaks.

There is a zoo in Tokyo where there are animals from all over the world. It is a large zoo, one of the largest. They have the most dangerous animals: lions, tigers, leopards, elephants, rhinos, hippopotamuses, every other wild animal and varieties of all types of animals. After going around the whole zoo, when you come to the very last cage you find a sign which says 'The Most Dangerous Animal of All'. You will naturally move quickly to see which animal is caged there. You will find only a mirror there in which you will see your own reflection. Otherwise, the cage is empty.

Man is indeed the most dangerous of all animals. Because he has the potential to rise high, there is also the possibility of falling low. If you do not rise, you will not be able to just stay where you are—you will fall lower. In this world, nothing is static. Nobody can be static here: either you will rise higher, or you will fall lower. Here, there is no way to stop in the middle. Hence, if you are not moving towards higher consciousness, you will gradually fall towards unconsciousness.

It is a very surprising and also very sad thing that small children are more conscious than old people. What happens? It should be the opposite: after a whole lifetime of experience an old man should be *more* aware, *more* alert. Instead, just the reverse happens—he only becomes more cunning. With all his experience he becomes more dishonest, more of a thief and more skilful in the ways of the world.

An old crow was teaching his young son, saying to him, 'Look, son, I am telling you from experience, beware of humans! Humans are not trustworthy. If you see a human bending down, fly away. He is sure to be picking up a stone to throw at you.'

The son asked, 'But what if he is already carrying a stone hidden in his pocket?'

Hearing this, the old crow immediately flew away, saying, 'This boy has already grown too smart! It is unsafe to stay around him.'

Old people don't become more aware because of their experience of life, they just become more cunning and clever. But what will they gain through their cunningness? There is nothing to gain in this world. There is nothing to lose here because of innocence, or to gain because of cunningness.

Whatever we build in this world is just like castles of sand—if they are built, they are bound to fall; if you could not build them, there is no harm.

Children seem to be more conscious. Look at them: their eyes seem to be more present, they are more alert, they seem to be more aware. We have to find ways to put them to sleep. We restrict their senses in every way so that their awareness becomes dulled. We don't allow them to laugh loudly or cry loudly; we don't allow them to run and skip as they please. We imprison their life energy from every direction. We want to force them to be dishonest, insincere, as quickly as possible.

I asked Mulla Nasruddin's son, 'How old are you?'

'Seven years at home, five on the bus,' he said.

This son has already been put on the right path by his father . . .

Once I was a guest in a household. One evening the hostess was putting her child to bed in the room next to mine. As she put him in bed I heard her telling him, 'Go to sleep now. If you need anything during the night—if you feel hungry or thirsty—just call out loudly for me and your father will come running.'

Call the mother, and the father will come running! All mothers are doing the same thing. But what is it that the child is being taught—lying, dishonesty, cunningness. We start feeding a child poison along with the mother's milk, and our whole effort is that the child becomes dishonest and cunning as soon as possible. Our effort is not to help him to become more conscious.

If culture is ever truly born on this earth and there is real education, the first thing that needs to be taught to a child is to become more aware, more conscious.

Turiya, the fourth state, is the only thing worth teaching, everything else is useless. All the rest just helps you to carry on your day-to-day life. And the child is so fresh! Just as you are fresh, a bit, in the morning, in the same way a child is very fresh because it is the morning of his life. And right at that time, if he can be shown the thread of turiya and is taught the art of witnessing, then by the time he becomes old he will have reached the peak—he will have attained buddhahood.

There is only one thing worth mastering, and that is to absorb the fourth state—consciousness, awareness, wakefulness, alertness, awakening—into the other three states, like oil into the body.

Through this delight, one enters one's own being.

Such a delighted person invariably slips into his own being. Once a person has known the delight of the fourth state, there is no delight deeper than this. All wines may delight you for a short while, but soon the delight will fade. The delight of the fourth state can never fade, that stream of bliss is eternal. The person who has delighted in it, who has danced in it, who has become filled with it, whose every fibre has become saturated with turiya, whose very way of being has become awareness; a person in whose sitting or standing, turiya sits and stands; a person in whose movements turiya moves, whose every particle of life has become bathed in turiya—only someone so immersed enters into his own being. Otherwise you will remain unknown to yourself. You will know the whole world, but you will be a stranger to yourself. This whole world will become your family, but you will remain a stranger to yourself.

You know much about others—their names, their homes, addresses, professions—but you know nothing about yourself. And until you know your own self, all your knowledge is of no value. Everything you know has no value at all because it is based in ignorance.

Through this delight, one enters one's own being. If you go on nurturing the fourth state into the other three states, soon you will find that the fourth state has seeped into the whole tree of your life. The way a buddha sits, stands up or walks is totally different. When he stands up, there is awareness in it, when he walks there is awareness in it. Whatsoever happens through him is not happening in unconsciousness, there is complete awareness. Whatever he is doing, it is conscious.

And whatever *you* have done up to now is unconscious. Although you say you have done a certain thing knowingly, that too is a lie. Your child comes home with a torn shirt or with a broken slate, and you scold him and beat him. If anyone asks you, you will say that you did it consciously to discipline the child for his own good. But have a little genuine introspection and ask yourself, did I really do it consciously? Were you really aware? Or did you simply become angry. Did you just take revenge on the child? The child has disobeyed you and you are angry with him. If you are angry with him, then whatever you are doing is out of unconsciousness because anger is unconsciousness. Whatever you are saying—that it is for his own good—is only a rationalization.

Mulla Nasruddin was beating his son and telling him, 'This is all for your own good.' He said to him. 'Look here! You are a child who does nothing right unless I beat you twice a day. I was also a child once, but my father never beat me!'

Looking at him, the son said, 'It proves that your father must have been a good man!'

You may beat your child and think that you are doing him a favour, but the child is taking it differently: he can see your anger, not just the act of beating. Whatsoever you are doing, you try to rationalize it in some way or another by spinning logic around it. You try to justify to yourself that what you are doing is absolutely right.

Only yesterday a friend came to me with his wife. His wife does not allow him to meditate. She doesn't think that this is really meditation, because she has very traditional ideas. But this is all only superficial: deep down in her unconscious the real reason is completely different. No wife ever wants her husband to meditate and no husband ever likes his wife to meditate, because the moment a person begins to meditate, the old relationships are in danger. The moment a person begins to meditate, his interest in sex becomes less and less. This is the real reason in the unconscious—the rest is just an excuse, it is just superficial.

A wife would rather have her husband go to a brothel because that will not make much of a difference to her. But if the husband is getting interested in meditation, that makes a difference. By going to a brothel he is not going too far away from his wife because he is still interested in women. But a growing interest in meditation means that he is losing interest in women.

If a wife has to choose between her husband going to a brothel or his taking sannyas, she will choose that he go to a brothel if these are the only choices. She will think that there are children at home and they have to be raised, if he starts meditating who will raise them?

But there is no conflict between meditating and raising a family or running your shop. In fact, a meditator does his work even more efficiently than others; meditation breaks your connection with the world deep inside you, not on the outside. On the outside, the show goes on as always, but now it becomes just a play. A new light begins to glow from within as the acting on the outside continues.

But a husband or a wife *does* feel troubled. Whatever they may say outwardly—and it may even be their feeling that this is the real reason they are creating obstacles to meditation—deep down, the reason is very different: it is connected to the sexual relationship. Going into meditation means that the sexual relationship will begin to weaken; the husband's or the wife's interest in sex will gradually diminish.

Every day friends with this sort of problem come to me and say, 'My wife was never interested in sex, but since the day I began to meditate she has become really sexually aggressive!'

Wives generally are not that interested in sex because they have no cause for concern, there is no fear, no danger. They don't show the least interest in sex. On the contrary, they act as if they are going into sex just for the sake of the other. This too is a lie, an absolute lie. But when the husband is falling all over her all by himself, why should she show any interest in it? So wives keep an aura of morality and virtuousness around themselves: that it is just because of their husbands that they have to participate in this contemptible act. But the moment the husband becomes interested in meditation, an anxiety arises. Now there is a danger and it is necessary to drag the husband into the body.

And the same thing also happens to the husband.

Just a few days ago a wife came to see me. She is really interested in meditation, and profound results are possible for her. Her husband burns my books and throws them out of the house. He says to her, 'When I am here, why do you need to go to someone else to ask? Ask me! What do you want to ask? If I can't answer something, then . . .!' And she knows him perfectly well, knows all that he has to say! But the husband's ego is hurt. If the wife becomes interested in a master, then the husband's ego is badly hurt because someone else is taking a higher place in his wife's heart. That is the real trouble, but that will not be said directly.

Whatever you are doing and whatever you are saying is not authentically real: deep down the reasons are different. A meditator should always look for the reasons deep within himself. He should find the root cause, because the root cause can be changed. If, instead of the root cause, you are thinking that something else is the cause, which is not true, then there is no possibility for any change.

As you become more and more aware, you will begin to see the root cause of all the actions and reactions in your life. Then you will realize that you are not angry with your son because he made a mistake, you are angry because you want to be angry—the mistake is only an excuse. You have come home angry from the office. You wanted to be angry at your boss, but you couldn't do that, because to be angry with your boss is a costly affair. Now you want to be angry somewhere, at anybody, anywhere. You can't be angry with your wife because ninety-nine times out of a hundred she will defeat you in being angry. It is also a bad bargain because if she becomes angry, then she will carry on with it for a few days—so your son becomes the target. And a son is after all a son: he is bound to come home with his books torn. He has not grown up yet. He is bound to play with the wrong type of children because, except for your own child, all other children are the wrong type!

Once I asked a small child, 'Tell me, are you a good child? Everyone says that you are.'

The child said, 'To tell you the truth, I am the kind of child that my mother would not allow me to play with.'

Except for your own child, all children are the wrong type. The son must have played with some of those children, might have torn his clothes, his books, he may even have hurt himself. You will immediately grab a hold of him—he is weak. You will transfer your anger on to him, but you will insist that you are doing it for his own good.

As you become more and more aware, you will find that you have started seeing the real reasons. And when the real reasons are seen, it is very easy to drop them. Then there is no difficulty in it. Then you will laugh about what a false life you have woven around yourself. You have become a lie. And with this lie you want to reach to truth, to godliness. You will never be able to do it.

In my heart, sannyas means to dissolve this web of lies that you have woven around yourself and to live authentically and realistically, exactly as you are. If you are bad then you are bad; if you are an angry person, you are an angry person. Don't try to whitewash and paint your anger to make it look beautiful. Covering the wound with flowers will not help, the wound will only become deeper. Don't cover yourself up; instead, expose yourself by saying, 'This is how I am. If I'm bad, then I am bad. If I'm good, then I am good.' Don't try to hide it by giving some rationalization or some logic or imposing some thought process on it.

Don't seek good explanations for evil deeds, because the evil will never be destroyed if you go on finding good explanations for it. Even when you are angry, you justify your anger by finding good reasons for it. But if you do this, then how can the anger ever be dissolved? You are supporting it with good reasons. You are trying to make the anger look good, you are decorating it. You have decorated the prison with flowers and leaves so that it looks like a home. Then you are satisfied. You are taking illness to be health—then you will never be able to get rid of it.

As a seeker begins to awaken more and more, he starts to realize that his waking state is false, his dreams are distorted and perverted, his sleep is filled with restlessness. There is restlessness and uneasiness on all three levels, a constant turmoil. As he begins to see the reality and drops all false rationalizations, he will discover that with the dropping of false reasons and with the truth coming to light, his awareness has begun to crystallize.

Your condition is like that of a man I heard about whose wife woke him up in the night during a hurricane. 'Wake up! I think the house is going to fall down.'

The man said, 'Don't worry, go back to sleep. It isn't our house, we have only rented it.'

The house you are living in may not be yours, but when it falls it is you who will die. The lies that you have built around yourself may not necessarily be your own, because you have borrowed many of them—some you have learned from the gurus, some you have picked up from the scriptures and some from the society; they are not even yours—but when they fall, it is you who is going to die. And you are surrounded by lies.

But the lies seem to be useful right now because they help you keep up a good front. Because of your lies, you always look poised and charming. Inside you are suffering and in pain, but on the surface you smile. It is all false. It is better if you cry and let the tears flow. Let all the paint and polish that you have applied be washed away. There is no harm in your tears, because you can find truth only by being authentic.

As you go on nurturing awareness all this paint and polish will start to wash off. Sannyas is the name of this washing away. As you become more and more authentic in yourself, you will find that it is not difficult at all to rid yourself of your illnesses—but it is very difficult to get rid of a false illness.

It is as if someone has cancer, but is too afraid to accept the fact. Instead, he insists that he is suffering from a chronic cold, nothing else, just a cold. And if he goes on treating himself for a cold, what good will it do? How long will you be able to deceive yourself?

Gurdjieff used to say to his disciples that the first, very important thing for a seeker is to find out what his problem really is—and all seekers try to hide it. But if you hide the real disease, a diagnosis can't happen and you will go on treating a false disease. In this way you will die; you can't be saved because the illness was never your real illness.

People come to me: some say they want to seek the ultimate truth, some say they want to search for their true self—their faces show no sign of this. Their search is false. They are searching for something else and hiding it in the name of ultimate truth.

One friend came to me—he is an old man—and he said, 'I have been searching for the ultimate truth for the last thirty years.'

I said, 'Thirty years is quite a long time! Unless the ultimate truth has been avoiding you, you should have found it by now. I am afraid the ultimate truth really is avoiding you. And if it is avoiding you, then even thirty lifetimes will not be enough. Or could it be that you are seeking it somewhere else and you don't go where it is? Either you are avoiding it, or it is avoiding you. Tell me exactly what the matter is.'

'No,' he said, 'I am really seeking the ultimate truth. I do my meditations and follow all the spiritual disciplines, but I don't get any results.'

'What results do you want?' I asked him.

'I don't attain any supernatural powers,' was his reply.

Now this man is not seeking the ultimate truth at all: this man is seeking supernatural powers. He has only given it the name 'ultimate truth', but deep inside he is seeking supernatural powers. He has simply labelled it 'ultimate truth'. It is not only in the supermarket that you find one ingredient on the label and something quite different inside the container, it happens in the temples too: on the container one thing is written, and there is something else inside.

A husband was in the kitchen looking for some salt. He was taking a very long time, so his wife called out, 'Why are you taking so long? Can't you find the salt?'

He said, 'I'm looking, but I can't find it.'

'It is right there in front of your eyes in the container labelled "turmeric". Are you blind?'

All searching is happening like this. You are not exactly sure about what you are seeking or why you are seeking it.

As you go on nurturing your awareness, a sense of direction will enter your life. What is meaningless will drop away and only the meaningful will be left. When only the meaningful is left, the destination is not far away.

Through this delight, one enters one's own being. And as the delight of the fourth state, turiya, fills you, as this ecstasy enters your life, you will find that this ecstasy is something totally different, but we have to use the same language to describe it. When a man drinks some wine, we also call it being in ecstasy, but in that ecstasy the man staggers. This ecstasy is just the opposite: here the staggering feet become absolutely steady. Wine has the effect of making you forget yourself. This ecstasy is the total opposite because here you remember yourself. You are filled with self-remembrance. One ecstasy comes from the wine; in it a man makes mistakes, he goes astray. Then there is the ecstasy of turiya, where it becomes impossible to commit any wrong.

One day the emperor Akbar was passing by on his elephant when a man standing on a rooftop began calling him names. Naturally, the man was immediately taken prisoner and brought to the court the next morning.

Akbar said to the man, 'You fool! Why did you behave like that yesterday?'

The man said, 'I wasn't there. I had drunk alcohol and it was the alcohol that was calling you names, it wasn't me! Now that I have come to my senses, I am repenting. Please don't punish me, because I was not there at all.'

Akbar understood the situation, because he himself was very interested in turiya, the fourth state. He wanted to find some clue to awakening. He understood the point, that it was useless to punish a man who was unconscious. It was natural that he would make mistakes. In that state, it would have been a miracle if he did anything right.

It is a miracle that sometimes you are able to do something right. It is simply natural that you do only wrong because you are not conscious. Gurdjieff used to say, 'God cannot send you to hell for your sins because you have committed them in unconsciousness.' Even a court of law forgives a man who is not in his senses. God cannot punish you for the wrongs that you have committed, because you have committed them in unconsciousness. He must be at least as wise as our courts! If it is proved that a man has committed murder under the influence of alcohol, even then the court will forgive him because he was not conscious; he will be punished more lightly. He may be punished for drinking, but why punish him for murder—the man was not there at all.

You have done evil in unconsciousness, and you have done good acts also in unconsciousness. Hence, there is almost no difference between your evil acts and your virtuous acts; their quality is almost the same. Whether you run a household, or renounce the home and become a so-called holy man, there is not much difference. You are unconscious. You are unconscious at your place of business and you will behave unconsciously even in the temple. You are unconscious in your office and you will also be unconscious in your monastery. It is not going to make any difference. You are unconscious wearing clothes and you will also be unconscious if you are a naked monk.

The real question is of breaking this unconsciousness, not of changing your activities. It is very easy to change your actions, but when there is unconsciousness in one action, the same unconsciousness will be there in the other actions too.

A person who joyously nurtures the fourth state will enter into his being. And as you enter into your being, for the first time in your life you will experience that life energy pervades all.

With the tidings of prana, life energy, that it is all-pervading, one knows all things and all beings to be equal.

As soon as someone enters within and comes to know his own being, he will also come to know that it is the same light present in all. The other seems to be separate only as long as you have not known yourself. As long as you have not recognized yourself, you believe others to be your enemies. The moment you have seen your own being, you will also see the same lamp lit in the inner shrine in everyone. You will know the vision of equality. Then there will be no friend or enemy, no 'mine' or 'yours'. Then it is you who permeates all. Then there is only the *one* present everywhere.

The Shiva Sutra calls this *prana samachar,* tidings of life energy; now you know that the same prana, the same life energy, is everywhere—the same light in every lamp, the same ocean in every drop. Some lamps may be black, some may be white, some may be made of red clay and some of yellow clay, some may have this shape and others that face; some may have this name and form and others that name or form, but the inner flame has no form and no name. A person who has known his self has also come to know his self to be in all.

The first thing that happens in the fourth state is that you come to know your own self. Simultaneously, a second thing happens: you come to know the universal self. You become aware of your being, and the universal being is revealed.

So don't try to seek the ultimate truth directly. If you do, it will be nothing but your own imagination. You can imagine that Krishna is playing on his flute, but in this way you will not experience the universal being. You are simply having a dream, a pleasant dream, but there is no difference between this dream and any other dream because your own mind is creating it. You can imagine that you are having a vision of Mahavira or Buddha or Rama. Many people are doing this: they just sit and dream. These may be religious dreams, but they are dreams just the same.

There is no way to seek the universal being directly, because you are the door to it. Until you pass through your own door, the door to it will remain closed. Your being is the door to the universal being. Here the door opens, here you know your own being, and the universal being

stands revealed. Then you will begin to see it everywhere—
it is present in the trees and in the rocks. Somewhere it is
asleep, somewhere it is awake, somewhere it is dreaming,
somewhere in deep sleep and, somewhere else, profoundly
awake—but it is the same universal being.

Shiva has called this experience of the one, 'the tidings
of prana'. This is the greatest of tidings, but it can only be
known by someone who has known their own being.

And when a person is settled in the vision of equality, he
becomes equal to Shiva.

One becomes equal to Shiva.

Then he himself has become the universal being. You are
an 'I' only because you don't know yourself. This seems to
be very contradictory. You go on saying 'I . . . I . . . I' only
as long as you don't know who you are. When you come to
know that, your 'I' will disappear and 'thou', 'you' will also
disappear. On that day, you will become equal to Shiva. On
that day, you are yourself the universal being. From that
day on, godliness will resonate in you each moment. Then
you will not be verbally repeating it, you will know it. Then
you will not have to understand it—it will be your very
existence, your very experience. Then all around you the air
will vibrate with only this music, the music of the 'one'. It is
like when the drop disappears into the ocean: all boundaries
dissolve and the drop becomes boundless. Then you have
become equal to Shiva.

Shiva's effort and the effort of all the buddhas is only
this—that you too become like them. The ultimate bliss
that they have known is also your treasure. You are still
a seed; they have flowered as trees, and these trees go
on saying only this: 'Don't remain seeds. You can also
become trees!'

You will never know peace until you become equal to Shiva; man cannot be satisfied with anything less. Man's being will not be fulfilled with less than this, his thirst will remain. No matter how much you try to quench it with the waters of this world, your thirst will not be quenched until you have drunk from the vessel of universal being. Then your thirst will be quenched forever. All desires, all ambitions, all hurry, all striving and struggling will end because you will have become that which is the ultimate. There is nothing beyond it.

Nurture turiya, the fourth, in all the three states like an oil, so that in your delight you enter into your own being, your own consciousness; so that you can hear the tidings of the life energy; so that you can know that the one is present in all; so that you can have the vision of equality; so that you become equal to Shiva.

Enough for today.

9

Hell Is Outside, Heaven Is Inside

> *Every utterance of such a one is japa, a recitation in prayerfulness.*
>
> *Enlightenment is his gift.*
>
> *He is the master of inner powers. He is the very source of knowing.*
>
> *Constant delight in his overflowing essential energy is his universe.*
>
> *Of his choosing he can merge into the void, or he can remain in this existence.*

PRAYER DOES NOT depend on what you say, but on what you are. Worship is not related to what you do, but to who you are. Religiousness is not related with your doing, but with your being. If there is love at your inner centre then there will be prayerfulness at your circumference. If there is a constant peace at your inner centre then there will be meditativeness at your circumference. If there is awareness at your inner centre every moment, then your life will be a shining purity.

The reverse is not possible: by bringing about a change at the circumference you cannot change your centre. But a change at the centre automatically brings about a change at your circumference, because the circumference is your shadow. By just changing your shadow you cannot change yourself, but if there is a change in yourself, the shadow will change on its own.

It is very important to know this, because the majority of people waste their lives just trying to change the periphery. They risk everything just changing their behaviour, although even if your outer behaviour changes, nothing really changes. No matter how much you change your behaviour, you will still remain you. If you were a thief you may become a saint, if you were amassing wealth, you may start giving it away in charity, but inside you will remain the same. The value of money will remain the same in your eyes: what it was when you stole it will be the same as when you give it away. When you were stealing you thought that money had tremendous value, and when you give it away you will still think that money has tremendous value.

Your money has not yet become worthless like dust, because who would want to give dust as charity? If money has really become rubbish in your eyes, then would you go on giving your rubbish away to others as charity? And if someone were to accept your money, would you think you have given something to him that he should be grateful for? Would you want him to thank you in return? If money has really become meaningless to you, it is you who should be grateful to the person who accepts your money. You will think yourself fortunate that someone has accepted your garbage and has not refused. But your so-called charitable people never think this way: even if they give you a single penny, they expect something in return.

A miserly businessman died, went straight to the gates of heaven and knocked. He was absolutely confident that the gates would open for him because he had given to charity. The gates opened and the sentry looked him over from head to toe, because in heaven no recognition is given to actions, a person is seen as he is. The sentry said, 'Perhaps you have knocked here by mistake. Knock at the door of hell which is right there in front of you.'

The businessman became annoyed and said, 'Haven't you received the information about me? Only yesterday I gave two pennies to an old beggar-woman, and the day before I gave one penny to a blind newspaper-boy.'

When he claimed to have given to charity, the guard had to check his ledger. He asked his associate to find the businessman's name. The three pennies were written under his name. The sentry became curious and asked, 'Have you done anything more than this?'

The businessman said, 'I don't recall anything else right now.'

Wouldn't he remember if he had done something more? He could remember three pennies, but couldn't remember if he had done any other act of charity. The ledger was looked into, but only those three pennies were written under his name. Only because of those three pennies he had knocked at the doors of heaven with arrogance.

The guard asked his associate, 'What should we do with this man?'

The colleague took three pennies out of his pocket and said, 'Give him back his three pennies and tell him to go to hell!'

Can the doors of heaven be opened by the power of money? Whether you hoard money or give it away in charity, in both cases its value for you doesn't change. Whether you live a worldly life or you escape from it, the importance of the 'world' remains the same in your eyes. Whether you turn your face towards something or away from it, your journey does not undergo any major change unless you are transformed at your very centre. The revolution is needed not in your outer behaviour but in your inner being. And the moment the inner changes, everything changes.

These sutras are for your inner transformation, so try to understand each sutra very carefully. If even a small particle of them finds its way inside you, it will be like a living spark. If there is even a little dry gunpowder within you, it is bound to catch fire. But if all your gunpowder is damp, then even if live embers fall on them they will be immediately extinguished.

Your problem is not that you don't have the opportunity to hear truth, but that you have become skilled at extinguishing it. All the gunpowder within you is wet, so even when a live ember falls on it, the gunpowder does not ignite and the ember itself is extinguished. How have you managed to dampen all your gunpowder? The more knowledgeable you are, the damper your gunpowder is. The more you think you know, the damper your gunpowder is.

It is because of your knowledge that you manage to even extinguish the spark of knowing. Your knowledge does not allow even a small spark of knowing to enter you: it stands right at the door and refuses entry at the door.

In all your knowledge, you are unconscious. And remember, it is difficult to find a drug more potent than the arrogance of knowledge, because nothing else gives you a more subtle ego. Even wealth does not give such a big ego, because wealth can be stolen: the government can change, the communists can take over—anything can happen. You can't be completely sure of wealth. But your knowledge can't be stolen; no one can take it away from you. Even if you are thrown into prison, your knowledge will be with you.

This is why even a rich man is not as arrogant as a pandit, a scholar. And it is this very arrogance that keeps the gunpowder inside you damp. Drop this arrogance and your gunpowder will dry out. Then even one tiny spark of truth will be enough to transform you, because not much fire is needed for that. If the gunpowder is ready, just one spark will ignite it. If it is ready, just one spark is enough, but if it is damp then even a big fire will not burn it.

These sutras are like sparks. Try to understand them, putting all your knowledge aside—because if you try to understand through your knowledge, you will never succeed.

The first sutra:

Every utterance of such a one is japa, a recitation in prayerfulness.

The person who has become 'equivalent to Shiva'—that was our last sutra yesterday—whatever such a person utters is . . . *japa, a recitation in prayerfulness*, a mantra. It is not a question of the words they say. Whatever they say is a recitation in prayerfulness, because now there is no 'world', no desires, no darkness in their hearts. Now their heart is a light, a flame, so whatever comes from such a heart is a recitation, a prayer. Only prayerfulness can come from such a heart. How can darkness come out of light? How can hatred come out of love? How can anger come out of compassion? Now whatever is said by such a person is japa.

There is a very well-known saying of Jesus: 'The kingdom of God is not reached by what you put into your mouth, but by what comes out of your mouth.' Nothing is decided by what you put inside yourself: only what comes out of you shows what you are. A person who has become like Shiva does not need to practise japa. There is no need for him to practise japa because whatsoever he says or does is japa.

Kabir has said, 'My sitting and standing have become acts of worship.'

Someone once said to Kabir, 'Nobody ever sees you doing any japa. When do you worship? When do you pray? People say you are a great devotee, but when do you perform the rituals of devotion and worship? We only see you busy working. You weave your cloth and you go to sell it in the market, but we have never seen you meditating, worshipping or going to the temple.'

Kabir said, 'Whatsoever I do is my worship. Whatsoever I speak is japa. My very existence is my meditation.'

What happens when *you* become interested in meditation? You devote a small part of your world of activities to meditation, whereas in reality, meditation is not an activity. You run your shop, you go to the market—you will have to, because your business, your routines of livelihood will have to continue on the periphery—and on that same periphery you also make a corner for meditation. You would like to go to the temple also for a few minutes before going to the market. Remember this difference well.

Whatever your activities are, add meditation to them. You are engaged in many activities and you add one more act: meditation. There are a thousand and one involvements in your 'world': add the search for ultimate reality as just one more involvement. Then you will never know the ultimate reality, because the ultimate reality simply cannot be an activity on the periphery. The ultimate reality has nothing to do with the dimensions of business, the market and the shop. The ultimate reality is the very core of your being, it is where *you* are. It is not in the world of your activities. Where all your activities have come to a stop and only you remain, where there is no doer, where only the witness remains—that is where the ultimate reality resides.

The ultimate reality is not just a part of you: it is the infinite, it is the all-pervading. Only if you are ready to be permeated by it totally will it permeate you. If you say, 'I will set aside a little time for you too,' then you are bound to go astray. Only when you give yourself totally to it will it permeate you.

This does not mean that you will not be able to do your work; rather, you will be able to do your work better, more efficiently. Then each of your tasks will resonate with the music of godliness. Then godliness will be within you . . . like your breathing. When you go to the market or when you are talking to somebody, you don't stop breathing. Breathing is not part of any action: you keep doing everything and your breathing continues inside you. In the same way, when godliness becomes a part of your very being, you will keep doing everything and the stream of godliness will keep constantly flowing inside you.

Godliness is not in any competition with your doing, with your action. Godliness is not a part of your mundane world. Your doing creates that world; your actions create that world. This is why we say that as long as a person is involved with action, he will remain attached to the world. When he is not the doer he is godliness itself. Non-doing is your very existence, where there is no question of doing, where you just are—a pure is-ness. Only if you connect from there . . .

Each utterance of the person who has become equivalent to Shiva is a recitation of prayerfulness. You will not find him praying, because now there is no need for him to pray separately. You will not find him worshipping, because, now, to him worship is no longer a part of doing. Now he himself *is* the worship. This is why if you look deeply into whatever he does, you will find worship there. Even when he breathes, it is worship; when he moves his hand, it is worship. Even when he just sits or when he stands, he is performing a sacred act.

All the actions of a person who has become equivalent to Shiva are meditative. And he does not have to practise it, because something that has to be practised can never be spontaneous. Sooner or later you will tire of what has to be practised. When you are tired, you will rest, and to rest means to go in the opposite direction.

Hence, if your goodness is practised, then after practising it for six days, on the seventh day you will have to rest. On that day you will move to the opposite. So your so-called saints are bound to have moments of un-saintliness in their lives, because they will get tired even of saintliness. They will have to take a holiday. No one can act continually because action causes tiredness. Hence, your saint also has to take a holiday, and if he doesn't, there is bound to be great tension.

So there are moments of un-saintliness in the lives of your saints, and moments of saintliness in the lives of your sinners. You will not be able to find a sinner who does not have moments of virtue in his life, because when he gets tired of sinning he takes a rest in the opposite direction. And you will not be able to find a saintly person who has no moments of sin in his life, because when he gets tired of his virtuous acts he will rest in sinning. You always have to go to the opposite so the mind can relax and become unburdened.

A saint is someone whose saintliness is not something practised, whose saintliness has become his spontaneous nature. Then there is no question of rest. You never need a rest from breathing. You never need a rest from existing. Whatever you do, it will be superficial until the state of Shiva-consciousness flowers in the very core of your being. It is as if you put on fine clothes, but underneath your body is dirty—how long can your fine clothes hide it? Or you may have sprayed perfume all over yourself, but a foul smell is emanating from inside—how will you hide that bad smell?

It is possible that you may succeed in hiding it from others, but how will you hide it from yourself?

This is why your so-called saints don't look happy, they don't look blissful. To others they look like saints, but to themselves they are aware of their un-saintliness all the time. No dance flows in their life. There is no change in their anger, they go on burning up inside. It will all remain hidden from you because you can only see the outer clothing, but someone who is hiding something from himself, how can he escape from it? He knows it is hidden there, and this very knowing goes on pricking him like a thorn. Until a saint is able to laugh and dance, know well that his saintliness is managed. Anything cultivated, managed, is false, only that which arises spontaneously is true. Hence, Kabir says again and again, '*Sadho, sahaj samadhi bhali*'—'Oh seeker, spontaneous enlightenment is best.'

Spontaneous enlightenment needs no managing. If it has to be managed, you will get tired of it. If not today, then tomorrow, it will become a burden. But when will it happen that enlightenment will be a natural, spontaneous phenomenon? Only when the Shiva-consciousness flows from your inner being, only when you become equivalent to Shiva.

And remember, this is not some ideal to be achieved some time in the future. If you can understand, then it can happen this very moment. Actions need time: if you have to *do* it, you will need time—but this is a leap, a realization, not a doing. You need not do it, you only need to *see* it. It is as if a man has a diamond in his pocket and, unaware of it, he goes on begging on the road. Then suddenly someone reminds him, 'You fool, why are you begging? There is something sparkling in your pocket! It looks like there is a diamond in your pocket,' and he puts his hand in his pocket and pulls out a diamond. It is just like this.

Shiva-consciousness is always there within you, it is your eternal treasure. There is no need for you to delay attaining it: you just have to see it by turning your eyes in. If it were somewhere in the future then it would be difficult, then it would take time to attain it—perhaps many lifetimes. But it is within you. This Shiva-consciousness is not something to be attained, it only has to be discovered, uncovered. It is like someone peeling an onion. What happens? You peel off one layer and another layer becomes visible. You go on uncovering layers, and a moment comes when there are no more layers and only emptiness remains. In the same way, you are also covered in many layers, and Shiva-consciousness is like ultimate emptiness.

Try to understand these layers so that it can become easy to peel them off, so that your life can also become Shiva-like and your every word can become a recitation of prayerfulness.

What is the first layer? The first layer is the body. Most people live their whole lives thinking themselves to be this first layer. It is as if they are living on the steps of a palace and making the steps their home. They don't realize that the steps are not the palace, they are only a means to lead into the palace. They eat, drink and live there; they marry and raise a family there, all on the outside porch. And their children don't even have an inkling of the existence of the palace, because they have been born on the steps. To them the steps are home and they will just go on living there. They never look back to see that these are just steps and they are only living on the porch and the palace is behind. They never knock on the palace doors. They have not knocked for so many lives that the door has almost become sealed up. Perhaps the door itself has started to look like a wall: now it is difficult to distinguish where the door is.

The first layer is the body, and you come to the end of your life living only in the body. There is an identification which makes you feel that you *are* the body. The body is yours, but it is not *you*, and what is yours can never be you. Whatever is yours can be possessed by you, but it is not you. If your foot is amputated, even then it is not you who is cut, it is just your foot. If you were your body, then if you were to lose your foot you would feel that now you are a little less. But if your foot is cut off or you lose your eyes or your ears or your hands, your wholeness will not be affected at all. The body can be crippled, but you remain whole.

Perhaps this is why even the ugliest man does not think himself ugly, because within each of us there is something which always remains beautiful. Perhaps this is why even the ugliest man doesn't agree that he is ugly, and even the worst sinner is not ready to accept that he is a sinner. Even the most evil person continues to have an inner echo of his goodness. If you watch even the most evil person carefully, you will find him saying, 'I have made a mistake, but I am not a bad person. It was only a mistake.' He says that his action was wrong, but he cannot accept that he is bad. This is true, but he doesn't know why he feels this way.

People around you—in your family, in your neighbourhood, in your town—die, but you are never overpowered by the feeling that you also will die. There must be some innate, deep-seated reason for it, because death is such a strong event that it is incredible that it doesn't make you aware of your own death. Even seeing the fact that everyone is dying does not affect you deep inside—that you too will die. Even if somebody tries to make you realize this, you think, 'Perhaps, yes,' but inside there is a voice that continues to say only others will die, you will not die. Otherwise, living would become difficult. Death happens all the time, everyone is standing in the queue awaiting death; you also are standing in that queue—yet you live without care, as if your life is eternal.

There is a deep reason for this. The reason is that there is something within you that can never die. No matter how much you become identified with the body, it still doesn't mean that you have become your body. This inner truth cannot be falsified no matter how much you try. No matter how identified you are, still the voice within you, the voice of truth, keeps on resonating.

One day I saw Mulla Nasruddin sitting outside his house. He was having a belly laugh, and he was so tremendously cheerful and ecstatic. I asked him, 'What has happened, Nasruddin? I have never seen you so happy before.'

He said, 'An amazing thing has happened, but you will not understand it unless I tell you the whole story.'

'Please tell me the story,' I said.

'We were twin brothers,' began Mulla. 'We looked so alike that it was difficult to tell who was who. And my whole life I was the one who suffered. He would throw a stone at someone in school, and I would be the one who was punished. He would steal something, and it was me who got caught. It was the same at home. He would create some trouble in the street, and the neighbours would catch me. And as if this were not enough, he ran away with the girl I was in love with.'

'Then what is there to be so happy about, Mulla?' I asked him.

'Seven days ago I got even with him,' said Nasruddin.

'How?' I asked.

'I died, and the people buried him!' exclaimed Nasruddin.

No one is as unconscious as this! However closely you might resemble somebody, still, such a mistake can't happen. Nasruddin was not dead, he was dead drunk.

You have also been drunk for many lives, but, still, you have never been so drunk that your awareness was totally lost. Your consciousness surfaces again and again. Somewhere deep within, you know that you will not die. All the facts suggest that death is inevitable, and yet you go on believing that you will not die.

You live as if you will be here forever, and most of your mistakes are only because of this. You build your house so solidly as if you have forever to live. Even in your mistakes, somewhere, there must be some glimpse of the reality behind them, otherwise they would have stopped. You build a house in such a way as if you believe you will live forever. You build strong walls, you make the foundation with rocks, and you are not aware that tomorrow you will die. Everyone else dies and you too will die: it is such simple, straightforward arithmetic. But there is something eternal within you; hence, the reflection of it is there in every situation in your life.

Your body belongs to you, but your body is not you. You are in your body but you are not only the body. The body is the first layer with which you have become identified. You have lived with it for a long time and an association has formed. It is as if you are twins, you were born together, so you become confused as to who is who.

You are unable to recognize your real face. And this mistake gets support, because the people who look at you from the outside see only your body, not you. They consider your physical face to be your real face, your physical form to be your real form. And they are many, and you are alone. They all believe that your body is you, and this collective belief influences you. If your body is ugly, they say you are ugly; if your body is beautiful, they say you are beautiful; if the body is old, they say you are old; if the body is young, they say you are young. Their numbers are great, and you are alone. Their collective opinion deepens your belief that you are the body because not a single one of them sees your being.

There is a very old story in the Upanishads about King Janak who once called a meeting of all the wise men of the country. Invitations were sent to all those who were considered well versed in spiritual knowledge. He wanted some essential things to be revealed about the ultimate truth. Arrangements were made to reward with much wealth and property the person who could reveal the essential truth. The invitations were sent only to those who were famous, naturally, to those who had thousands of disciples, who were well known, who had written scriptures and were known for their scholarliness and who were experts in the art of debating.

There was one man who did not receive an invitation; perhaps he was deliberately left out. His name was Ashtavakra. His body was crooked, crippled in eight different places. You would be repulsed just looking at him. How could someone with such a distorted body be a self-realized one? However, his father had received an invitation.

For some reason, Ashtavakra had to go to Janak's court to call his father. When he entered the court, a great number of pandits who had gathered there started laughing when they saw him. He was certainly a funny sight: his body was certainly ugly, crooked at eight different places. His walk, his speech, everything about him evoked laughter. He was more of a cartoon than a man. He could have been a clown in a circus. Seeing everyone laughing at him, at his camel-like gait, he also had a belly laugh and his belly laughter silenced them all.

They were all amazed—why was he laughing? At last Janak asked him, 'I can understand why these people are laughing, Ashtavakra, but what made you laugh?'

Ashtavakra said, 'I laughed because you have taken this gathering of cobblers to be a gathering of the wise ones. They are all skin-dealers and shoemakers. They can see only the body, only the skin. I, who am the most straight of all, appear to them to be crooked in eight places. And they are all deformed, they are not straight! Janak, if you are expecting the wisdom of self-realization from them, then you are trying to squeeze oil out of sand. If you want self-realization, come to me.'

Ashtavakra was absolutely right. But this happens because the outer eye can see only the outside. You are also troubled by outer eyes, because all around you there are eyes and eyes, and they all see only your body—if the body is beautiful then you are beautiful; if the body is ugly then you are ugly. And their voices are so loud and their beliefs so strong because they are in the majority and you are a minority—alone, single. It is not surprising that you are defeated by them. It is not surprising if you also start believing that you are the body. What actually is surprising is when you manage to escape from those eyes and recognize that you are not the body.

This is what being free from society means. Freedom from society does not mean escaping to the Himalayas. Freedom from society means to be liberated from what the eyes of the crowd around you say to you. It is very difficult, because when everyone repeats the same thing, this constant repetition makes even an untruth start looking like a truth. However healthy you may be, if the whole village decides to repeat that you are ill, and whenever you pass by someone tells you that you are ill, soon you *will* become ill. It becomes a powerful mantra, a suggestion. When so many people are saying something, it will be very difficult to survive without being affected by it.

The whole world says that you are the body. Not only human beings, but even stones and rocks, the earth and sky, all say that you are the body. When a thorn pierces you, it pierces the body, not the being. If someone hurls a stone at you, the blood will flow from the body not from the being. Pebbles, stones, thorns, the earth, the sky—all are saying that you are the body. It is very difficult to overcome such a powerful repetition.

And you are alone! Against all, you are alone, because only you are inside yourself and the rest of the world is outside of you. Besides, they are not wrong in what they are saying because they only see your body, the outer layer. Your neighbours only see the fence around your house, not the rooms inside—they might think that this fence is your house. What they think is right from their side, but when you also start believing this, there the delusion starts.

To be free from society is to be freed from the influence of external eyes. A person who becomes free from the eyes of the society will begin to see clearly that he is within the body, but he is not the body.

Start breaking the first layer. Slowly, slowly intensify this remembrance that you are not the body. Experience it! Just repetition won't do. When a thorn pierces you, remember that it has pierced the foot—the pain is in the foot and you are only a watcher. A thorn cannot pierce you, the pain cannot reach you: you are the light that knows. This is why when you become unconscious you don't notice the piercing of a thorn. If a doctor has to perform surgery, then he gives you anaesthesia to make you unconscious. Then he can cut your feet, your hands, he may cut your whole body. He can cut your body into pieces and you will not be aware of it. If you were the body, you would be bound to become aware of it—but you are not the body, you are consciousness. The surgeon has only severed the connection between the body and the consciousness. He has made you unconscious: now anything can be done to your body and you will not know about it.

Those who have carried out intensive research on life and death have experienced—and I endorse their experience—that for three or four days after you have died you are not sure that you have died. Normally, it takes three days for you to realize that you are dead. The reason is that death happens in unconsciousness when the outer physical body drops, but you have an inner body exactly like the form of the outer body, the mental body, and that remains with you. It takes at least three days, sometimes longer, for you to realize that you are dead. Until then you wander around your house, around your friends, around your family.

The soul wanders around for three days. It is perplexed: 'What has happened? No one seems to see me or to recognize me.' You are standing at the door and your wife passes by, crying, and you don't understand what has happened: 'What is the matter?' You are as you have always been, complete; nothing has become less in you. Nothing has been lost with the loss of the body. It is just as if you have removed your clothes: if you remove your clothes, you will stand naked, but what has changed? You will remain the same. This is a subtler body that stays with you, it has the same shape and the same perceptions. It takes time. When you die, you don't immediately know that you are dead.

There are processes in Tibet called bardo. Buddhist monks help the dying person pass through the bardo process. When the person is dying, they give him suggestions: 'Look! Now you are leaving your body. Now be full of awareness that the body is falling away, that you are leaving your body. Soon this body will fall away. Remember yourself, die with awareness that the body that is with you now is not your physical body, it is the subtle body. Now you have left the physical body. Now you have choices about what kind of womb you want to enter.' These suggestions are given to a dying person in the bardo process.

No other culture has done such extensive research into death as Tibet. A person is dying and the monk continues giving these suggestions. Until the last moment, as the body is dropping away, the person is listening to the monk. Now the person is dead and the monk goes on speaking. You will wonder whom he is talking to. 'Stop now,' you will say, because for you the man is dead. But the monk will continue to speak, because for the monk the man is not yet dead, he is still listening. It does not make any difference that the physical body has fallen away—*he* is still listening. And his next life can be influenced as to what kind of womb he should enter. He can then be freed from the attachments and infatuations of this life.

In these moments, the person can be made completely aware of the fact that he is not the physical body, which is very difficult to be aware of at any other time. Now he can see clearly that the body is lying there, separate, and he still is. And the monk will say, 'Look, now you are above and the body is lying below. Look carefully! This is the body you had identified yourself with. And now your dear ones, your friends, will take this body to the burning ground. Follow them! See your body burning there! It will burn to ashes there, yet it will make no difference at all to your is-ness. Remember this on your journey ahead and don't become identified and obsessed with the body again. From the very first moment of your next birth, remember that you are not the body. Everyone will tell you that you are the body, but don't lose your remembrance; don't let your remembrance be covered by their suggestions.'

If you could throw off others' suggestions, your self-realization is not far away.

Picasso was a great painter. No one else in this century can be compared to him, but there was no shortage of people giving him free advice. The truth is that only a fool gives unsolicited advice. To get the advice of a wise man you have to work hard—you have to ask for it, earn it. Only a fool gives free advice. And it is good that people don't follow each other's advice, otherwise they would be in great trouble. Free advice is the thing most given in the world and the least taken.

People would go to Picasso, people who didn't even know the ABC of painting, and say, 'If only you had used this colour a little more. If only you had made this painting that way. You should have done the background in a different colour!'

Picasso was tired of talking to these foolish people. So what did he do? You should do the same—he made a beautiful box and printed the words 'suggestion box' on it, and he wrote on it: 'Kindly put all your suggestions in this box.'

So far so good—but the box had no bottom and he kept a wastebasket under it! People were thrilled that their suggestions had so much value. They would put their suggestions into the box and the suggestions would go straight into the trash. He would never even read them. You should do the same.

If you want to be free from society—and that is what sannyas means—then free yourself from other people's suggestions. They are outside of you, and their suggestions will also be of the outside. This can only be a hindrance on the path of inner realization. Don't listen to them. If you want to hear the voice of godliness within you then save yourself from society. If you want to hear your inner voice, then shut out all the outer voices. Otherwise the outer voices are so loud and so sharp that your still, small, soft inner-voice will be lost in the din and you will not be able to hear it. Each moment this inner voice is reverberating, but you are standing in the marketplace where there is too much noise.

The first layer is the body. And there is only one key—it can be called the master key because it opens all the locks, and all locks are alike. The key is: become aware of the body. When you walk, be aware that the body is walking, not you. When you are hungry, watch that the body is hungry, not you. When you become thirsty, watch that the body is thirsty, not you. Let this awareness always be with you. Slowly, slowly you will find that this awareness has started creating a gap between you and the body. As this awareness deepens, the gap between you and the body will become greater and greater. There is an infinite gap between you and the body, an infinite distance.

As your awareness deepens, the bridge between you and your body will break, the connection will break. One day you will be able to see with great depth that the body is just a shell. *You* are life, the body is death; *you* are consciousness, the body is matter. The body is a play of atoms, a collection of atoms—there today; tomorrow it will not be. It is ever-changing. You are not a collection of anything, you are indivisible consciousness: you always were and always will be.

As soon as the first layer, the body, is peeled off, like the first layer of an onion, the second layer will appear. This second layer is your mind. This ailment is more deeply rooted, because the body is far away, but the mind is closer. The body is a collection of atoms and the mind is a collection of thoughts. If the body is matter then the mind is subtle matter. Thoughts are subtle sounds, and sound is matter. Thoughts are closer to you; you are so much in their grip. They are not only like clothes. If the body is like your clothing, then thoughts are like your skin. Your thoughts are as close as your skin, closer than clothes. It is all the more difficult to be free of them because you have always been under the illusion that thoughts are really yours.

You often argue and quarrel saying, 'This is my thought.' Whether right or wrong, you always try to uphold your thoughts, you try to prove them, because you are always afraid that if your thinking is wrong then *you* are wrong. Your identification with your thoughts is much stronger than your identification with your body.

If you are told to go to a doctor because your body is ill, you won't be offended; but if you are told that your mind is sick and you need a psychiatrist, you will immediately be offended. There is no problem if you call somebody ill, but if you call somebody mad you invite trouble. This is because there is some distance between you and your body, but your identification with the mind is very deep-rooted. If someone says, 'You are crazy,' you are offended. 'I am mad? What are you saying?' No madman is ready to accept that he is mad. 'You must be mad,' he will say. The reason is that your thoughts have enveloped you from all sides like smoke, and as long as these thoughts persist your vision will remain blind.

So the second, more difficult, experiment—and it is an arduous inner discipline—is to become aware of your thoughts, all your thoughts. It doesn't matter what kind of thoughts—good, bad, right or wrong; whether they come from the scriptures; whether they are traditional or non-traditional—just know that 'I am not these thoughts.' Thoughts are also borrowed. *All* thoughts are borrowed: they also are given to you by society; they too have come from others. You have learned them.

In reality, you are the untaught that is within you. You are only consciousness, not the thoughts. Thoughts are like waves over you. Just as rubbish floats on the surface of a river, so are thoughts. But you are the river, the stream of consciousness.

Slowly, slowly you also have to peel off the layer of thoughts. Whenever a thought catches hold of you, remember, you are not it. It is only the outer dust. Just as dust gathers on a mirror, thoughts have gathered on you.

Never make any thought so much your own that you are ready to fight over it. If people were to break their identification with their thoughts, there would be no more wars in the world. All wars, all conflicts, all violence is caused by identification with thoughts. Someone is a Hindu, someone is a Jaina, someone else is a Mohammedan; someone is a communist, another is a socialist, someone is something else—all of them have become identified with their thoughts. You are only godliness—you are neither Hindu nor Jaina nor Buddhist nor Mohammedan. Your pure being, your pure is-ness is Shiva-consciousness.

But you get entangled in what is worthless: you think that it is more important to be a Hindu or a Mohammedan than to be godly. Your being a Hindu or a Mohammedan only results in fights between the temples and the mosques, hence this earth becomes more and more deprived of religiousness rather than being filled with it. All religions cause fights because all religions turn into thoughts. There is one and only one religion, and that is your Shiva-consciousness. You are godliness, divine, and this is the only true religion. It can never cause any fights, because how can there be fights when there are no thoughts? How can there be prejudice? How can there be opposition?

The body has separated you from others, but thoughts do that even more deeply. Understand one thing, although it may appear to be contradictory, whatever disconnects you from yourself also disconnects you from others. The body has separated you from yourself, it has also estranged you from others. Thoughts have disconnected you from yourself even more deeply, and just as much from others. On the day you throw off the layers of both the body and thoughts and are rooted in your own intrinsic nature—where only pure life remains without any wall—on that day you will find you have become one with all, because there are not two godlinesses. Then godliness outside of you and the godliness within you have merged into one. Then the inner sky of the vessel and the outer sky have become one. The walls of the vessel have fallen away. It is identification with the walls that creates the vessel.

As you go on removing the layers . . . And 'layer' means identification with something you are not. Identification is taking yourself to be what you are not. To break the identification with what you are not is meditation. Meditation is the key. By and by, only what you really are remains. All the layers of the onion have been removed; and only nothingness is in your hands. This nothingness, this void, is your godliness, your Shiva-consciousness.

Have you noticed that the image of Shiva we have created is almost spherical, the shape of zero? We have intentionally made it this way. Shiva does not have any face. No statue is as beautiful as one of Shiva, because it has no face—it is just a form of the void. As you go deeper and deeper and deeper into yourself, you will find this same form of the void is beginning to arise within you: you are moving closer and closer to Shiva. When you are just a luminous void, a light that is formless and nameless, from then on, whatever you speak is japa, sacred recitation in prayerfulness.

As you are now, whatever you speak is a deception. Right now, even your religious actions are irreligious. You can't do otherwise. You try to save yourself from one mistake and you commit a thousand others. Right now, the best thing would be to do nothing: just break your identification, just be aware, and do nothing. Otherwise, in trying to save yourself from making one mistake, you make another one.

Mulla Nasruddin was sitting at the seashore. Just nearby, a man was sitting, looking very upset. Finally, when he couldn't restrain himself any more, he said to Mulla, 'Excuse me, but is that your son who is throwing sand on my clothes?' By now the man was very angry.

'No, brother,' said the Mulla with a kindly smile. 'That's my nephew. The one who just broke your umbrella and is now busy filling your shoes with water is my son.'

You try to take care here and something else goes wrong there. The reasons you give to justify your mistakes turn out to be bigger mistakes. In ancient times emperors always kept a great fool in their courts to remind them of the fact that man's intelligence is not much of an intelligence.

One day, a king who kept a jester at his court was standing before a mirror when the jester suddenly came from behind him and gave him a sound kick on his back. The king fell forward on to the mirror and was badly bruised and bled when the mirror fell and broke.

The king said, 'This is the limit! I have come across many fools before you, but I have never seen a fool like you. Why did you do that? If you can't give an even more foolish explanation for the stupid thing you did, I will have you hanged!'

The fool said, 'Your majesty, I thought it was the queen standing there.' That was the reason he gave! 'I didn't realize it was you standing there, I thought it was the queen.' The king had to let him go because the excuse he gave was even more idiotic.

Where you are, you are standing in darkness. You make one mistake and whatever reason you find to explain it away results in another mistake. In this way you create a vicious circle of mistakes. To avoid going to your business you go to the temple, but you never get to the temple because the temple becomes your business—a bigger business! You try to save yourself here, but you get caught somewhere else, because the cause is not outside you, it is inside you. You are in darkness, so wherever you go there will be trouble.

Once Mulla Nasruddin was arrested and put in jail. I went to see him. We have an old relationship, so it was necessary to go to see him.

I said to him, 'You are so clever, Nasruddin, how come you got caught?'

'What can I say?' said the Mulla. 'I was caught stealing, but all because of my own mistake.'

'And what was that?' I asked.

He said, 'For three months I worked hard at befriending the dog in the rich man's house that I planned to rob, but as luck would have it, as soon as I got inside I stepped on the cat's tail.'

You spend your whole life like this—getting friendly with the dog and then stepping on the cat. You have no eyes to see. You go on groping around in darkness from here to there. The real question is not that you seek; the real question is whether there is light. By groping in darkness you will never arrive. If there were light, then you would see the door right now and you would walk through it.

A person who goes on trying to change his behaviour is groping in the dark. Before he used to eat too much and now he is fasting, but he is still groping for the same thing—he is still stuck with food. Fasting is just another way of eating; it is still related to food. It makes no difference. At the most, he will start doing just the opposite of what he was doing yesterday. He looked in one direction and didn't find it there, so he started looking in the opposite direction. But if your eyes are closed here, they will be closed there too. You are not lost because your direction is wrong, you are lost because your eyes are closed.

Open your eyes! And when I say 'eyes' I mean your awareness. Your unconsciousness has to break and your awareness has to grow. Don't walk around like a somnambulist—wake up! The moment you wake up you will be the same consciousness as Shiva.

> *Every utterance of such a one is japa, a recitation in prayerfulness.*
> *Enlightenment is his gift.*

He does not give away money, because money is rubbish; and giving money has no meaning either. What is the point in giving something he himself has let go of? There is no sense in sharing something he has found to be worthless. He does not serve your body. He can give you only one thing, which in fact is the only thing worth giving, and that is enlightenment. This is his gift.

Just look at it! You don't keep an account of such things, but if you ask the Jainas, they have kept a full account of exactly how many horses and elephants and chariots, how many precious stones and jewels Mahavira gave to charity. And they have greatly exaggerated the number! He didn't even have that much because he was the king of one small state; it was not a big empire, not larger than a district. There couldn't have been as many elephants and horses as the Jainas have mentioned. By their account he appears to be the emperor of a great kingdom, which is absolutely wrong. His position was not more than that of the king of Sikkim. In Mahavira's time there were about two thousand kingdoms in India, so Mahavira would have been roughly at the level of a deputy collector—the chief administrator of a district today.

Now why do they exaggerate the figures? Because the Jainas think that if his renunciation is small then how would it be possible to make him a great tirthankara? So inflate the figures—hundreds of thousands of horses and elephants, diamonds and jewels worth billions—so that you can see the extent of his renunciation. These blind people don't know that Mahavira has nothing to do with that kind of charity or renunciation. The real diamond that Mahavira shared is enlightenment. But that has never been mentioned at all.

You can only see through the lens of your desires. You see only what interests you. 'Enlightenment'—this word doesn't sound so valuable to you. If I have a world-famous diamond in one hand and enlightenment in the other, ask yourself, in all honesty, which one would you choose? You would say to yourself, 'I can seek enlightenment any time. What's the rush? What's the hurry? There are so many lifetimes available for that, but a great diamond . . . Who knows if it will come my way again or not?' You will invariably choose the diamond because your interest is in things that are of no use. You are blind!

One who has become as Shiva has only one gift to share and that is enlightenment. He shares what he has found. He offers the taste of what he has tasted to you also. He shares his very self. He doesn't distribute wealth, he gives of himself. He makes you a participant in his inner wealth. External wealth has no longer any value to him.

It makes no big difference whether you die a prince or a pauper, whether you die on a comfortable bed having eaten good food or if you die hungry on the road—the only thing that makes a difference is that you live in total awareness and that you die in total awareness. Everything else depends on this. Your whole life's outcome will depend on it; it is this that will decide the essence of your existence. Everything else has no meaning at all.

> *Enlightenment is his gift.*
> *He is the master of inner powers. He is the very source*
> *of knowing.*

Enlightenment itself will make you the master of inner powers. Enlightenment itself will fill your life with light, wisdom and radiance. And on the day you are able to know, are able to wake up, you will find that you have always been an emperor. You will laugh at how you believed yourself to be a beggar! You will wonder at how you had remained buried in a nightmare.

Many times you have seen nightmares. That's how your whole life is. Sometimes it happens that while you are asleep your hand may come to rest on your chest and then you will dream that someone is sitting on your chest. There is nothing there, just your hand resting there, but you will only become aware of this when you wake up. In sleep you may feel that someone is sitting on your chest or that someone has placed a rock on your chest or that someone is throwing you down from a mountain: you are scared, you are soaked in perspiration, completely frightened. In that panic, you will wake up. Then you will be astonished, amazed that it is only your hand on your chest, not a rock. How exaggerated things can become in a dream. What an exaggeration a dream is, where your own hands can become mountains and rocks. If your hand hangs down from the bed, you feel as if you are falling into an abyss.

Try a few experiments. You can induce dreams in another person who is asleep. Place a small flame close to someone's feet, and soon he will dream that he is walking in a desert, almost dying of heat and thirst, sweating profusely. Or if you touch his feet with a little ice, he will dream that he has reached Everest, that his feet are frozen and he is dying of cold. Or just put a pillow on his chest—he might dream the devil is sitting on him! Try putting his hand around his neck and he might dream that he is being hanged. He will only know the reality when he wakes up. Dreams are great exaggerations. He is bound to laugh when he wakes up and sees how much he was suffering, and for no reason at all. There was nothing there! A slight hint and the mind swings into action, the imagination runs wild.

You never actually suffer as much as you imagine you suffer. You never suffer the illnesses that you keep suspecting or the miseries that you are constantly afraid of. 90 per cent of the suffering in your life is psychological, the imagination of your mind. Only 10 per cent is real, but 90 per cent is total imagination—and because of this 90 per cent you cannot solve the 10 per cent. If that 90 per cent is eliminated and the false suffering is removed, then whatever real misery there is in life has a solution. It is possible to get rid of it. There is a way to step out of it. You are always bigger than your sufferings; you can use them as stepping stones. But you magnify them so much that the suffering becomes so large and you so small: then you tremble and think that you can't do anything.

The moment the ray of inner knowing awakens and the lamp within is lit, you become the master of all your energies. And that is the seed of enlightenment. Enlightenment is the ultimate happening. Enlightenment is the inner eye, the ability to see, the ability to see through and through. Then there is no misery in life, there is only bliss. Misery is because

of your blindness. Your dreams have become nightmares
because of your own sleep. Consciousness knows no misery;
consciousness knows only bliss.

> *Constant delight in his overflowing essential energy is his*
> *universe.*

The person who attains enlightenment is in a constant
loving dance of his own energies. He is in constant bliss. The
overflow of his own energy gives rise to endless pleasure.
This bliss is arising in him each moment. This bliss flows
through him like a constantly flowing stream.

Infinite springs of bliss are flowing in you every moment,
but you remain oblivious to them. And remember, religion
is not renunciation, religion is ultimate rejoicing. God is not
sitting somewhere weeping, the divine is dancing. Don't
seek a weeping God, because you will never find it. And if
you do find such a God, it will be one of you acting as God.

The divine is always dancing. This whole life is a
celebration of bliss. Life has not known any misery at
all. Misery is your imagination, you have created it. It is
something that you have thought up, it is produced by you.
But a blind man cannot do any better—wherever he goes he
will bump into things. He may even think that the whole
world is ready to bump into him—but why would anyone be
interested in bumping into him? Does a wall or a door have
some interest in bumping into you? But wherever a blind man
goes, he hits either a wall or a door, and thinks that the whole
world is out to hit him. No one bumps into people who have
eyes. Certainly, there is no one sitting there ready to collide
with you: it is you who are blind and bump into everybody
and everything. You put the blame on others, but, in reality,
you, yourself, are to blame. You throw the responsibility on
others, but except for you, no one else has any responsibility.

This statement is worth understanding: *Constant delight in his overflowing essential energy is his universe.* When this state of knowing is attained, then in every moment there is only bliss. Only flowers blossom there, there are no thorns there. Only the elixir of life showers there, there is no death there. Not even a ray of misery can enter there.

There is a kingdom of supreme bliss inside you. It is what you are searching for, but you are searching on the outside. Your search is right, but your direction is wrong. The awakened one gives you the direction, and that is his gift. He takes you in the direction he has taken, where he found the ultimate. The awakened one does not try to make you understand, because there is no way to explain it. He simply takes you by the hand and leads you towards it.

But you are so afraid that you are afraid to even hold someone's hand. You can't surrender, you can't trust, you can't have faith in someone. Your fear has made you so insecure that you can't even trust someone who offers to lead you out of your misery. You think he may lead you into some new problems. You have been getting into so many problems that now you can only see problems everywhere.

If you are not ready to hold the hand of the awakened one, then there is no way he can give you the gift. You will have to extend your hand and accept his gift. If you are standing with your fists clenched, not ready to accept the gift, even the awakened one will move away from your door without giving you anything.

Constant delight in his overflowing essential energy is his universe. A constant loving dance of consciousness is going on there, and you are in constant misery.

Of his choosing he can merge into the void, or he can remain in this existence.

It is very difficult to understand this because it can only be understood through experience. It can't be understood without experience. Still, if you have some introduction to it, some day it will be helpful.

As soon as a person comes to know himself, he is filled with a unique power. It is the greatest power; there is no bigger miracle than this. The miracle is that whenever he wishes he can be, and whenever he wishes he can choose not to be. He can be in existence when he chooses, and he can merge into the ultimate void when he chooses. Just as you sleep and wake up—except even that is not of your own free will. In the morning, when you have woken up from your sleep, then what will you do? You can't go back to sleep again. When you find yourself falling asleep at night, you can't stay awake. But just as you sleep and wake up, an awakened one can disappear into the void or remain in existence of his free will. This is his freedom. He is not bound by anything. If he decides he wants to disappear into the ultimate void, he does so. If he decides he wants to remain in this existence, he remains in existence.

There is a story in the life of Buddha that when he reached heaven the guard opened the gate, but Buddha turned his back to the gates of heaven. He said, 'I will wait at the gate until each and every person is liberated. Only the day the last person enters the supreme bliss of heaven, will I follow behind him.'

This story is tremendously beautiful. It means that in this world there are two types of awakened ones. All the religions have understood there to be these two kinds. One type, after becoming enlightened, becomes one with the void. The other type becomes enlightened, but still remains in existence to help others. The Jainas have called the first

type of enlightened one *kewali*, one who has known the
ultimate aloneness. There have been numerous kewalis: they
have reached their ultimate destination and disappeared
into the void. They enter heaven, they don't wait at the gate.
The Jainas have called twenty-four of the enlightened ones
tirthankaras. A tirthankara is a kewali who waits at the gate
to pave the way for others.

Buddhists have also recognized these two types of
awakened ones. One they call *arhata* and the others are
called bodhisattva. An arhata attains enlightenment and
merges into the void, and the bodhisattva is the one who
waits for others. All religions have recognized two types of
enlightened ones because there *are* two types.

When you reach the ultimate state, then either a desire
to help others will remain in your heart, in your being—this
must also be called a desire—or even this desire will not
be there and then you will disappear into the void. This is
why great masters try to create tirthankaras or bodhisattvas
from disciples who have more the quality of compassion.

There are two qualities that remain at the end:
compassion and wisdom. Wisdom means knowing, and
compassion means kindness. There are only two types
of people among you: those who have more compassion
within and those who have more of wisdom. Those who
have more wisdom will disappear into the void; they cannot
become masters. They will remain disciples only, and when
they become enlightened they will disappear. They will
never become masters. The ones who have more of the
quality of compassion in their being can become masters—
tirthankaras and bodhisattvas.

So it will depend on the master, how he prepares his
disciples. He will prepare those in whom he sees more of
the quality of love, compassion and service in such a way
that the desire of compassion stays with them till the very

end. This desire of compassion and love will still be there when their enlightenment happens. When their ship is ready to sail, one anchor will still hold the line—the anchor of compassion. But if there is no compassion in them, only a clear, dry wisdom, then there is no need to keep the anchor. The moment their ship is ready to sail, they will set out on their journey and disappear into the great void.

A person who has attained Shiva-consciousness will either merge into the void or stay in this existence, according to his own free will. Either he can remain in existence to serve, or he can disappear into the void. It is his choice. And remember, only such a person has free will; *you* don't have any free will. You are not present in your being, so how can your actions be from your own choice? You may say, 'I am doing this out of my own free will,' but it is not true. Whatever you do is caused by the pressure of some desire.

What free will do you have? Free will is when somebody insults you, abuses you, and you don't get angry. It is possible that you may not show your anger, but the moment someone insults you, anger arises in you. You possess free will if you are as calm inside when someone insults you, as if no insult has been made. It is also free will when someone praises you, and you are as calm and unaffected by the praise as if no praise has been made. You are as you were before, it has not made the slightest difference. Only then can you say that you are your own master. For the possessor of such mastery, the final decision happens in his last moment.

On the basis of this, Buddhism was divided into two major sects, Hinayana and Mahayana. 'Hinayana' means 'the small vessel'—the small boat that can carry only one person, not more than that. This is the boat of the arhata. The arhata enters his boat and sails away. 'Mahayana' means 'the great vessel'—the great boat, the boat of the bodhisattva. Even after the bodhisattva has entered his boat, he waits so that others can also get into his boat before he sails off.

It is not possible to say who is right and who is wrong, the arhata or the bodhisattva. At this stage it is impossible to judge; it is whatever suits a person's intrinsic nature. Those who have a feminine quality in their hearts will become bodhisattvas, and those who have a masculine quality in their hearts will become arhatas.

There are these two types of hearts, and in the ultimate moment also these two types of hearts will be decisive. You either have the masculine heart of dry wisdom or the feminine heart of overflowing compassion; you are either full of love or full of wisdom; either a sage or a devotee. This world is made of these two opposites. All things of the world are part of duality: darkness and light, female and male, birth and death. In the same way, there is compassion and there is wisdom.

In the final moment also, both will be there on the shore—whichever is stronger will be the deciding factor. Then it will be a choice of his own free will, because a liberated person has no attachments, he has free will. Free will is born for the very first time. For the first time the capacity to decide is born. It is only an awakened person who can use free will to decide. You are carried away by your desires, but he will be someone who can decide. This is the only decisiveness; before this there is no capacity to decide. Before this you simply get carried away, you are not the decider.

Someone once asked Gurdjieff, 'Please tell me what I should do.'

Gurdjieff's answer was, 'If only you *could* do something, I would surely tell you! Right now, you can't do anything. Right now you are just moving blindly. Right now, you are like a straw drifting on the waves that goes wherever the waves take it. Right now, you aren't there.'

Someone once told Buddha that he wanted to serve people. Buddha looked at him very closely and said to him compassionately, 'You don't yet exist, so how will you serve?'

Choice comes into your own hands only at the last moment. Only after enlightenment do you have the capacity to decide things, because then you have become equal to Shiva. Then you are no longer the creation, you have become the creator. Then you are no longer a part of this universe, you are the universal self itself. Now the whole play is in your hands and you are in control. Now is when the time comes for the final decision: either you would like to wait for others to enter your boat and you will become a bodhisattva, or you will simply not be bothered. The very idea will not arise in you because you will think that each one finds his own path, each one arrives by his own path. Who can guide anybody? And you will just set your sails and leave.

Of his choosing he can merge into the void, or he can remain in this existence. It will be good to remember this sutra, because just by listening to it the idea will begin to arise in you too: 'What will I do if given the opportunity to choose?' This thought will invariably arise in you. And that is useful, because in the final moment this same seed of a thought will sprout and become the tree.

Enough for today.

10

Om: A Taste of Bliss

*Happiness and unhappiness are peripheral events—this is
his constant awareness.*

*Freed from these, he becomes rooted in the ultimate
aloneness.*

*The yogin who is rooted in such aloneness and whose
desiring has ceased goes beyond birth and death.*

*Having dropped all layers, this bhutakanchuki, this
liberated one, is Shiva—the image of ultimate consciousness.*

Om

May this be an offering to blessed Shiva.

BEFORE WE ENTER into the sutras, earlier I had told you that
I would say something about mantras. It would be good to
understand a few things about mantras. If you know how
to use them properly, it can bring about a revolution in
your life.

The first thing is, as I said yesterday, your personality is
made up of layers upon layers, like an onion. You have to
peel off each layer so that you can reach the centre hidden
deep within. The diamond is hidden, you have not lost it.
You can't lose it because you, yourself, are that diamond.
You may be covered under deep layers; a diamond also gets

covered under layers of dirt. It may look like a stone, but nothing inside is destroyed.

Perhaps you don't know why diamonds are so valuable: behind its value lies man's search for the eternal. The diamond is the most enduring object in the world. Everything changes, but a diamond remains as it is, without any change. Even after tens of millions of years it does not deteriorate. In this ever-changing world, the diamond is the symbol of an unchanging existence. This is why the diamond has so much value; otherwise it is just a stone. Its value lies in its imperishability, its endurability.

To be a diamond is your eternal nature. All your sadhana, your spiritual discipline, consists in removing the layers of dirt that have settled on you. Since the layers are made of dirt, it isn't difficult to remove them. Because the layers on your diamond are of dirt, because they cover the eternal and consist of the transient, it will not be a very difficult task. Mantras are a method for removing these layers.

Let me tell you about a small incident. Mulla Nasruddin met a friend he had not seen for many years. His friend first asked Mulla about his family and then he asked, 'What about your daughter, Nasruddin?'

Mulla said, 'Believe it or not, my daughter is married, and not just to an ordinary man, but to a famous doctor.'

The friend couldn't believe a word of it. He said, 'Forgive me, Mulla, but I find that difficult to believe. Don't be offended, but you also know that your daughter was, well, not beautiful. In fact she was definitely ugly, really ugly. She had a body like an army tent! It is hard enough to believe that she got married at all—and to a doctor, a famous doctor! It is a very mysterious happening. How did she hoodwink a doctor?'

'All right, all right!' exclaimed the Mulla. 'So maybe he is not such a big doctor . . . maybe he's not a doctor at all. But one thing I must tell you: he has relieved me of my headache, so for me he is a doctor.'

The person who takes away your headache is a doctor; and what removes your very head is mantra. If there is no bamboo, there will be no flute. As long as there is a head there will be headaches. And there is a technique to remove the head. All your troubles are caused by your head—your thoughts, your debating, your worrying. If there is no thought then there is no mind. Then *you* will be, but the mind will no longer be!

What kills the mind is mantra. What causes the death of the mind is mantra. And when the mind is not there, the bridge between you and the body is broken. It is the mind that is connecting you to the body. If the bridge, the connecting link, breaks then the body is separate and you are separate. And a person who has known himself to be separate from the body and without the mind, attains Shiva-consciousness. He becomes someone who is rooted in ultimate aloneness.

So try to understand what mantras are. The definition of a mantra is: something that destroys the 'head' so that the mind is no longer there. It is a method for cutting through the layers of the body and the mind. It is essential to go step by step. And you have to be very patient, because mantra is a method that demands immense patience. Impatient people will not benefit from mantra; it might even be harmful. It is good to understand this first: as it is, you have enough problems, and mantra will just be an added problem for you if you are impatient.

I was once at a train station where a man was selling toys, shouting himself hoarse, 'No child can possibly break this toy, it is unbreakable!' So I thought to buy it for Nasruddin's son because his wife was always complaining that her nasty child breaks his toys as soon as they arrive. I bought the toy. It was costly and it also looked very durable. I gave it to Nasruddin's wife for the child. Both he and his wife were happy that the child would not be able to break it, and even they would not be able to break it. The toy was really strong.

A week later I went to visit them again. No sooner had I entered than the Mulla's wife said, 'We are in great trouble.'

'What happened,' I asked. 'Has your son broken the new toy also?'

'No,' she answered, 'he has not been able to break that toy. But with it he has broken all his other toys, every mirror in the house, and now we have to do something for our own self-protection because he's using the toy as a weapon!'

As it is, you are already in a state of insanity. Mantra can either destroy the insanity or it can even increase it. You are already burdened, and mantra may just bring an additional burden. This is why a strange thing happens: the people you call religious often look more troubled than a normal worldly person. It is because a worldly person carries only worldly troubles; this religious person has the same worldly troubles, but he has added another burden to them—his religious trouble. It is not a plus. It doesn't reduce the troubles, it increases them. His mind continues all its old activities, and added to this is the new activity, which makes the mind even busier.

With mantras, immense patience is needed. Otherwise it is better you don't bother yourself with it. It is just like medicine that has to be taken in doses: you wouldn't drink the whole bottle in one go to instantly cure your sickness. You could die like that and the sickness will not disappear. You will have to take it in doses. The doses of mantra are

very homeopathic, very subtle. Great patience is needed—
that is the first requirement.

Don't expect quick results. The results of mantra
happen very slowly, because it is the ultimate result. It is
not a seasonal flower that you plant and within two weeks
the flowers are there; it can take lifetimes. Another difficult
thing to understand is that the more patient you are, the
sooner the results, and the more impatient you are, the
longer will be the delay.

A man was walking along a road swearing at his shoes,
which were hurting him because they were too tight. He
was very upset. Nasruddin happened to pass by and asked,
'Where did you buy such a tight pair of shoes?' The man
was already in a bad mood, already angry.

He said, 'Where did I buy them? I plucked them off a
tree!'

Nasruddin said, 'Well, my friend, if you had waited a
little, then they would have grown to the right size. You
picked an unripe shoe!'

Don't ever pluck an unripe mantra or you will be in a mess.
It is easy to throw away a pair of shoes, but it is really
difficult to get rid of a mantra, because the shoes are on the
outside, but the mantra is a process inside you. If you get
involved in the world of mantra by mistake, it becomes very
difficult to get out of it. Many so-called religious people go
mad, and the reason is that they got caught up in a mantra,
and they were in such a hurry that they tried to pluck the
fruit before it was ripe. A ripe fruit has become very sweet;
an unripe fruit will be very bitter, very acrid—poisonous.

The first layer is the body. So it is necessary to start the
first experiment of mantra at the body level, because that
is where you are, in the body. The cure has to begin from

there. If you try to skip this layer your illness will not go away, and soon you will have an unripe fruit in your hands. Remember, you can only start the journey from where you are. If you start from somewhere else, you are just dreaming. Right now you are only a body, so the mantra will have to start at the body level.

Now understand the technique: first, sit silently for ten minutes. But before that—because it is not easy to sit silently—dance, jump, skip, sway and shake for five minutes. Do this totally, wholeheartedly, so that the restlessness in every pore, in every part of your body, is released. Only then will you be able to sit in silence for ten minutes. This catharsis is necessary before you can sit in silence. It will need from five to ten minutes, depending on the extent of your restlessness. Let your body dance, jump or shake— move your body in every possible way so that for the next ten minutes the body will have no need to move. Satisfy its craving for activity. Move your body for ten minutes—sway, dance, jump or run—and then sit down. Now sit absolutely still. The body should not move for ten minutes. Keep your eyes half-closed.

It would be better not to do this experiment in the open. Do it indoors, in a small, closed room, preferably totally empty. There should be nothing inside the room. Hence, a church or a temple or a mosque is a very good place, where there is nothing, no furniture or anything else. Or clear a corner of your house so that there is nothing left. Don't even keep any pictures of gods or goddesses there, because they are also a hindrance. Make it totally empty. Emptiness is the only godliness there is; everything else is only your mind game.

And the mind is so crazy! If you look at the little corners that people set up in their houses to use as a prayer room, you will see their madness. You will find pictures of hundreds of gods and goddesses cut from old calendars hanging on the walls. Wherever they can find a picture of a god or goddess in an old newspaper or magazine or any trash, they stick it up on the wall. The walls are covered with them! And then they bow down to each one of them in a hurried way and sprinkle some holy water, or they do whatever other empty gestures of worship have to be observed. And thinking the gods are now satisfied, off they go! But, truly, not one god has ever been satisfied. If you could truly satisfy even one, most probably they would all be satisfied. But in your effort to satisfy them all, not even one is satisfied. Win one and you have won them all—and that *one* is within you, not outside of you.

So keep the room completely empty. The emptier it is, the better, because it is the same emptiness that you are seeking within. Let the room be a symbol of your inner emptiness. And the room should be small; this will help the mantra. It should also be empty; this will help too. Let your eyes be half-open, because when they are completely open it is as if you are standing at the door of your house with your back to the house and your face towards the world. You can't suddenly make a complete about-face. A sudden change is not easy, so keep the eyes half-open. Let them be half-closed to the world and half-opened towards yourself. This is the meaning of half-opened eyes—that you are looking half at the world and half at your inner being. Begin from here. And there is no need to hurry.

When the eyes are half-opened, you will experience a state of drowsiness. Keep looking at the tip of your nose and keep your eyes open only to that extent. You are not to concentrate, you are just to look at the tip of your nose peacefully.

Then begin to chant om loudly. You are starting from the body because that is where you are right now. So make the om loud enough so that the sound starts bouncing off the walls and falling back on you. This is why an empty room is essential. That resonance is only possible in an empty room, and the greater the echo, the better it is. If you have been in Christian cathedrals, you will find that they were designed for mantras. Whatever is said there reverberates and echoes a thousandfold from all sides and falls back on you. The Hindu temple also is constructed with a rounded ceiling just for the purpose of allowing sound to bounce back after hitting the dome. The dome serves the same purpose because sound bounces back after it hits the dome. No sound escapes from inside a circular place, it goes back towards the centre. These architectural designs were made for mantra chanting.

So sit down and repeat om as loud as possible, because you have to use the body. Let your whole body be bathed in the sound of om. You should feel that you have put all your life energy into chanting om, that you have not held anything back. Do it as if your life and death depend on it. No mantra can ripen with anything less than this. If you repeat it softly, half-heartedly, like a half-dead person, then nothing is going to happen. Totally! As if your life depends on it, as if only when you chant om totally will you live, or else you will die. Risk your all, as if om has become like a lion's roar!

With your eyes half-closed and half-open, repeat om loudly. It is just like when a person throws a stone into a silent lake: ripples spread in all directions. When you chant om, you have thrown a stone into that silent emptiness of the room and the vibrations will spread all around. The sound will strike against the walls and then come back to you.

And you should repeat om so quickly that an overlapping happens, that the second om overlaps with the first one—om . . . om . . . om . . . Leave no space between two oms.

Use all your strength until you are wet with perspiration. In a few days you will find that the whole room is charged with om and that the whole room is supporting you. All the sound will be returning back to you. If you can find a circular room, it will be better. If you can find one with a dome, it will be even better. The room should be absolutely empty so that the sound rains back on you from all sides. Your whole body will be bathed in those vibrations, and you will find a freshness, a coolness that you have never experienced after bathing in water.

Scientists are carrying out extensive research on vibrations. They have discovered that trees grow faster and bear flowers and fruit earlier and more abundantly if they are exposed to music of a particular vibration. Both in Russia and in America, music is being used in fields to promote richer and earlier harvests. The results of these experiments have been quite successful.

Ravi Shankar played his sitar in an experiment in Canada. He played the sitar and some seeds were sown on one side, and more seeds of different plants were sown on the other side, at different distances. The result was surprising: when the seeds sprouted, all the sprouts were leaning towards the place where Ravi Shankar had been playing. The plants grew, and they grew twice as quickly! Just as a deaf person leans forward and brings his ear closer to hear better, all the plants had leaned towards where the sitar had been playing. The growth that would have taken three months took just one-and-a-half months, and the plants looked very happy. A plant is only body, in which everything is still asleep, deeply asleep. But the body also vibrates when there is sound and is affected by it.

When *omkar*, the sound of om, begins to shower on you from all sides and its vibrations start falling back on you—when a circle of sound is formed—you will feel every pore of your body filled with bliss. You will feel all your sickness is being shaken off from every pore of your body, and a peace, a profound sense of well-being, is deepening in you. You will be amazed to discover that many sicknesses of your body have disappeared on their own because of this profound bathing which penetrates very deep within you.

The body is nothing but a manifestation of sounds. And there is no other sound more profound than om. Chant om loudly for ten minutes through the medium of the body. Then close your eyes and your lips and let the tip of your tongue touch the roof of your closed mouth. Close your mouth as if you are closing it for good, leaving no space for anything, because, now, neither the tongue nor the lips are to be used.

The next step is to repeat om inwardly for ten minutes. Up till now the room was surrounding you on all sides, now it is the body that is all around you. Until now you were in a room, now your body is the room. For the next ten minutes, hum the mantra within you. You are not to use your lips or your tongue or your throat at all. Only inside, om . . . om . . . Inside you let the mind repeat om . . . om . . . but keep the same speed and the same intensity. Just as you had filled the room with om, now you fill the body with om from within, so that the vibrations happen from within the body. Let om resonate from your head to your toes.

Repeat om as fast as you can. Allow no gap between two oms, because it is a rule of the mind that it cannot think two thoughts simultaneously; to think two thoughts at the same time is impossible. If your repetition is so fast and intense that there is no gap between two oms, then no other thought will be able to come in. If you allow the slightest gap, other thoughts will creep in and create their own space in that gap. Don't leave any gap—chant without any gaps! Don't even be bothered that one om is overlapping the next om. Let your oms pile up on top of one another like wagons of a goods train in an accident; don't leave any gap between them.

And remember, you are not to use your body any more. This is why the eyes are closed now and the body is still. The chanting is to be done only in the mind. The echoes will bounce back from the walls of the body and fall on the mind in the same way that they had been bouncing back from the walls of the room and falling on the body. With those sounds the body was purified, and with these internal sounds the mind will be cleansed. And as the vibrations begin to deepen, you will find that the mind is beginning to fade. You will begin to have the taste of a deep silence that you have never known before.

Hum within for ten minutes. After ten minutes, drop your head so that your chin touches your chest. For a few days you might feel a strain in your neck, but don't pay any attention to it and, soon, it will go away. So in the third step, let your chin fall down and touch your chest, as if your neck has been cut off, as if it has no life. Now don't repeat om even in your mind: now just try to hear it, as if the om is already resounding within you and you are only its listener, not the doer. You can step completely outside your mind only when the doer is no more. Now you become the witness; now with your neck dropped to your chest, simply listen to the om resonating within.

There is a famous verse by Ghalib:

In the mirror of my heart is the picture of my beloved,
Whenever I bow my head even slightly, I see it.

This bowing down of the head is necessary. The moment you bow your head, the mirror of the heart comes in front of you, and the image, the reflection of your most beloved, is there. But you don't know how to bow your head, you walk around with a stiff neck. When it is a question of bowing your head, you become even stiffer. If you have failed to experience godliness up to now, the only reason is that you are not ready to bow your head, you are not ready to surrender. Dropping the head is only symbolic: let your head hang down as if it is severed from your body, so that you will be able to bow down. And the moment you bow your head, it becomes easier to see inside; as soon as you bow your head, thinking becomes difficult.

Try to listen: until now you have been chanting the mantra; now, try to become a witness to the mantra. You will be amazed to discover that there is a very subtle chanting of the mantra happening inside. It is something like om, but it is not exactly om, because it is difficult to reduce it to any language. It is almost like om. If you listen very silently, you will now be able to hear it.

Now you have become separate from the body. Chanting the mantra out loud was the first step, and this made you separate from the body. The second step, chanting the mantra inside, has separated you from your mind. Now, the third step of the mantra is to become a witness to it.

This is why there is no mantra more unique than om, more amazing than om. Rama, Krishna, Mahavira and Buddha are all beautiful, but they can't take you beyond the mind because they have an image, a form. Om is formless. You have certain affection for Buddha, for Krishna and for Jesus; you have a feeling, a love, an attachment, a fondness for them. This will not allow you to go beyond your mind.

Om is completely without any meaning. Om is really unique: it has no meaning, no form, no image, not even an outline. It is not even part of the alphabet. And it is closest to the sound that continuously resonates within you and is the very nature of your existence. It is like the babble of a brook: a brook doesn't have to babble because babbling is intrinsic to its flow, or the rustling sound of the breeze passing through the trees—the breeze doesn't have to create the rustling sound, it is intrinsic to its passing through the trees. In the same way, your existence is such that om resounds within you. Om is the sound of your being.

This is why no religion has any claim over om. It doesn't belong to the Hindus or the Jainas or the Buddhists or the Christians or the Muslims. Om is a non-sectarian mantra; all other mantras are sectarian. You will be surprised to know that the Jainas, the Buddhists, the Christians and the Muslims all use om, just with slight variations. The Muslims say *aamin*, the Christians say amen—these are just altered forms of om. On the course of its journey from India to distant lands, this mutation took place because om is not connected with any thought process. Whoever has submerged themselves in the state of no-thought has always heard it.

So in the first two steps you chant the mantra and in the third step you will just listen to it. You will become a shravaka, a listener; you will become a witness. In the first two steps you are the doer because the body and mind are parts of doing. The third step is witnessing. In the third step you listen, you just listen. The body is transcended, the mind is transcended, and only you are left there. Layers of the onion are peeled off, now only pure is-ness remains. And that is the state of Shiva-consciousness.

Once you have a taste of it, you will want to experience it more and more. That taste itself will start pulling you, it will become a magnet. We are drawn towards things that appeal to us, we naturally move towards them. The difficulty arises only where you haven't yet had a taste. You try to meditate, but you are unable to get into it because you haven't yet had a taste of it. Once you have had the first taste then there will be no difficulty, then the mind will go there again and again on its own. When you have a little time, as soon as you close your eyes you will feel it: 'In the mirror of my heart is the image of my beloved . . .'

Then in the marketplace, at your shop, wherever you have a little free time, give it a try: 'Whenever I bow my head even slightly, I see it.'

It is only the first step that is difficult. It is just a question of having your first taste. When you have taken the first step, half the work is done. Once you have had a taste, then like a bee with nectar, the mind goes back there again and again. It is the very nature of mind to go again and again to the place where there is nectar. It is only because you have not had the first taste of that nectar yet that you have to find ways to persuade the mind towards meditation.

You ask the mind to meditate, to remember your godliness, and the mind says, 'Let's go to the market! Why are you wasting time just sitting here? In this time you could have earned something! And you can do all this later when you have the time. What's the hurry for it? Now is the time for the shop or the office.' The mind only takes you to the place that it has found juicy, the mind is not to blame in this whole business. Once you have a taste of the inner world, you will find that it becomes more and more difficult to come out. Right now it is difficult for you to go in, and then it becomes difficult to come out.

Sariputta, Buddha's disciple, attained the ultimate state of mantra when he heard the sound of om within. The day this happened, Buddha said to him, 'Now go out and teach people.'

Sariputta said, 'But now I don't feel any desire to go anywhere.'

Buddha replied, 'That is exactly why I want you to go. First, you were held by the outer; that was one form of bondage. Now don't get held by the inner, because that too is bondage. Just as before there was difficulty to go in, now there is difficulty to go out.'

The perfect enlightened one has no difficulty either way: he can go in or out like a soft breeze. For him there is no problem to go in and no problem to go out. Now the in is no longer in, and the out is no longer out—they have both become one. Just as easily as you go in and out of your house, in the same way your inner world is your house, you should have no difficulty going in and out of it.

So there are people who are attached to the world and there are people who are attached to the spiritual world—but both are attached and both are in bondage. The ultimate freedom has not yet happened to them. The enlightened person is one who has no attachments to the inside or the outside, who has a natural flow.

So this is the process of the mantra. Try to maintain the third stage of the mantra as long as possible. The first step is to sit silently. The prelude to this silent sitting is to shake your body up by dancing and jumping around for about ten minutes to throw all the body's restlessness out. The body is always full of tension. When I say this, I am simply stating a scientific fact—the body is always filled with restlessness.

For instance, you want to slap a person, so your whole body energy immediately rushes to your hand—and this is why when even a very weak person slaps, the slap is really hard. You could not have imagined that this person could slap so hard, but now his hand is no longer an ordinary hand, because all his energy has moved into it. But life is complex, and there could be a thousand and one reasons why you can't slap the person. Perhaps you have some vested interest you need to fulfil through that person, so you stop yourself from slapping him—but there is no way for the energy to go back.

This is the latest scientific research—absolutely the latest—that there are paths for energy to move out from the body, but there is no path to pull that energy back once it has moved out. If you did not use it to hit or slap somebody or something, the energy that had moved to the hand will remain there. It doesn't matter who you slap—even if you hit an empty space, the energy will be released. There are no channels to draw that energy back to the centre, it will remain stuck in the hand.

In this way, during a twenty-four-hour period, you block lots of your energy in various parts of your body. Then when you sit for meditation, that blocked energy is bound to create problems. This is why you complain of aching in your feet, or a feeling of ants crawling over you, or something seems to be happening in your back, or suddenly you feel an itch in your neck. All this is not your imagination. You are not imagining it, it is really happening. But normally you never sit still, you are always busy doing something, your energy is occupied. Now that you are sitting and not doing anything, there will be restlessness in the areas where your energy is blocked.

Observe a small child. If you ask him to sit quietly, he may sit down with his eyes closed, but just see how difficult it is for him to sit still. He will press his hands together or massage his feet or cover his mouth or blink his eyes, because everywhere there is a flow of energy in him. His legs want to run, his hands want to move, his eyes want to see, his ears want to listen—these are all old habits. This is the way his energy has always moved.

This is why I always emphasize that catharsis is needed before any meditation. Catharsis will be very helpful for you in this meditation too. You just run, jump and skip around for ten minutes to release the blocked energy, and then sit down. Just as there is a peace that comes after a storm, in the same way the body becomes light when its restlessness is released. But this is only a prelude, it is not an actual stage of this meditation. It is the steps to the doorway outside the house.

The real journey starts inside the house: ten minutes of chanting the sound om through the body, ten minutes of chanting the sound om through the mind, and then ten minutes of listening to the sound om that is already happening in existence. Then you only have to listen to it, not make it.

This is why I say that to chant the names of Rama, Krishna or Buddha will not be so deep, because these will only take you up to the second step, they will not take you to the third step. The sound that is resonating in the third step is om. But sometimes by chanting Rama . . . Rama . . . Rama . . . a person also reaches the third stage. It is like when you are travelling in a train and you hear the wheels going *chucka . . . chucka*, you can imagine that sound being anything you like. If you want to hear Allah . . . Allah in it, then by and by you will not hear *chucka . . . chucka*, you will hear Allah . . . Allah, or Rama . . . Rama if that is what you want to hear. In reality, it is *chucka . . . chucka . . . chucka . . .*

Om is the pure sound, but if you insist on clinging to Rama, Rama, you will begin to hear Rama, Rama there, although it is just a projection. And projection is an indication that the mind is still alive to some extent.

If we want to experience only what is, if we want to know only that which is and don't want to impose our minds on it and colour it, then the ultimate mantra is om. All other mantras are inferior. They can take you as far as the second step, but they will become a hindrance in the third step.

So there is no need for other mantras: just use om in the way I have described. Don't worry at all about results for at least three months. Don't even think about results, simply keep doing it. Don't think about whether something is happening or not, whether anything has happened yet or not. Don't think about it for three months. Fix a date beyond three months, that on such and such a date you will look back and see if anything has happened or not. Until then, don't even think about any results.

If you can have this much courage and patience . . . This patience is not like when a child sows a mango seed and half an hour later digs it up to see whether it has begun to sprout, then puts it back, disappointed, that nothing has happened yet, then again digs it up an hour later. This seed will never sprout, because to sprout it must lie buried in darkness in the earth for a certain period of time.

Your meditation also fails to bear fruit, because again and again you dig the seed up to check whether anything has happened or not. Before it has reached the depth of your heart, you dig it up to take a look. Jesus has said, 'Let not your left hand know what your right hand is doing.' Bury the mantra deep inside you; don't dig it up again and again because it is a seed. This is the reason a mantra is referred to as *beej*, a seed. To call it a seed means that you don't keep digging it up over and over again to take a look; it has its own time. It will sprout in its own good time, not with your impatience. Your impatience may bring about a completely opposite result—perhaps it may never sprout.

Take this ultimate mantra away with you from this meditation camp and experiment with it. If you do it with patience for three months, you will be filled with a sweet nectar, what Kabir has called '*gunge keri sarkara*'—'the taste of sweetness to a voiceless person'—because he cannot describe it. Once the sweetness has been tasted, then there is no problem. Then wherever you are it is perfectly fine, whatever you do is perfectly fine. Then for you, the world becomes like a dream; life is no more than a play, and you become a witness. And this state of witnessing itself is Shiva-consciousness.

Now let us go into the sutras.

> *Happiness and unhappiness are peripheral events—this is*
> *his constant awareness.*

A person who has become a witness knows that happiness and unhappiness are all on the periphery. Happiness happens outside of you and so does unhappiness; they cannot penetrate your inner being. But you are disturbed by both: you cling to happiness; you become identified with it and then you think *you* are happy—but now sorrow is not far away because you have created the possibility of sorrow. This is the starting point of suffering.

The moment you say, 'I am happy,' you have sown the seeds of unhappiness. Now it will not be long before suffering arrives, because suffering is nothing but identification with your emotions. Later on, when the suffering comes, you will become identified with that too. Your problem is that you become identified with whatever comes before you. Whatever you see, you no longer remain a watcher of it, you become an identified participant in it. When sorrow comes, you beat your chest and cry; when happiness comes, you dance and jump with joy. Happiness and unhappiness come from the outside and they have no way of entering inside you—it is you who identifies yourself with them on your own and suffer. The moment you go beyond the mind, you begin to see that all this happens outside the temple, nothing enters within.

Happiness and unhappiness are peripheral events—this is his constant awareness. Here, the word 'constant' is significant. You know about the occasional—and when it is a question of advising others, then you *certainly* know it. If only you could be as wise for yourself as you are for others. If only you would have the same understanding about your own life's journey as you have when you give advice to others.

What could be the reason you are so wise with others? If someone is suffering, you will say, 'Why upset yourself? This is life! This is the way the world is. Don't get so involved with it, keep a little distance.' But when you find yourself suffering in the same way, it is very possible that this same person will give you the same advice. He will say to you 'Brother, don't worry. Happiness and unhappiness are only outer attitudes.'

Why is this so? What is the reason behind it? It is simply that when others suffer, you are a witness, so it is easy for you to understand. The suffering has happened to someone else, not to you; you are just a watcher. When you become a similar watcher to your own suffering, then you will have the same understanding towards yourself too. Until now, you have only given your understanding to others.

Mulla Nasruddin went to a psychiatrist and said, 'My wife's condition is very serious. You will have to do something now.'

The psychiatrist studied her for a few weeks and then told the Mulla, 'She has completely lost her mind. There is no brain left in her.'

'I knew it would happen!' exclaimed the Mulla. 'Every day she used to give me a piece of her mind, and eventually everything has to come to an end. Every day, little by little, she kept on giving me a piece of her mind until now she has no more left.'

You are giving your understanding to others, but you are not able to use it for yourself. Now the next time happiness comes into your life, observe it as if it were happening to someone else. Try to stand a little apart from it and observe it. A little distance is needed. Even a little distance is enough. Just don't stand so close to yourself—be your own neighbour and don't stand so close.

Once I said to Nasruddin, 'Mulla, the owner of the restaurant at the end of the street says that he is a close relative of yours, very close.'

'He certainly isn't! He's wrong,' replied the Mulla. 'There is a relationship, but very distant.'

I asked, 'What is the relationship?'

Nasruddin said, 'We are twelve sons with the same father. He is the first child and I am the twelfth. There is a big distance!'

You are your neighbour, and that is enough distance. Don't stand too close, keep a little distance. Without distance, the perspective is lost. To be able to see anything you need some distance from it. If you hold a flower right against your eyes, can you see it? If you press your face right up against a mirror you will not be able to see anything at all. A little distance is needed, a little distance from yourself.

This is what spiritual discipline is all about; creating a little distance from yourself. As this distance grows, you will be surprised to see how meaningless all your troubles were. Things that had never happened to you, which were actually happening outside of you and were merely reflected in you, whose mere shadows formed inside you, whose mere echoes reached you only because of your closeness to them . . . and you suffered because you thought that echo belongs to you.

A house was on fire and the owner was beating his chest and crying. A man standing next to him said, 'You are unnecessarily tormenting yourself, because I know that only yesterday your son sold this house.'

The man could not believe his ears! And today his son had gone to another village. He stopped crying, even though the house was still burning. In fact, it flared up even more and everything was in flames. But the man looked on unconcerned: being at a distance; he was no longer the owner of the house.

Just then his son came running, 'Oh my God, what has happened? How did the house catch fire? I had made the deal on the house, but the payment is still to come. Now who will pay for this ruined house?' Again the father began to wail and beat his chest.

The house was still where it was, nothing had changed about the reality of its situation, but it could never have imagined that now happiness has happened, now sadness has happened over it. And it can all change again: if the buyer comes and says, 'It doesn't matter. Although the house is ruined, being a man of my word, I will pay for it since I had agreed to buy it,' then everything will change again for the man.

Everything is happening outside of you, but you stand so close to it and that is what creates the problem. Create some distance! When happiness comes, stand a little apart and watch. When unhappiness comes, stand a little apart and watch—but start with happiness. Remember, don't start with unhappiness. People try to dissociate themselves from unhappiness to escape from it. Then you will not succeed because that is a difficult way. Try to create a distance when there is happiness. Everyone wants to escape from unhappiness because it is the natural tendency of the mind. It is best not to begin by trying to be detached from suffering, because that is what you have always done and nothing has come out of it. You have to begin from just the opposite.

The way you have travelled up to now has only taken you astray. You will have to go back and retrace your steps. Mahavira has called this turning back *pratyakramana*, and Patanjali has used the word *pratyahar*, returning to the source. You will have to turn back a few steps.

Retrace a few of your steps so when happiness comes, you take a little distance and watch. Don't let your heart beat faster, don't dance with joy—just know that this has come, and this too will pass. It is not going to last because nothing in this world lasts. It is like a gust of wind that comes and goes and you are hardly aware of it before it is gone. Just stand at a distance and watch.

What can happen? What is the fear? Why don't you look at happiness and be a witness to it? There is a deep reason behind it: as soon as you look at happiness as a witness, it can no longer remain happiness. It was happiness only because of your closeness to it. The more you forget yourself, the more intense your happiness is; the more you remember yourself, the less anything at all remains. This is why no one wants to be a witness to their happiness—but the journey can begin only from there.

When happiness comes, witness it. As you witness it, soon you will find that happiness will fade and only *you* will remain. And if you can succeed with happiness, you will also be able to succeed with unhappiness. Then the key is in your hands. When sorrow comes, you will be able to witness it from a distance. And you can stand apart, because you and your body are separate. No two things can have more distance than you and your body.

What can be more distant from each other than matter and consciousness? Even the stars and the moon are not as distant from each other as you are from your own body. One is material and the other is consciousness; one is made of elements and is perishable, and the other is made of consciousness and is imperishable, immortal. The distance is enormous; there cannot be two more opposite extremes.

So begin with happiness and then work towards unhappiness, remembering only one thing: that you are outside. You will have to practise this as a discipline—that happiness and unhappiness are both events outside of you. Again and again you will forget it, it cannot be constant. This remembrance can only be constant when you are centred in your being, when the mantra has succeeded and the mind has disappeared. Until then, practise it as a discipline for as long as you can. This practice clears the way.

The seed may not yet be sown, but at least the ground will be cleared. Then when it is time to sow the seed, you will find a ready soil for it. Your remembrance will disappear again and again, it cannot be constant. And when you lose awareness even slightly, happiness will again overwhelm you, unhappiness will again catch hold of you.

Happiness and unhappiness are peripheral events— this is his constant awareness. Happiness and sorrow are peripheral events, and the meditator who has touched his own being knows this constantly. 'Constantly' means without a moment's interruption. Only something which is your very nature can be constant. Something which is not your nature cannot be constant. For how long do you think you can remain in a state of anger?

When Bodhidharma went to China, the emperor went to visit him. He said, 'I have much anger in me. What should I do?'

Bodhidharma asked, 'When you are angry, how long can you be in it?'

The emperor said, 'How long? What sort of a question is that? Maybe half an hour, an hour at the most.'

Bodhidharma said, 'What can be done for only half an hour or an hour is not your nature. Can you be angry for twenty-four hours a day? Can you do it constantly?'

The emperor said, 'I am troubled enough already by doing it for half an hour or an hour! And I haven't come here to ask you how I can be constantly angry!'

Bodhidharma said, 'I am saying this to make it clear to you that only what you can do constantly is your nature. Why are you offended?'

What can you do constantly? Think about it a little. You can't even be happy constantly. You may find this difficult to understand, but I say to you that you can't be constantly happy. Think a little: for how long are you able to remain happy? Whatever happens, after a while, happiness begins to fade and eventually you start feeling unhappy. And if nothing happens to disturb your happiness, you start becoming bored with happiness: a palace to live in, good food to eat, a wife—you have everything, no troubles, no problems—then what will you do? How long will you remain happy? After a while you will be fed up, you will want a change of taste.

It often happens that even a man with a beautiful wife has an affair with an ordinary girl, the housemaid. Others are amazed about this, because others are only witnesses to what is happening: 'Such a beautiful wife! A rare beauty! And leaving her for an ugly maid! What has gone wrong with this man?' He only wants a change of taste. He is bored.

Even beauty makes you feel bored. For how long can you keep looking even at a beautiful woman? In a short while you will start to feel bored. Even the most melodious of songs, how many times can you hear it? Your head will start spinning. You will say, 'Now stop it!' And if the song continues to be played, it will become sheer hell.

The mind can't tolerate anything constantly; it can't even bear happiness for too long. This is why whenever you feel happy, the mind immediately looks for ways to create unhappiness. It wants a change in taste, then again you are ready to be happy. You can't even sit in silence for a little while: soon, your mind will start creating restlessness because the silence will also become boring.

Bertrand Russell has written that he would not like to go to moksha, the ultimate realm of the liberated ones, because he has heard that the people there are sitting on their enlightenment thrones for eternity. There is nothing to do there because doing is part of the world. What would Mahavira be doing? Just sitting on his throne! Just sitting for so long . . . and there is no end to how long he will have to sit there. And there is no work. There are no newspapers to waste away the day there with. No news ever happens there because news only happens in the wrong sorts of places. In hell there must be lots of news. There must be more things happening there than here in this world! Perhaps they publish ten or twelve editions of newspapers a day because something or the other keeps on happening there: killings, arson, looting, all kinds of violence continue. Nothing is ever happening in heaven, everyone is sitting on their enlightenment thrones.

Bertrand Russell says that his mind dreads so much to think of heaven that he feels hell would be preferable. His mind is right, but what Bertrand Russell doesn't know is that as long as the mind exists you cannot enter the realm of ultimate liberation. It is the mind that asks for change and it is left behind; only the no-mind enters there. Liberation exists only for those who have become constant.

Is there anything that you can live all the time with, constantly? You can tolerate neither suffering nor happiness constantly, because they both cause excitement and tension. You can only be peaceful constantly, because it is not a state of excitement; it is a state exactly between the two, and beyond the two.

Once I was a guest at Mulla Nasruddin's house, and his son was eating with us at the table. At first he started eating the meal with his left hand, but after a while he switched over to his right hand. I was a little surprised. Then I saw that he again started to eat with his left hand. Nasruddin said, 'Son, how many times have I told you to eat only with your right hand?'

The boy said, 'What difference does it make which hand I use? Either way, my mouth is exactly in the middle. The trip to my mouth is the same either way, because my mouth is right in the middle.'

Look for a point exactly between happiness and unhappiness; only that can be constant. The balance is right in the middle. This extreme or that extreme are not there. Just like the arrow of a scale is balanced right in the middle, you can only be in balance like that. Any slight weight on either side and you will soon be tired, and you will have to put more weight on the other side to balance it.

When people carry a dead body to the crematorium, they get tired and change shoulders. One shoulder starts hurting so they carry the body on the other shoulder. The weight doesn't become less, but changing shoulders brings relief. Happiness and unhappiness are your two shoulders, and the belief that you are the doer is the corpse that you are carrying, that you keep changing shoulders under— sometimes you identify with happiness and sometimes you identify with unhappiness. Be a witness, stay in the middle. Only then will you be able to remain constant.

Enlightenment can be constant because it is a state of peace. There is bliss there, but that bliss is not like the intense rays of the sun, it is like the peaceful rays of the moon. There is bliss there, but it is not like a burning fire, it is like a cool light. There is no tension in it, no restlessness.

Have you ever noticed that a happy person can die of a heart attack? A sudden, overwhelming happiness in his life—suddenly the man wins the lottery and he is extremely happy—and he drops dead! Winning the lottery is trouble, and not winning the lottery is trouble.

I have heard about a man who won a million dollars in the lottery. He was not home when the news came. His wife was terribly upset because she knew that if her husband were to hear that he had won even a small amount, he might die of a heart attack. A million dollars! She went running around the neighbourhood to find the priest from the church because she thought he was a wise man.

She said to him, 'Please help me! Before my husband comes home, do something. He has won a million dollars in the lottery!'

He told her, 'Don't worry. I will break the news to him in instalments. Let your husband return home; I am coming.'

The priest waited. The husband came home. The priest thought that to tell him about a million would be too much; it would be better to start with a smaller amount. So he said, 'Listen, I want to tell you that you have won a hundred thousand dollars in the lottery.'

The husband said, 'Really? If that's true, then I will donate fifty thousand dollars to your church.'

Then and there the priest dropped dead of a heart attack! He had never even imagined it—fifty thousand dollars!

Happiness can also kill you. There is no doubt that sorrow can kill, but happiness also can kill because of the excitement. Wherever there is too much excitement, something is bound to snap. The only thing that can be constant is your self-nature which is non-excitable. Only your true nature, which needs no practice, can remain constantly with you. Only something which you can't leave behind can remain constantly there.

Hence, the whole search of religion is the search for self-nature, intrinsic nature. Religion is the search for your true nature, because that alone is forever. You can never become bored with it because it is you! There just is no way for you to be separate from it. There is no way to step away from it and watch it. Whatever you can step away from and look at, you will ultimately get bored with because it is not your true nature.

Once the mantra kills the mind, once the mind commits suicide through the mantra, this constant stream will start flowing within you. And when this constant stream has happened, the individual, liberated from the external states of happiness and unhappiness, knows the ultimate aloneness. Now he is alone. Now alone, he is drunk with himself. Now he needs nothing. All his desiring has ended. Because both happiness and unhappiness are outside of him, he does not desire happiness or want to escape from unhappiness. His ties with everything outside are simply broken and he is settled in his own self. He is constantly in bliss, so there is no question of having any desires. He dwells in each moment in the bliss of his own consciousness. Truth-consciousness-bliss is now his constant state. It is there in his every breath, in every atom of his being.

> *Freed from these, he becomes rooted in the ultimate aloneness.*
>   *The yogin who is rooted in such aloneness and whose desiring has ceased, goes beyond birth and death.*

Then there is no birth and there is no death, because birth and death exist in the search for happiness. We desire happiness, and happiness can be found only through the body, so we have no choice but to be reborn into a body. The happiness that we desire decides what kind of body we are born into. Then the desire for happiness continues up until the moment of death. You go on dying again and again, but the desire for happiness does not leave you and it is this desire that becomes the seed for the next birth.

When a tree starts dying, what happens? Before it dies, the tree gathers all its life energy and collects it into its seeds. The seeds are the desire of that tree to go on living after it dies. And a seed is a very unique phenomenon because the tree is so big, but it collects its whole essence in its seed and sends the seed on the journey of life. This tree will die, this 'body' will die, but it has made arrangements to live once again in a new body. This explains why even though a tree is born from a single seed, it leaves millions of seeds before it dies. Because who knows whether or not one single seed will find the right soil? It may fall on a rock, it may not get enough water, some animal might eat it or somebody may crush it. The tree cannot take the risk by leaving only one seed, because it may survive, it may not survive. This is why it produces millions of seeds, and through various means sends them far and wide to places where at least some of them can find the right soil.

Just watch—have you ever seen a flower of the kapok tree? One of the characteristics of this tree is that nothing can grow underneath it because its roots suck all the water away. So the tree has a wonderful way to scatter its seeds: it attaches silk cotton to the seedpods to give them wings so that they can fly away from the tree when the wind comes. Don't think that the kapok tree puts silk cotton on its seeds to stuff your beds and pillows with. It puts silk cotton to give its seeds wings to fly far away with the wind. This ensures that the seeds won't remain on the ground right beneath it because that would be certain death for them.

It is difficult for any plant to grow under a big tree, so all trees devise their own ways. They are not so simple—trees are very skilful and clever. They are not so plain and simple because no one in this world can afford to be. The moment you become plain and simple, you disappear. You can only survive here if you are crooked; to be crooked is the prerequisite to being here. That is the qualification for being here. So the tree devises thousands of ways to survive.

If you study trees, you will be amazed how many different ways they have devised to survive. They attract butterflies, and they survive with the help of these butterflies. Butterflies settle on the flowers to suck the nectar. They must be thinking that this sweet-flowing nectar has been provided especially for them, but they are mistaken: they are just being bribed by the trees. The tree is putting hundreds of seeds on the butterflies' legs and wings in the form of pollen.

Trees devise thousands of ways to survive. And when even trees are devising so many ways to survive, then how many ways must you be inventing? There is no limit to your cleverness.

If only one man could use all his sperm, he could father as many people as there are on this earth. An ordinary person, just normal, who is neither celibate nor promiscuous, has intercourse at least four thousand times in his lifetime. In each sex act, about a hundred million sperms or seeds are ejected. Imagine if all his seeds succeeded in creating life—which perhaps will happen one day. It has not been possible up to now because a woman's capacity is limited to maturing one seed in nine months. A woman can give birth to twelve or fifteen, or at the most twenty-four babies in her lifetime, so there is a limit. This is why kings used to keep so many wives, so the limit could be exceeded.

Science is now making it possible for the semen of a single individual to fertilize all the women in the world—those sperms can be injected. This is a real possibility, because no matter how dangerous a scientific idea may sound, sooner or later it becomes an accepted norm. Some scientists maintain that not everyone should have the right to give birth to children, that it would be good to use the sperm of a person like Einstein or people of his stature—and they are right. When we are so careful about the quality of plants in our gardens, we take so much care to improve the quality of flowers, then why don't we start to think the same way about the human race? After all, a gardener looks for the best seeds possible; he doesn't sow just any useless seeds.

If not today, then tomorrow, it is possible that scientists will decide which people should be given the right to procreate according to various factors such as health, intelligence, age, alertness or genius, and only their seed will be used. Their sperm could then be available in packets that you would be able to buy.

So, one single man produces so many sperms that he can populate the whole earth. This is also part of the survival instinct of life.

You will be amazed to hear this, and you have not read this anywhere else because it has not yet been written anywhere else: when a man goes beyond happiness and unhappiness, when he has attained the ultimate aloneness, his body stops producing sperm. And only a man whose body has stopped producing sperm has reached real celibacy. But sperm production stops only when the desire for survival is completely extinguished. The body will go on producing sperm as long as the lust for life exists, as long as the desire to survive is there—the desire that I must survive in any form; it doesn't matter if this body dies, I can live on in another body, but live I must. On the one hand, your body will live, and on the other hand, your desiring mind will drive your being to go on seeking new wombs.

You will wander as long as you are identified with happiness and unhappiness. Until that point, you will do everything possible to avoid unhappiness and to invite happiness, always desiring more and more journeys into happiness, more and more exploration into happiness. These dreams and desires are what will lead you into new births.

The yogin who is rooted in such aloneness and whose desiring has ceased, goes beyond birth and death. One who has no desires cannot be born, and one who has not been born cannot die. You can die only if you have been born. Death is just the other side of birth, they are two sides of the same coin—on one side is birth, on the other side is death. Here you are born and here also you will die. If you want to be free from death, you will have to be free from birth.

Everyone wants to be free of death, but nobody wants to be free of birth. This is your difficulty. Everyone wants to be free of suffering and misery, but no one wants to be free of happiness. The day you are ready to seek freedom from happiness, your life will have undergone a revolution—you will have become truly religious.

Mulla Nasruddin and his wife went on a sea voyage for the first time and Mulla was terribly seasick with nausea, dizziness and vomiting. One morning there was a violent storm. The sea was rough and the ship was tossing about wildly, which made things even worse for him. He was very afraid. He called his wife and said to her, 'Listen, before starting on this journey I made my will. I have transferred everything to your name. My will is in the bank with all the necessary papers. Bury me on the shore when I arrive, whether I am dead or alive, because I can't take another sea voyage! Dead or alive, I just can't take another sea voyage, so just bury me when we arrive. Everything is in the bank, you take care of it.'

When this life starts looking that absurd to you, when life appears so meaningless to you that it makes no difference whether you are dead or alive, and under no circumstances do you want to make this journey again, when you start seeing this life as a fate worse than death—and so it is—there will be a revolution in your life. Right now, even if you are interested in religion, it is only part of your search for happiness. This is the reason why you never become truly religious.

Your religious search will become authentic only when under no circumstances do you want to go any more on this journey of birth and death. You have seen it all and found it all to be meaningless. You have experienced happiness and have found that in the end, this too becomes unhappiness. You have experienced unhappiness and found it to be full of suffering. Misery is misery, true—but in this world even happiness is misery. Here, even what has a sweet taste is poison. Poison is poison, true, but what is labelled as nectar is also just a trick to hide the poison. When you are ready to recognize the meaninglessness of it all, that it is all outside of you, futile, only then will real religiousness be born in your life.

Remember, look inside yourself sincerely to see whether you have become interested in religion only to find happiness. If so, then you are not interested in religion at all. Your interest in religion is authentic only when your search is for peace—not for happiness. Happiness has become futile, unhappiness has become futile, and now you want to be free of both.

The yogin who is rooted in such aloneness and whose desiring has ceased, goes beyond birth and death. Now he has no desires; now he doesn't want to go on any new life-journeys. Journeying into birth and death as such has become meaningless to him. It is here that the cycle of birth and death comes to an end.

Having dropped all layers, this bhutakanchuki, this liberated one is Shiva—the image of ultimate consciousness.

Such a one is Brahman, such a one is ultimate godliness.

This 'bhutakanchuki' . . . it is a beautiful word. 'Bhutakanchuki' means 'someone for whom this body, made up of the five elements, has become like a sheath, and he has dropped it.' The body and the mind are made up of five elements—the gross aspect of the five elements forms the body and the subtle aspect of the same five elements forms the mind. When both body and mind have become like sheaths, layers, and the person has seen himself as the one hidden behind the two—when he has peeled off all the layers of the onion, when he has come to know the inner Shiva-consciousness, the inner void—such a bhutakanchuki, such a liberated one, becomes the ultimate godliness.

In India we don't believe in a single God sitting somewhere up in the sky and managing the universe, no. In

India we believe that all life journeys end in God, godliness. Passing through all the stages of flowering, everyone becomes a reflection of godliness, existence. God is not an entity, a person—godliness is everyone's future.

Try to understand this more deeply.

Judaism, Christianity and Islam are the three major religions born outside India, and Hinduism, Buddhism and Jainism are the three major religions born in India— and there is a fundamental difference between the two. Judaism, Christianity and Islam put God at the beginning, as the primal cause, as the one who created the universe. We in India see God, godliness, as something ahead, as our ultimate fruition. This makes a great difference—it is the future, not the past; it is the flower, not the seed. This is why we have placed statues of the buddhas, the awakened ones, on a flower, a lotus flower with all its thousand petals opened.

If God is at the beginning of everything, if he is the creator, then he is a single entity. Then this world is under a kind of dictatorship. Then there cannot be any liberation, because how can there be freedom if you have been created? How can a thing that has been created have freedom, because the day the creator chooses, he can de-create! If he could create you, what is the problem to uncreate you? Then you are just toys, puppets. Then your being, your freedom, have no meaning. This is why in India we don't look upon 'God' as the creator; we look upon it as the ultimate culmination, as the ultimate outcome. It is your ultimate flowering.

God, godliness, is not at the first step of evolution; it is the ultimate peak. It is the Gourishankar of consciousness, the Everest, the Kailash of consciousness, the ultimate peak where all consciousness will ultimately reach, to where all are heading. Sooner or later, everyone has to reach this state. You are godliness in process each day. God is not an event that has already happened; it is a flow that is happening every moment. Godliness is happening each moment; it is growing within you, you are its womb.

Hence, the Shiva Sutra concludes with this ultimate statement. All scriptures end here. They begin with you and end with godliness. As you are now, is the first step; as you will ultimately be, is the last and final step. Your wandering is you as a seed; your culmination, your fulfilment will be you flowered as a tree in its totality. That will be the state of your total contentment, all is fulfilled.

When a flower blooms, the tree's being comes to its culmination, its fulfilment. In the blooming of the flower the tree has attained its full fragrance. What the tree was born for, has happened. When the flowers bloom, the tree is filled with a dance, each atom of its being is thrilled. Its life has not been a waste; it has realized its meaning, its fulfilment; fragrance and beauty have flowered in its life.

And when a tree is filled with so much bliss at the blooming of just one flower—a flower that will last for a moment and then wither away, a flower that blooms now and will die by the evening—then how much more bliss must there be in the universe when a Vardhamana becomes Mahavir—the flower has bloomed; or a Gautam Siddhartha becomes Buddha—the flower has bloomed? And this is a flower that will never wither away. This very flowering that will never fade is called Shiva-consciousness, and that is the only 'God'.

Use the mantra, so that all that is useless in you drops away, and all that is meaningful blossoms. Make use of the mantra so that what you are right now shatters and scatters on the ground, and that which is your intrinsic potential can sprout.

You are carrying godliness hidden within you, so walk carefully, move carefully! Just as a pregnant woman walks carefully, so must a seeker walk, alert with every step, because it is not a question of just your life, the whole existence has staked everything in you. The whole of existence is eager to blossom in you.

The responsibility is great! Take each step with great care, caution and alertness—because godliness is to be born through you.

Enough for today.

Osho International Meditation Resort

Each year the Meditation Resort welcomes thousands of people from more than 100 countries. The unique campus provides an opportunity for a direct personal experience of a new way of living—with more awareness, relaxation, celebration and creativity. A great variety of around-the-clock and around-the-year programme options are available. Doing nothing and just relaxing is one of them!

All of the programmes are based on Osho's vision of 'Zorba the Buddha'—a qualitatively new kind of human being who is able to *both* participate creatively in everyday life *and* relax into silence and meditation.

Location
Located 100 miles south-east of Mumbai in the thriving modern city of Pune, India, the OSHO International Meditation Resort is a holiday destination with a difference. The Meditation Resort is spread over 28 acres of spectacular gardens in a beautiful tree-lined residential area.

OSHO Meditations
A full daily schedule of meditations for every type of person includes both traditional and revolutionary methods, and particularly the OSHO Active Meditations™. The daily meditation programme takes place in what must be the world's largest meditation hall, the OSHO Auditorium.

OSHO Multiversity

Individual sessions, courses and workshops cover everything from creative arts to holistic health, personal transformation, relationship and life transition, transforming meditation into a lifestyle for life and work, esoteric sciences, and the 'Zen' approach to sports and recreation. The secret of the OSHO Multiversity's success lies in the fact that all its programmes are combined with meditation, supporting the understanding that as human beings we are far more than the sum of our parts.

OSHO Basho Spa

The luxurious Basho Spa provides for leisurely open-air swimming surrounded by trees and tropical green. The uniquely styled spacious Jacuzzi, the saunas, gym, tennis courts ... all these are enhanced by their stunningly beautiful setting.

Cuisine

A variety of different eating areas serve delicious Western, Asian and Indian vegetarian food—most of it organically grown especially for the Meditation Resort. Breads and cakes are baked in the resort's own bakery.

Nightlife

There are many evening events to choose from—dancing being at the top of the list! Other activities include full-moon meditations beneath the stars, variety shows, music performances and meditations for daily life.

Facilities

You can buy all of your basic necessities and toiletries in the Galleria. The Multimedia Gallery sells a large range of OSHO media products. There is also a bank, a travel agency and a Cyber Café on campus. For those who enjoy shopping, Pune provides all the options, ranging from traditional and ethnic Indian products to all of the global brand-name stores.

Accommodation
You can choose to stay in the elegant rooms of the OSHO Guesthouse, or for longer stays on campus you can select one of the OSHO Living-In programmes. Additionally there is a plentiful variety of nearby hotels and serviced apartments.

www.osho.com/meditationresort
www.osho.com/guesthouse
www.osho.com/livingin

For more information

For a full selection of OSHO multilingual online destinations, see www.osho.com/allaboutosho.

The official and comprehensive website of OSHO International is www.osho.com.

For more OSHO unique content and formats see:

— OSHO Active Meditations: www.osho.com/meditate.
— iOsho, a bouquet of digital OSHO experiences featuring OSHO Zen Tarot, TV, Library, Horoscope, eGreetings and Radio. Please take a moment to do a one-time registration which will allow you a universal login. Registration is free and open to anyone with a valid email address: www. osho.com/iosho.
— The OSHO online shop: www.osho.com/shop.

113 - 117
223
239